Text Book Of

POWER ELECTRONICS

SEMESTER VI
FOR
THIRD YEAR DEGREE IN ELECTRONICS
AND TELECOMMUNICATION ENGINEERING GROUP
AS PER NEW REVISED SYLLABUS OF NORTH MAHARASHTRA
UNIVERSITY, JALGAON

K. P. AKOLE
B. E. (E & TC), M.E. (Comp.), M.I.E.T.E., M.I.E.
Lecturer in Electronics Department,
Government Polytechnic

N3352

POWER ELECTRONICS (SEM. VI) (NMU)
First Edition : **January 2015**
© : **Authors**
ISBN 978-93-5164-405-7

The text of this publication, or any part thereof, should not be reproduced or transmitted in any form or stored in any computer storage system or device for distribution including photocopy, recording, taping or information retrieval system or reproduced on any disc, tape, perforated media or other information storage device etc., without the written permission of Authors with whom the rights are reserved. Breach of this condition is liable for legal action.

Every effort has been made to avoid errors or omissions in this publication. In spite of this, errors may have crept in. Any mistake, error or discrepancy so noted and shall be brought to our notice shall be taken care of in the next edition. It is notified that neither the publisher nor the authors or seller shall be responsible for any damage or loss of action to any one, of any kind, in any manner, therefrom.

Published By :
NIRALI PRAKASHAN
Abhyudaya Pragati, 1312, Shivaji Nagar,
Off J.M. Road, PUNE – 411005
Tel - (020) 25512336/37/39, Fax - (020) 25511379
Email : niralipune@pragationline.com

Printed By :
REPRO INDIA LTD,
Mumbai.

DISTRIBUTION CENTRES

PUNE
Nirali Prakashan
119, Budhwar Peth, Jogeshwari Mandir Lane
Pune 411002, Maharashtra
Tel : (020) 2445 2044, 66022708
Fax : (020) 2445 1538
Email : bookorder@pragationline.com

MUMBAI
Nirali Prakashan
385, S.V.P. Road, Rasdhara Co-op. Hsg. Society Ltd.,
Girgaum, Mumbai 400004, Maharashtra
Tel : (022) 2385 6339 / 2386 9976,
Fax : (022) 2386 9976
Email : niralimumbai@pragationline.com

DISTRIBUTION BRANCHES

NAGPUR
Pratibha Book Distributors
Above Maratha Mandir, Shop No. 3, First Floor,
Rani Jhanshi Square, Sitabuldi, Nagpur 440012,
Maharashtra, Tel : (0712) 254 7129

BENGALURU
Pragati Book House
House No. 1, Sanjeevappa Lane, Avenue Road Cross,
Opp. Rice Church, Bengaluru – 560002.
Tel . (080) 64513344, 64513355,
Mob : 9880582331, 9845021552
Email:bharatsavla@yahoo.com

JALGAON
Nirali Prakashan
34, V. V. Golani Market, Navi Peth, Jalgaon 425001,
Maharashtra, Tel : (0257) 222 0395
Mob : 94234 91860

KOLHAPUR
Nirali Prakashan
New Mahadvar Road,
Kedar Plaza, 1st Floor Opp. IDBI Bank
Kolhapur 416 012, Maharashtra. Mob : 9855046155

CHENNAI
Pragati Books
9/1, Montieth Road, Behind Taas Mahal, Egmore,
Chennai 600008 Tamil Nadu, Tel : (044) 6518 3535,
Mob : 94440 01782 / 98450 21552 / 98805 82331
Email : bharatsavla@yahoo.com

RETAIL OUTLETS
PUNE

Pragati Book Centre
157, Budhwar Peth, Opp. Ratan Talkies,
Pune 411002, Maharashtra
Tel : (020) 2445 8887 / 6602 2707, Fax : (020) 2445 8887
Pragati Book Centre
Amber Chamber, 28/A, Budhwar Peth,
Appa Balwant Chowk, Pune : 411002, Maharashtra,
Tel : (020) 20240335 / 66281669
Email : pbcpune@pragationline.com

Pragati Book Centre
676/B, Budhwar Peth, Opp. Jogeshwari Mandir,
Pune 411002, Maharashtra
Tel : (020) 6601 7784 / 6602 0855
Pragati Book Centre
917/22, Sai Complex, F.C. Road, Opp. Hotel Roopali,
Shivajinagar, Pune 411004, Maharashtra
Tel : (020) 2566 3372 / 6602 2728

PBC Book Sellers & Stationers
152, Budhwar Peth, Pune 411002, Maharashtra
Tel : (020) 2445 2254 / 6609 2463

MUMBAI
Pragati Book Corner
Indira Niwas, 111 - A, Bhavani Shankar Road, Dadar (W), Mumbai 400028, Maharashtra
Tel : (022) 2422 3526 / 6662 5254
Email : pbcmumbai@pragationline.com

www.pragationline.com   info@pragationline.com

Dedicated to

My Father and Mother

Akole K. P.

Preface ...

With tremendous advancement in Power Electronics since last few decades a number of semiconductor devices have come up in power electronic field. This rapid development made significant change in the field of electronics and telecommunication group. The field of E & TC is generally segmented into three major areas electronics and telecommunication group. The function of power electronics is to process and control the electrical energy by supplying voltage and current in a form that is optimally suited to the load. **Power Electronics** plays a vital role in many domestic and industrial appliances. Electrical machines are controlled by power electronics. Various conventional controls and relays are replaced by electronic system consisting of power electronic circuits.

Power electronics is popular for technical as well as economical reasons. Electrical power generation, transformation, transmission and distribution are in A.C. but almost all terminal equipments used in industries, laboratories, agriculture and domestic require D.C. power. In order to satisfy these requirements, easy conversion of power is essential. Power electronics provides solution for all such requirements.

By considering these facts, power electronics subject is included in the curriculum of degree and diploma engineering in Electrical and Electronics Engineering group. This book is intended for imparting fundamental knowledge to degree students of electronics and telecommunication engineering group for studying power electronics related subjects such as power electronics and drives, industrial electronics, power electronics etc. This book is mainly designed as per the semester pattern curriculum for sixth semester degree in electronics and telecommunication engineering group. This book is an outcome of the author's realization of the fact that the important subject power electronics must be learnt by the students with clarity and ease. It is written in a simple straightforward style, emphasizing the core concepts underlying various power electronic circuits without deriving complex mathematical equations. This book is expected to serve as a student friendly text to students of electrical and electronics engineering degree programme.

The book is divided into five chapters. The book begins with introductory chapter related to power electronic devices with main focus on SCR. The next four chapters explain basic concepts of converter, inverter and AC controllers, UPS and Simulation of Inverter.

Every care has been taken to check mistakes and misprints. Yet it is very difficult to claim perfection. Any constructive criticism and suggestions from professionals, teachers and students are most welcome that help us in improving this book.

Pune **Author**

Acknowledgement

Author is very much thankful to Dineshbhai Furia of Nirali Prakashan and Shri. M. P. Munde and Shri P. M. More whose inspiration and constant motivation are responsible for producing this book within a short period of time. Author is also very much thankful to Shri Jigneshbhai Furia who has contributed quite a lot for this publication.

We hope that this book will prove to be useful to all readers. Any errors, omissions and suggestions for the improvement of this book, brought to our notice will be thankfully acknowledged and incorporated in the next edition.

Pune **K. P. Akole**

Syllabus

UNIT – I : INTRODUCTION TO POWER DEVICES (No. of Lect. 09, 16 Marks)

(a) **Silicon controlled Rectifier (SCR)** : Structure, Symbolic representation, Working principle, Two transistor analogy of SCR, Characteristics (Static and Dynamic), Turn-ON methods, Gate triggering circuits of SCR (R, RC, UJT).

(b) **Commutation Methods** : Class A, B, C, D, E, F commutation (Circuit diagram, Working principle and Waveforms).

(c) **Protection Circuit of SCR** : $\frac{di}{dt}$ and $\frac{dv}{dt}$ protection and Snubber circuit.

(d) **IGBT, GTO, DIAC, TRIAC** : Structure, Symbolic representation, Working principle, Characteristics.

UNIT – II : LINE FREQUENCY CONTROLLED CONVERTERS/RECTIFIERS (No. of Lect. 09, 16 Marks)

(a) **Single-Phase Half Controlled Bridge Rectifier (R and RL Load)** : Circuit diagram, Waveforms, Average load voltage, RMS load voltage, Average load power, Active power, Reactive power, Current distortion factor, Displacement factor, Input power factor, Efficiency, Ripple factor, Form factor.

(b) **Single-Phase Full Controlled Bridge Rectifier (R and RL Load)** : Circuit diagram, Waveforms, Average load voltage, RMS load voltage, Average load power, Active power, Reactive power, Current distortion factor, Displacement factor, Input power factor, Efficiency, Ripple factor, Form factor.

(c) **Three Phase Half and Full Controlled Converter (R and RL Load)** : Circuit diagram, Waveforms, Average load voltage, RMS load voltage, Average load current, Operating modes.

(d) **Effect of Source Inductance** : 1-phase and 3-phase fully controlled rectifier.

UNIT – III : DC-DC CONVERTER (No. of Lect. 07, 16 Marks)

(a) Classification of choppers, Control strategies of dc-dc-converter.

(b) **Step Down and Step Up dc-dc Converter** : Circuit diagram, Waveform and Output voltage calculations. Continuous conduction mode, Boundary between continuous and discontinuous conduction, Mode and Discontinuous conduction mode.

(c) **Full Bridge dc-dc Converter** : PWM with bipolar voltage switching (Derivation of output voltage).

(d) **Switch Mode Power Supply** : Block diagram and explain.

UNIT – IV : INVERTERS   (No. of Lect. 08, 16 Marks)

(a) **Inverters :** Basic series and Parallel inverters, Construction and Principle of operation.

(b) **Square and PWM Bridge Inverters :** Single phase half bridge and full bridge inverters with R and R-L load, Output voltage calculations. Square wave, Quasi-square wave and sinusoidal PWM switching, Selection of frequency modulation ratio and Amplitude modulation ratio.

(c) **Harmonic reduction techniques.**

(d) **Three Phase Bridge Inverter :** With balanced star resistive load, 120 degree and 180 degree conduction mode for line and phase voltages.

UNIT – V : AC CONTROLLERS, UPS AND SIMULATION OF CONVERTERS
               (No. of Lect. 09, 16 Marks)

(a) **AC Controllers :** Principle of ON-OFF control or integral cycle and phase angle control.

(b) 1-phase half wave and full wave AC control with R and R-L load, Derivation of output voltage.

(c) **UPS :** Basic principle, Different configurations/Types of UPS – OFF-line, ON-line, Line interactive, their comparison.

   Battery : AH, back-up time and battery charger rating calculations.

(d) Simulation of Single phase full converter, Single phase semi-converter, Single phase full bridge inverter, Single phase AC voltage controller.

•••

Contents

1. Introduction to Power Devices — 1.1 – 1.52

2. Line Frequency Controlled Converter/Rectifier — 2.1 – 2.40

3. DC-DC Converter — 3.1 – 3.40

4. Inverter — 4.1 – 4.40

5. AC Controllers, UPS and Simulation of Converters — 5.1 – 5.34

Appendix – A — A.1 – A.4

Appendix – B — B.1 – B.20

Chapter 1

INTRODUCTION TO POWER DEVICES

Weightage of Marks = 16, Teaching Hours = 09

Contents

- Review of electronic components
- Introduction to power electronics
- Silicon controlled rectifier
  - Structure
  - Symbol
  - Working
  - Two transistor analogy
  - Characteristics
  - Turn-ON methods
  - Gate triggering circuits
- SCR commutation methods
- SCR protection circuits
- SCR rating and selection factors
- SCR testing
- Other thyristor family devices
  - DIAC
  - TRIAC
  - IGBT
  - GTO

Objectives

After learning this chapter reader will be able to :
- Know importance and area of applications of power electronic devices.
- Sketch constructional details of planar and mesa SCR, its technical symbol
- Know SCR operation.
- Sketch static and dynamic characteristics of SCR.
- Illustrate two transistor analogy of SCR.
- Understand the process of thyristor triggering circuit i.e. turn-ON circuits.
- Classify commutation methods and state working of various commutation methods.
- Know importance, working principle and circuit for SCR protection.
- State selection factors and rating of SCR.
- Test given by SCR.
- Know structure, symbol, working and applications of other thyristor devices such as DIAC, TRIAC, IGBT, GTO.

1.1 REVIEW OF ELECTRONIC COMPONENTS

- To understand power electronic devices and circuits, it is essential to have knowledge about basic electronic components. Two main categories of electronic components are (a) Passive components, (b) Active components. For passive components, biasing supply is not essential. Their working does not depend on external biasing supply. Examples of passive components are resistor, capacitor and inductor. For the operation of active component, external biasing supply is essential. Their operation changes as per biasing supply amplitude. Biasing means application of external supply for device operation. For stable operation of device, biasing supply must be DC supply. Examples of active devices are diode, BJT, FET, UJT, SCR, TRIAC, CRT etc.

- Electronic devices can be classified as tube devices and solid state or semiconductor devices. In early days of electronics (1900 to 1940), tube devices were most commonly used. Tube devices can be further classified as vacuum tube devices and gas filled tube devices. Vacuum tube diode, triode, tetrode, pentrode, cathode ray tube (CRT) are few examples of vacuum tube devices. Thermionic emission is the basic principle of vacuum tube devices. Emission of electrons due to heating of cathode is known as thermionic emission. Gas filled tube devices operate on the principle of gas ionization. Examples of gas filled tube devices are thyratron, ignitron, mercury arc rectifier, neon lamp etc. In this type of devices, gas ionization occurs due to applied very high potential. These are high power electronic devices. Due to technological development, these are replaced by thyristor devices.

- Semiconductor components are also known as solid state components. Semiconductor materials are having specific electrical conductivity between that of good conductor and that of good insulator. The ability of carrying electrical current can be enhanced by the addition of certain chemical impurities from third and fifth group of atomic table. Semiconductor materials in pure form are called as intrinsic semiconductors. These are from fourth group. The most commonly used semiconductor is Si and less frequently used is Ge. The process of addition of impurity material to pure semiconductor is called as doping. Due to addition of impurity, impure semiconductor is formed. This impure semiconductor is called as extrinsic semiconductor. Two types of extrinsic semiconductors are P-type semiconductor and N-type semiconductor. By using these extrinsic semiconductors, various electronic devices are manufactured. Table 1.1 shows symbol, terminal names and applications of basic semiconductor devices.

Table 1.1

(Chap. 1.2)

Device	Symbol	Applications
P-N Junction Diode	A ──▷|── K	1. Rectifier 2. Clipping circuit 3. Clamping circuit 4. Digital circuit
Zener Diode	A ──▷|── K	1. Voltage regulation 2. Meter protection 3. Over voltage detection 4. Battery charger
Light Emitting Diode	A ──▷|── K	1. Indicator 2. Display device 3. 7-segment display 4. In matrix display
Bipolar Junction Transistor (BJT) NPN PNP	(NPN symbol with B, C, E) (PNP symbol with B, C, E)	1. Amplifier 2. Series and shunt voltage regulator 3. Oscillator 4. Multivibrator 5. Digital circuits 6. Transistorized voltmeter (TVM) 7. Operational amplifier 8. Switching element
Junction Field Effect Transistor (JFET) N-channel P-channel	(N-channel JFET symbol with G, D, S) (P-channel JFET symbol with G, D, S)	1. Amplifier 2. Oscillator 3. Multivibrator 4. Digital circuits 5. TVM 6. Digital memory 7. Switching element 8. High power applications

... *Contd.*

Device	Symbol	Applications
Metal Oxide Semiconductor Field Effect Transistor (MOSFET) N-channel P-channel	(N-channel MOSFET symbol with D, G, S, sub) (P-channel MOSFET symbol with D, G, S, sub)	1. In power electronics 2. Inverter 3. Digital circuits 4. VLSI ICs 5. Amplifier
Uni Junction Transistor (UJT)	(UJT symbol with E, B_1, B_2)	1. For triggering of SCR 2. Relaxation oscillator 3. Time base generator 4. Beam deflection circuit of CRO and TV

1.2 INTRODUCTION TO POWER ELECTRONICS

- Power electronics deals with the application of electronic devices in the control and conversion of electrical power. It is partly in power engineering and partly in electronics. Power engineering deals with high electrical power generation, transmission and utilization at higher frequency. Electronics deals with low power signal level and data signal. During last three decades, power electronics achieved phenomenal growth to occupy an important place in modern technology.

- In broad consideration, electrical engineering field may be divided into three areas :

    (1) Electronics, (2) Power, (3) Control.

- Electrical power generation is a basic need for domestic and industrial applications. To generate electrical power, conventional and non-conventional methods are used. AC electrical power generation and transmission is more efficient than DC electric power. For power conversion rectifier, control rectifier, inverter, chopper, cycloinverter, cycloconverter and other circuits are suitable. Power electronic equipment involves interaction between the source and the load. It utilizes small signal electronic control circuits as well as power semiconductor devices. In early days before 1975, thyratron, ignitron, mercury arc rectifier like gas filled tubes were used for power conversion and control. Now-a-days the major component of power electronic circuit is the thyristor. Thyristor is a fast switching semiconductor and its function is to modulate the power in AC and DC systems.

- Power electronic circuits are also called as thyristorised power controllers. The power controllers are generally classified into five categories.

- **Phase controlled rectifier :** These are also called as AC to DC converters. For these power controller source is single phase or three phase. These are used in DC drives, metallurgical and chemical industries, excitation system for synchronous system etc.
- **Chopper :** These are DC to DC converters. It converts fixed DC input voltage to variable and controllable DC output voltage. Choppers are commonly used for DC drive, railway cars, trolley trucks, battery operated vehicles.
- **Inverter :** These are DC to AC converters. Output may be variable voltage and variable frequency. Inverters are widely used in induction motor drive, synchronous motor drive, induction heating, UPS, HVDC transmission etc.
- **Cycloconverter :** These circuits convert input power at one frequency to output power at a different frequency. These are basically used for low speed large AC drive like rotary kiln etc.
- **AC voltage controller :** These converter circuits convert fixed AC voltage directly to a variable AC voltage at the same frequency. These are used for lighting control, speed control of fans, pumps etc.

1.3 ROLE OF POWER ELECTRONICS

- A power station is also called as generating station, power plant, power house or generating plant. Electrical power generation is the process of generating electronic power from other sources of primary energy. The fundamental principle of electricity generation were discovered during 1820 by the British scientist Michael Faraday.

Merits of Power Electronic Converters :

1. High efficiency due to low loss in power semiconductor devices.
2. High reliability of power electronic component and converter system.
3. Long life and less maintenance due to absence of moving parts.
4. Fast dynamic response compared to electromechanical converter system.
5. Small size and less weight, so less installation cost.
6. Mass production of power semiconductor devices has brought down the cost of converter equipment.

Demerits of Power Electronic Converters :

1. It generates harmonics into the supply and load system, adversely affecting the performance of the load and other equipment.
2. A.C. to D.C. and A.C. to A.C. converters operate at low input power factor.
3. Power electronic controllers have low overload capacity.

Applications of Power Electronic Converters :

1. Arc and industrial furnace
2. Blowers and fans
3. Pumps and compressors
4. Transformer tap changer
5. Rolling mills
6. Battery charger
7. A.C. and D.C. motor speed control
8. Static circuit breaker
9. Induction and dielectric heating control
10. Electric welding control
11. Static excitation system for alternators
12. Traction control of electric vehicles, electric locomotives
13. Light dimmers
14. Washing machines
15. SMPS and UPS
16. HVDC transmission
17. Fan speed regulator
18. Automatic power factor correction
19. Process control
20. Satellite power supply.
21. Battery monitoring power converter in laptop computers
22. High performance and compact switching regulators
23. Power electronics boost converter for automobiles
24. Replacement of spark plug and ignition coil of automobiles

25. Power steering

26. Power converter in space system

27. Flexible AC transmission system (FACTS)

28. Electrochemical process

29. Portable hand set tool drive

30. Power conditioning function in renewable sources of energy

Fig. 1.1 shows multidisciplinary nature of power electronics.

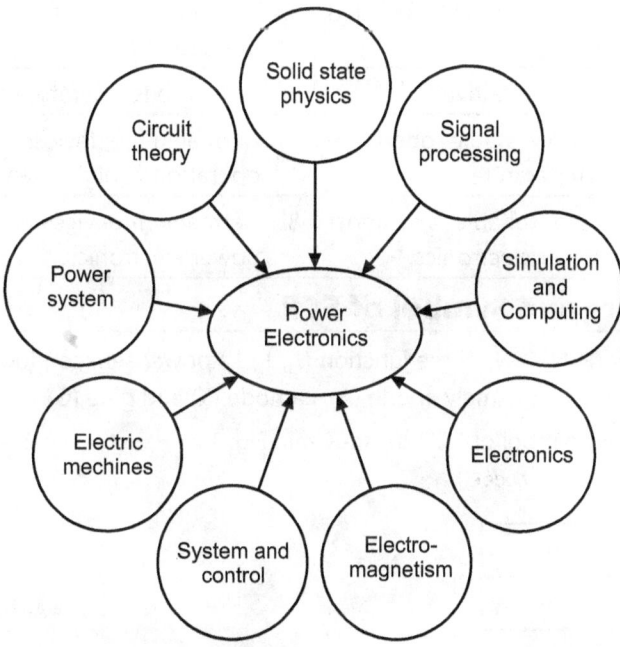

Fig. 1.1 : Multidisciplinary nature of power electronics

1.4 SILICON CONTROLLED RECTIFIER

- Silicon Controlled Rectifier (SCR) being the first amongst the thyristor family, it is also as thyristor. This device is called as SCR because silicon is used for its manufacturing and it performs controlled rectification. (Note that for controlled rectification, germanium cannot be used because Ge is more temperature sensitive than Si. In Ge devices, leakage current is more. So in power electronics applications, Ge devices are not preferable.) As SCR conducts only in one direction, so it is a unidirectional device and it is suitable for rectification. Table 1.2 shows comparison between silicon and germanium.

Table 1.2 : Comparison between Silicon and Germanium

Silicon	Germanium
1. Silicon (Si) atomic number is 14.	1. Germanium (Ge) atomic number is 32.
2. Valence electrons are available in third orbit.	2. Valence electrons are available in fourth orbit.
3. Forbidden energy gap is 1.12 eV at room temperature.	3. Forbidden energy gap is 0.72 eV at room temperature.
4. Valence electrons are nearer to nucleus as compared to Ge.	4. Valence electrons are at larger distance from nucleus than Si.
5. Valence electrons are closely bonded with the nucleus.	5. Valence electrons are more loosely bonded to the nucleus.
6. It is less temperature sensitive.	6. It is more temperature sensitive.
7. Silicon devices show stable operation even at higher temperature.	7. Germanium devices show unstable operation at higher temperature.
8. Silicon devices are suitable and most widely used in power electronics.	8. Germanium devices are not suitable for power electronics.

1.4.1 Structure and Symbol of SCR

- It is a four layer (P–N–P–N), three junction (J_1, J_2, J_3) power semiconductor (silicon) device having three terminals, namely anode (A), cathode (K) and gate (G).
- The structure and symbol of SCR are shown in Fig. 1.2.

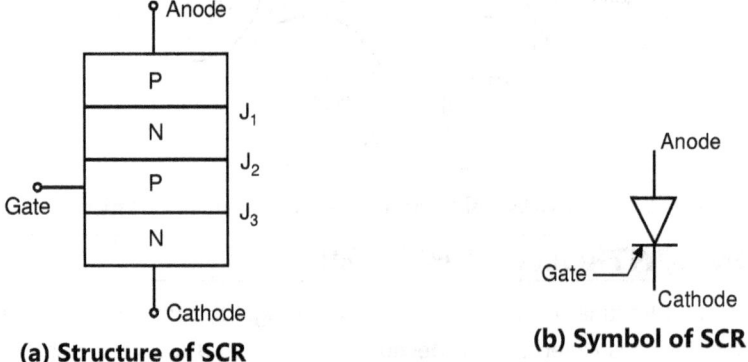

(a) Structure of SCR (b) Symbol of SCR

Fig. 1.2

- Anode is connected to the outer P layer, the cathode is connected to the outer N layer and gate is connected to the inner P layer.
- It is a switching device i.e. it shows 'ON' state and 'OFF' state operation.

- It is also known as cathode gate SCR because gate is connected to P region near to cathode. [**Note** : Anode gate SCR is the another device. It is known as PUT (Programmable Unijunction Transistor).]
- Anode and cathode are connected to the main power circuit.
- Gate terminal carries low level gate current for triggering of SCR.

Construction :
- SCR operation and rating depend on design and fabrication of the device.
- SCR is a four layered device.
- Junctions are fabricated either by diffusion method or by alloying method.
- Two basic construction techniques for SCR are (a) Planar SCR and (b) Mesa SCR.

Features of Planar SCR :
- All three junctions are diffused type.
- Single silicon pellet is used.
- More protected from outside environment.
- Suitable for low current applications.
- More silicon is required to increase current capability.
- Smaller size.

- Fig. 1.3 shows cross-sectional view of planar type SCR. For planar SCR temperature compensation heat sink is used. It can be attached to base using mechanical coupling.
- Most commonly used planar SCRs are 2P4M (2 Amp 400 V), 4A600 (4 Amp 600V), C38.

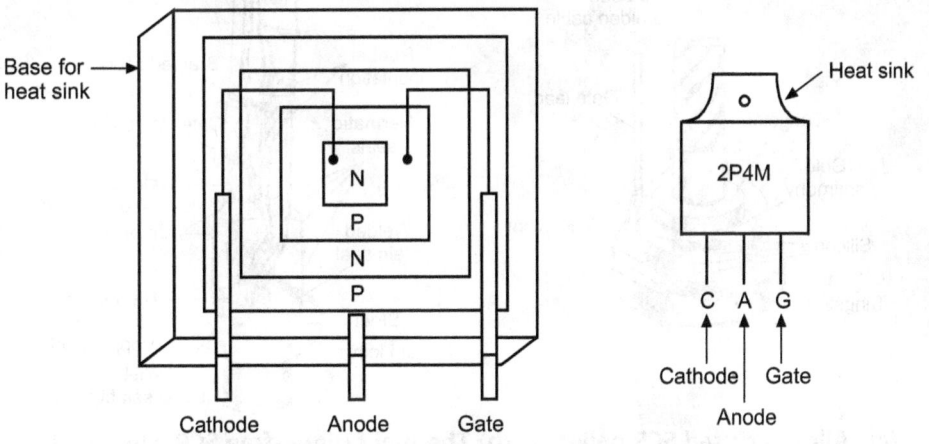

Fig. 1.3 : Cross-sectional view of planar SCR

Features of Mesa Type SCR :

- Inner junction J_2 is obtained by diffusion.
- Outer two junctions are alloyed.
- For mechanical strength, tungsten or molybdenum bracing is done.
- Copper or aluminium stud is used with heat sink attachment.
- High power SCR.
- In very high power mesa SCR, for thermal compensation, water or air cooling is used.

• Fig. 1.4 shows cross-sectional view of mesa type SCR.
• Depending upon the power rating, mesa SCRs are available in various sizes and shapes.

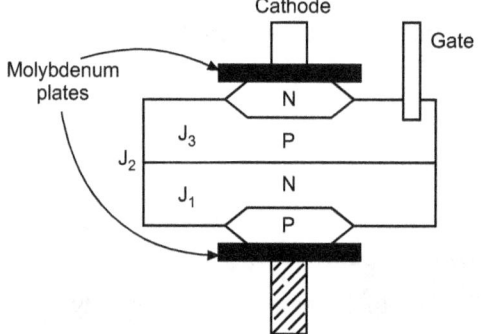

Fig. 1.4 : Cross-sectional view of mesa type SCR

• Commercially available mesa SCRs are 30A400 (30 Amp, 400 V), 100 A 1000 (100 Amp, 1000 V), BHt P46 133 (2000 V, 600 A), BHt P61 337 (500 V, 1100 A).

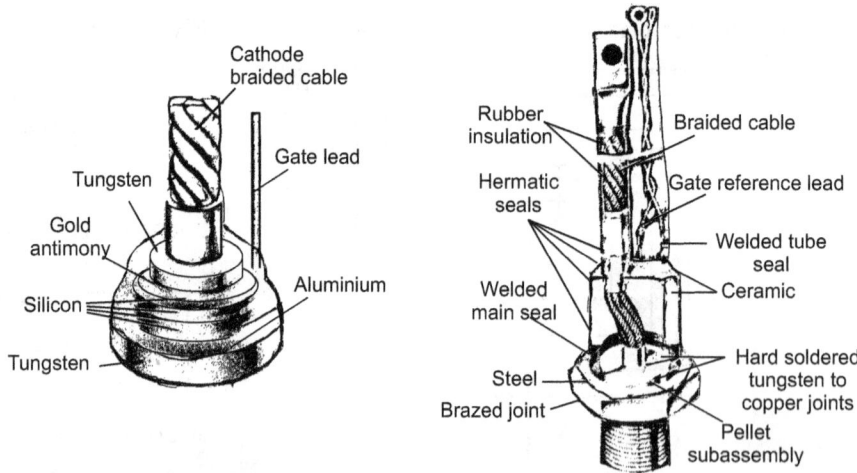

(a) **Alloy-diffused SCR pellet**   (b) **Thermal fatigue-free SCR construction**

Fig. 1.5

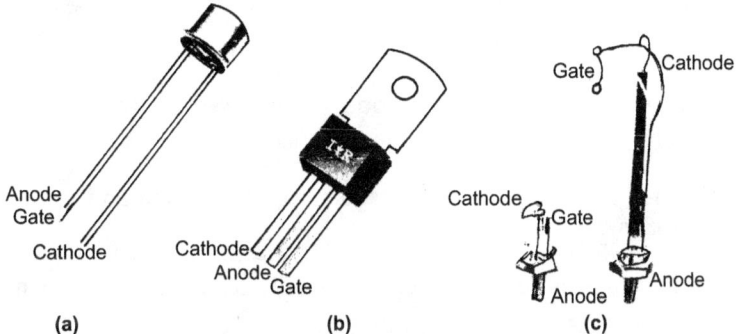

(a) (b) (c)

Fig. 1.6 : SCR case construction and terminal identification

1.4.2 Working Principe and V-I Characteristics

Working Principle :

- The SCR shows the property of switch. It has only two stable states - ON state and OFF state.
- During ON state, device shows very low resistance (1 Ω). During OFF state, the device offers a very high resistance as large as 1 MΩ.

Fig. 1.7 shows circuit diagram for operating SCR in various state. Same circuit is suitable to plot V-I characteristics of SCR.

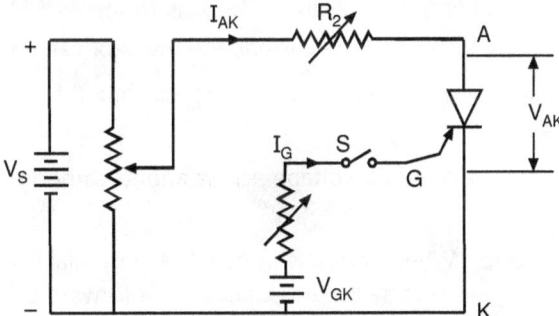

Fig. 1.7 : Circuit connection for SCR operation

- The anode is connected to positive terminal of main source and cathode is connected to negative terminal of main source.
- Main source is a variable D.C. power supply. R_2 is a variable load resistance connected in series with anode of SCR. V_{GK} D.C. supply is used to provide positive gate current.
- The thyristor has three basic modes of operation, namely forward blocking state (OFF state), reverse blocking state (OFF state) and forward conducting state (ON state).
- **Forward Blocking State :** Thyristor remains in forward blocking state when anode is positive with respect to cathode, but gate signal is insufficient or absent ($I_G = 0$).

- Junctions J_1 and J_3 of SCR are forward biased. Junction J_2 remains in reverse biased state. So very small leakage current flows from anode to cathode.

- If voltage across the anode and cathode is increased to high value then reverse breakdown (avalanche breakdown) occurs for junction J_2.

- Now SCR switches to ON state. This voltage across the anode and cathode is called as breakover voltage (V_{BO}).

- When forward voltage is less than V_{BO} then SCR offers high impedance in forward blocking state.

- **Forward Conduction State :** Thyristor can be switched from forward blocking state to forward conducting state even without gate current (I_G = 0) by increasing anode - cathode voltage to the level of forward breakover voltage. SCR can be switched ON at a lower forward voltage by applying gate current. Turning ON SCR is also called **Firing of SCR** or **Triggering of SCR**. When SCR is in ON state, then even gate current is reduced, current flowing through it is greater than the latching current. Latching current is the minimum value of anode current for the SCR to stay in conduction. In this mode SCR offers less resistance. Voltage drop across SCR in ON state is 1 V to 2 V. If load impedance is increased gradually, the anode current falls. If the anode current reduces to a value below the holding current, the SCR turns to forward blocking state. Holding current is the minimum value of anode current, the thyristor can conduct in 'ON' state.

- Holding current (I_H) is always less than latching current (I_L). I_H and I_L are always in mA range.

- As gate current increases, required voltage across anode-cathode decreases to turn ON SCR.

- **Reverse Blocking State :** When anode is at negative potential with respect to cathode, then junctions J_1 and J_3 are reverse biased. Junction J_2 is forward biased.

- A small leakage current flows (in the order of mA) from cathode to anode.

- This is called as reverse blocking state.

- The thyristor is in OFF and non-conducting state.

- If the reverse voltage is increased, then at critical voltage avalanche breakdown occurs and reverse leakage current increases rapidly.

- This reverse biased voltage is called as reverse breakdown voltage (V_{BR}).

- This large reverse leakage current gives more losses. It should therefore be ensured that maximum working reverse voltage across the thyristor does not exceed V_{BR}.

Fig. 1.8 shows V-I characteristics of SCR. From V-I characteristics, it is clear that I_H is always less than I_L and as I_G increases, required voltage across anode-cathode decreases.

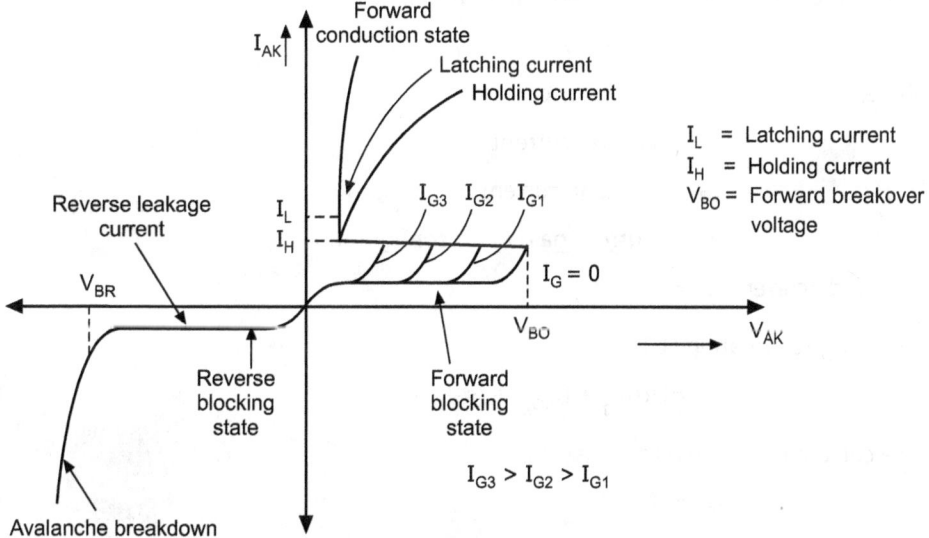

Fig. 1.8 : V-I characteristics of SCR

- Latching current is the minimum value of 'ON' state current.

- Holding current is the maximum value of 'OFF' state current.

1.4.3 Two Transistor Analogy

- Transistor model of SCR consists of two-transistor N-P-N and P-N-P connected back to back. Fig. 1.9 shows the two-transistor model of SCR.

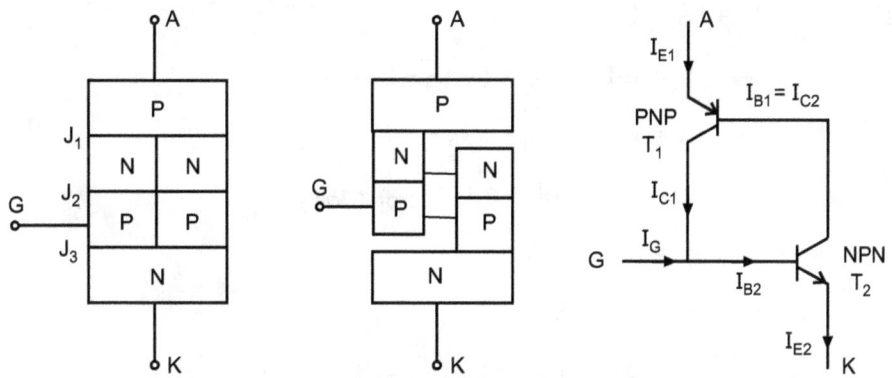

Fig. 1.9 : Two-transistor model of SCR

- Transistor T_1 is P-N-P with emitter as a anode. Transistor T_2 is N-P-N with emitter as a cathode of SCR. Both the transistors are connected in CB configuration. According to transistor current equation for CB configuration,

$$I_C = \alpha I_E + I_{CBO} \quad \ldots (1.1)$$

where,
I_C = Collector current
I_E = Emitter current
I_{CBO} = Leakage current
α = Current gain in CB configuration

The anode current, $I_a = I_{C_1} + I_{C_2}$ ... (1.2)

According to equation (1.1),

$$I_a = (\alpha_1 I_{E_1} + I_{CBO_1}) + (\alpha_2 I_{E_2} + I_{CBO_2}) \quad \ldots (1.3)$$

Base current of T_2 transistor

$$I_{B_2} = I_G + I_{C_1} \quad \ldots (1.4)$$

As $I_{E_1} = I_a$ and $I_{E_2} = I_K$, putting these values of I_{E_1} and I_{E_2} in equation (1.3)

$$I_a = \alpha_1 I_a + I_{CBO_1} + \alpha_2 I_K + I_{CBO_2} \quad \ldots (1.5)$$

As $\quad I_E = I_B + I_C$

So, $\quad I_K = I_{B_2} + I_{C_2}$ According to equation (1.4)

$\quad I_K = I_G + I_{C_1} + I_{C_2}$

$\therefore \quad I_a = \alpha_1 I_a + I_{CBO_1} + [\alpha_2 (I_G + I_{C_1} + I_{C_2}) + I_{CBO_2}]$

As $\quad I_{C_1} + I_{C_2} = I_a$ ... (1.6)

$\therefore \quad I_a = \alpha_1 I_a + I_{CBO_1} + [\alpha_2 (I_G + I_a) + I_{CBO_2}]$ ... (1.7)

$\therefore \quad I_a = \alpha_1 I_a + I_{CBO_1} + \alpha_2 I_G + \alpha_2 I_a + I_{CBO_2}$

$\quad I_a = \alpha_1 I_a + \alpha_2 I_a + \alpha_2 I_G + I_{CBO_1} + I_{CBO_2}$

$\therefore \quad I_a - \alpha_1 I_a - \alpha_2 I_a = \alpha_2 I_G + I_{CBO_1} + I_{CBO_2}$

$\quad I_a (1 - \alpha_1 - \alpha_2) = \alpha_2 I_G + I_{CBO_1} + I_{CBO_2}$

$$\therefore \quad I_a = \frac{\alpha_2 I_G + I_{CBO_1} + I_{CBO_2}}{1 - (\alpha_1 + \alpha_2)} \quad \ldots (1.8)$$

- In equation (1.8), when $\alpha_1 + \alpha_2$ equals to one, then I_a becomes infinity. This is called as firing, triggering or turn ON process of SCR.

- The thyristor operation can be explained using two transistors. SCR turns ON due to internal regenerative feedback. Emitter of P-N-P transistor acts as anode and emitter of N-P-N transistor acts as cathode.

- Both transistors are operated in common base configuration. Collector current of T_1 acts as base current of T_2. Two transistor model of SCR explain the internal phenomenon of building up of forward anode current inside the SCR.

1.4.4 Turn ON Methods

- Turn ON methods are also known as triggering methods.

- Turn ON process of thyristor is a dynamic process in which the device voltage and current simultaneously vary with time. Turn ON is the process describing the transition from forward blocking state to the conduction state. The transition time, called thyristor turn ON time is defined as the time during which it changes from forward blocking state to the final ON state. Total turn ON time of SCR is equal to the sum of delay time, rise time and spread time. Total turn ON time depends upon the anode circuit parameters, gate signal amplitude and gate signal rise time. The turn on time is of the order of 2-4 microsec.

- A forward biased thyristor can be turned ON by
    (a) Forward voltage triggering,
    (b) Gate triggering,
    (c) dv/dt triggering,
    (d) Temperature triggering,
    (e) Light triggering.

- These methods are used to increase leakage current in forward biased thyristor. It initiates the regeneration ultimately leading to the turn ON of the thyristor. From these five turn-ON methods, gate triggering and light triggering are recommended.

Forward Voltage Triggering :

- In this method, gate current $I_G = 0$, anode is at positive potential w.r.t. cathode. Anode voltage is increased to breakover voltage, V_{BO}. This method is known as forward voltage triggering. In practice, this method is not employed because it requires large anode to cathode voltage and also large current generation occurs. It may cause damage to the thyristor. In this method avalanche breakdown occurs.

dv/dt Triggering :

- When anode to cathode voltage is positive, outer junctions J_1 and J_3 get forward biased and inner junction J_2 reverse biased. Junction J_2 behaves as a capacitor.
- Charging current of this capacitor depends on the rate of rise of forward voltage.
- If forward voltage is suddenly applied then charging current would be large. Due to this phenomenon SCR turns to ON state. However, this dv/dt turn ON has to be avoided. Rate of change of applied voltage is kept below the specified rated limit.

Light Triggering (Radiation Triggering) :

- Light can be used to turn ON SCR by causing breakdown of the junction J_2 with junctions J_1 and J_3 forward biased.
- In light triggered SCR, gate region is of light sensitive material. When light rays of appropriate wavelength and intensity falls on gate region, gate current increases. It causes forward biased SCR to turn ON. A SCR turn ON by light radiation is known as light activated SCR (LASCR). Fig. 1.10 shows basic construction and symbol of LASCR.

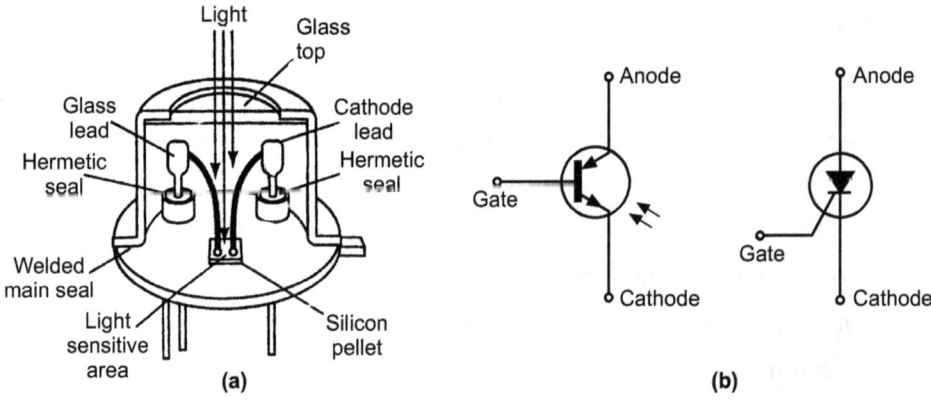

Fig. 1.10 : Light-activated SCR (LASCR) : (a) Basic construction, (b) Symbol of SCR shows light rays falling on SCR

1.4.5 Gate Triggering

- Gate triggering is a simple, reliable and efficient method. At a desired moment of turn-ON, a suitable positive gate voltage is applied. This results in gate current. As the value of I_G increases, required anode-cathode voltage decreases.
- Gate current magnitudes are of the order of 20 to 200 mA. Fig. 1.11 shows variation of breakover voltage with respect to gate current.
- Once the SCR start conducting, gate current is no longer required. Gate current may be removed after firing of SCR.
- If gate current is removed before raising anode current, attain the latching current value, the thyristor will return to forward blocking state.

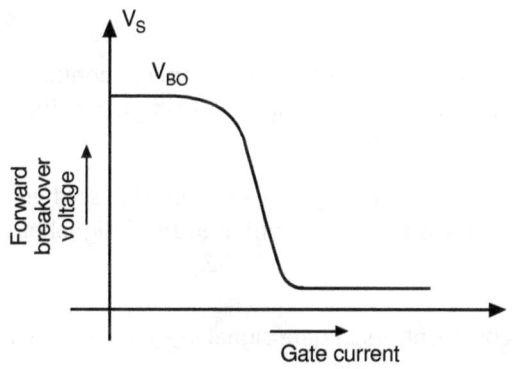

Fig. 1.11 : Variation of breakover voltage with respect to gate current

- This problem mainly arises with inductive load. Three types of signals can be used for this purpose. They are either D.C. signals, pulse signals or A.C. signals.
- The gate triggering circuits are also called as firing circuits.
- These are low power electronic circuits. Gate trigger circuit commonly consists of power supply, pulse generator with synchronizing command and feedback signals, pulse amplifier and pulse transformer.
- After pulse transformer, clamping circuit is used. Fig. 1.12 shows general layout of gate control circuit.

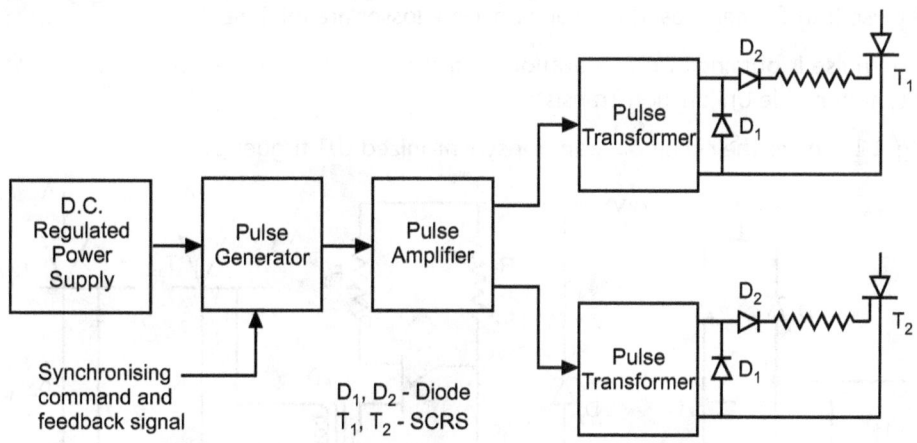

Fig. 1.12 : General layout of gate control circuit

Gate Control Methods :

- Three types of signals can be used for gate triggering. They are either D.C. signal, A.C. signal or pulse signal.

D.C. Gate Triggering :

- In this type of triggering, a D.C. voltage of proper magnitude and polarity is applied between the gate and cathode. When applied voltage is sufficient to produce required gate current, the device starts conducting.

- In this method, power circuit and trigger circuit are D.C. so there is no isolation between both circuits. Another drawback is that continuous D.C. signal has to be applied.

A.C. Gate Triggering :

- A.C. source is most commonly used gate signal in all applications of thyristor control A.C. application.

- This scheme provides proper isolation between power and control circuits. The firing angle control is obtained very conventionally by changing phase angle of the control signal. The drive is maintained for one half cycle after the device is turned ON. The drawback of this scheme is that a separate transformer is required to step down the a.c. supply.

Pulse Gate Griggering :

- This method is most commonly used. In this method, the gate drive consists of pulse generating circuit.

- High frequency pulses are applied. This is known as carrier frequency gating.

- A pulse transformer is used for isolation. Gate losses are minimized.

- Gate pulse is obtained from relaxation oscillator circuit which may consist of UJT or PUT (Programmable Unijunction Transistor).

    Fig. 1.13 shows the circuit diagram for synchronized UJT trigger circuit.

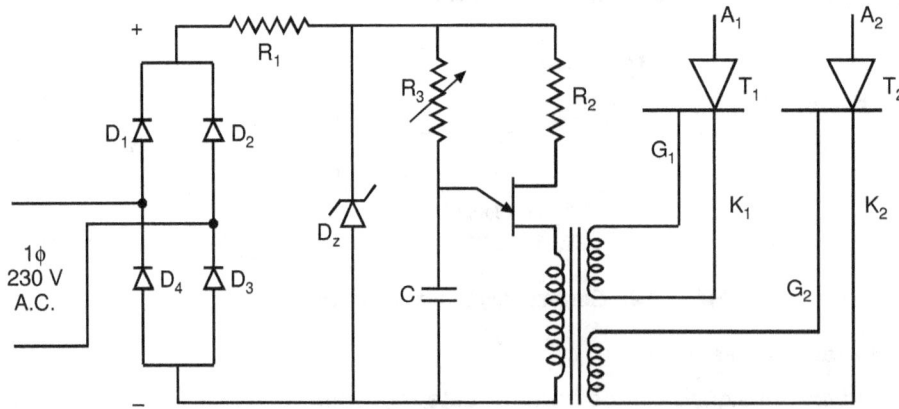

Fig. 1.13 : Synchronized UJT trigger circuit

(Chap. 1.18)

- Diodes D_1, D_2, D_3 and D_4 form bridge rectifier which convert A.C. to D.C. The zener diode D_Z is used to clip the rectified voltage to a fixed value V_Z. This V_Z voltage is used for charging R_3C circuit. Capacitor C charges through R_3 to peak point voltage of UJT. Then UJT turns ON and C discharges through UJT emitter and primary of pulse transformer. Pulses at the secondary winding feed pulse to two SCRs T_1 and T_2. SCR with positive anode voltage would turn ON. The firing angle can be controlled upto about 150°. This method is also called as ramp control.
- The proper triggering of SCR requires that the source of trigger should supply sufficient gate current and voltage without exceeding the SCR gate current and voltage rating. The performance of the SCR depends on magnitude and waveshape of the trigger signal.
- For proper firing of SCR, gate signal should be of :
  (1) Proper amplitude with short rise time.
  (2) Sufficient duration.
  (3) Occurred at appropriate time of mains circuit condition i.e. Anode positive and cathode negative.
- For SCR $I_{g\ min}$ indicates minimum gate current required to fire all SCR of same type. Practically for firing of SCR with minimum turn-ON time, $1.4\ I_{g\ min}$ current is applied. The gate voltage must exceed firing voltage $V_{g\ min}$ rating of SCR.
- Gate pulse duration must be large enough, for the anode current to rise to latching current level and to avoid turn off mechanism during initial trigger due to oscillations, disturbance and reflections. Normally pulse duration is 30 to 60 μsec. It is not essential to maintain high-amplitude gate pulse for whole pulse duration. In practice, pulse waveform with a leading edge of required amplitude and rise time followed by a tail of not more than $1.14\ I_{g\ min}$ amplitude. Fig. 1.14 shows nature of practical pulse.

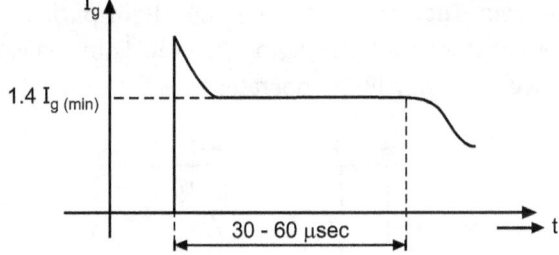

Fig. 1.14 : Gate firing pulse

- To couple a source of pulse of electrical energy to a load with its shape and other properties, unchanged pulse transformer is used. Pulse transformer is used in communication, digital electronics, fast pulse generation, power electronics etc. It provides electrical isolation. These are either 1 : 1 two winding type or 1 : 1 : 1 three winding type.

- Fig. 1.15 shows the use of pulse transformer for coupling the trigger signal to SCR. In this circuit, 1 : 1 two winding pulse transformer is used. Diode D ensures only application of positive pulses and blocks if any negative pulse is occurred. It prevents reverse gate current and reduces the holding current of the SCR.

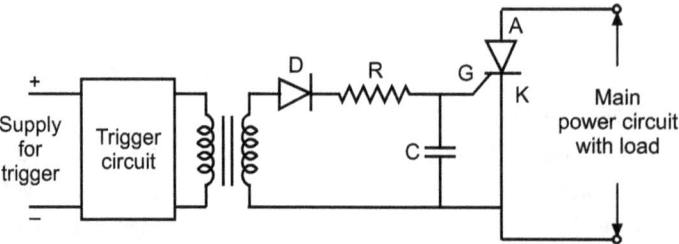

Fig. 1.15 : Gate triggering with pulse transformer

- When a low voltage, low current logic circuit such as microcontroller, computer is used to control the SCR operated large power rating load electrical isolation is done. It avoids the coupling of noise from high current circuit into the logic circuit through common ground line. For this type of isolation either electromechanical relay or opto isolators are used. Electromechanical relays are widely used in industrial applications but they are having some drawbacks such as :

(1) The contacts create sparking.

(2) They create magnetic field.

(3) More expensive, larger size and shorter life with lower reliability.

(4) Larger time for operation.

- To overcome these drawbacks, opto isolators are used. In opto isolator, light source and light detectors are used. They are available in light tight package. It consists of IRLED with either phototransistor, photodarlington, LASCR, light activated LASCR or other photosensitive device. Normally IRLED operates at + 5 V. Fig. 1.16 shows opto isolator with LASCR.

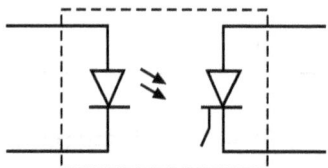

Fig. 1.16 : Opto isolator IRLED and LASCR

- In thyristor (SCR) based circuit, SCR is at line potential and trigger circuit must be referenced with respect to a logic ground associated with the control input. Therefore the zero crossing detection of a line voltage synchronization and gate pulse generated with gate trigger circuit must be isolated from the line potential by means of transformer. Delay for firing pulse can be varied over the range of 0° to 180°. Most commonly used triggering methods are :

(1) Resistance firing circuit.
(2) Resistance capacitance firing circuit.
(3) UJT based firing circuit.

1.4.5.1 Resistance Gate Trigger Circuit

- It is the simplest method of triggering the SCR. In this method, very few components are required. Trigger current is applied for complete duration of positive half cycle instead of pulse. So in this method pulse is not generated. The major drawback of this method is the firing angle α to $I_{g\,(min)}$ dependent. Again α can be varied in between 0° to 90° only. Because at 90°, source voltage is maximum. Therefore, source voltage waveform can only be varied from $\alpha = 0°$ to $\alpha = 90°$. Fig. 1.17 shows the circuit diagram for resistance triggering method of SCR. In this circuit, gate current is applied by an A.C. source through resistances R_{min}, R_v and diode D. R_v is the variable resistance to control the firing angle.

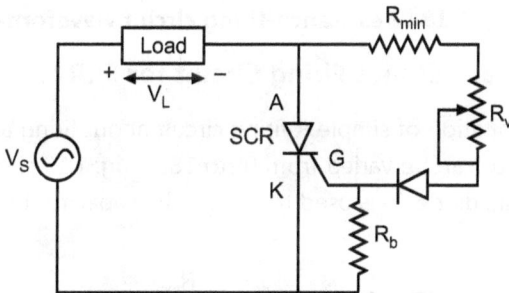

Fig. 1.17 : Resistance triggering circuit for SCR

- R_{min} is selected, such that peak gate current of SCR $I_{g\,max}$ is not exceeded, even when the supply voltage reaches to the maximum value V_{max}.

$$R_{min} \geq \frac{V_{max}}{I_{g\,max}} \quad \ldots (1.9)$$

- R_b is the stabilizing resistor. It is selected such that the maximum voltage drop across it does not exceed maximum possible gate voltage rating of SCR $V_{g\,max}$.

$$R_b \leq \frac{(R_v + R_{min})\,V_{g\,max}}{V_{max} - V_{g\,max}} \quad \ldots (1.10)$$

- SCR triggering occurs when input source voltage is positive and I_g is more than $I_{g\,min}$. Input source voltage at which SCR fires is V_s.

$$V_s = I_{g\,(min)}\,(R_v + R_{min}) + V_d + V_{g\,min}$$
$$V_d = \text{Voltage drop across the diode} \cong 0.6\,V$$
$$V_{g\,(min)} = \text{Gate voltage to trigger the SCR}$$

- After triggering of SCR it remains in 'ON' state till input voltage decreases to the point where the load current is below SCR holding current. Diode D is used in gate circuit to prevent the gate cathode reverse bias from exceeding peak reverse gate voltage during the negative half cycle. Fig. 1.18 shows the waveform for input AC voltage, voltage across the load and voltage across the SCR.

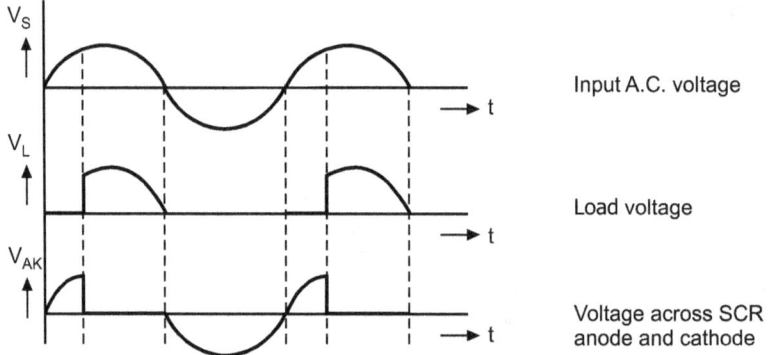

Fig. 1.18 : Resistance-firing circuit waveform

1.4.5.2 Resistance-Capacitance Firing Circuit for SCR

- To overcome the limitation of simple R firing circuit about firing angle, RC firing circuit is used. In this circuit, α can be varied from 0° to 180°. Fig. 1.19 shows the RC firing circuit for SCR. In this circuit, diode D_2 is used to charge the capacitor during negative half cycle to $-V_{max}$ level.

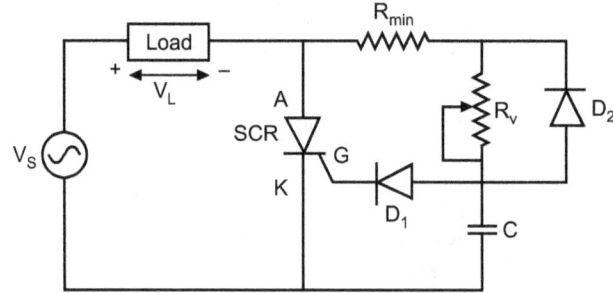

Fig. 1.19 : Resistance-capacitance firing circuit for SCR

- When supply voltage becomes positive, capacitor C begins to charge through $(R_{min} + R_v)$ from initial voltage $-V_{max}$ when voltage across the capacitor $V_C \geq V_{g\ min} + V_D$, SCR is triggered. Maximum value of $R_{min} + R_v$ depends on V_s, V_D, $V_{g\ min}$ and $I_{g\ min}$.

$$(R_{min} + R_v) \leq \frac{V_s - V_{g\ (min)} - V_{D_1}}{I_{g\ min}}$$

- R_{min} is used to limit I_g upto $I_{g\ max}$ value. Fig. 1.20 shows the waveforms of signal from source, capacitor voltage and load voltage.

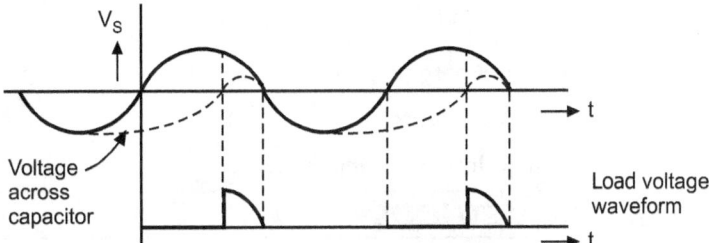

Fig. 1.20 : Resistance-capacitance firing waveform

1.4.5.3 UJT Firing Circuit for SCR

- In this circuit, UJT is operated in relaxation oscillator mode. This circuit facilitates 0° to 180° variation in the firing angle. Negative resistance property of UJT is used. For isolation, if required pulse transformer may be used. Fig. 1.21 shows the UJT firing circuit for SCR.

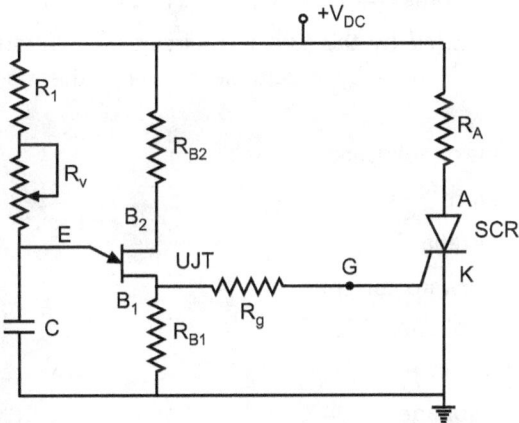

Fig. 1.21 : UJT relaxation oscillator as SCR triggers

- UJT is a switching device. For UJT the basic parameter is intrinsic stand off ratio η (etc.).

$$\eta = \frac{r_{b_1}}{r_{b_1} + r_{b_2}} \qquad \ldots (1.11)$$

r_{b_1} and r_{b_2} are internal resistances of UJT. Typical range of η is 0.5 to 0.8. When voltage across the capacitor C is more than peak point voltage of UJT, then UJT turns ON.

$$V_p = \eta\, V_{B_1, B_2} + V_D$$
$$= \eta\, V_{B_1 B_2} + 0.7 \qquad \ldots (1.12)$$
$$V_p = 0.7 \text{ for silicon}$$
$$V_{B_1 B_2} = \text{Voltage across the UJT}$$

Trigger pulse is obtained from UJT after T time duration.

$$T = (R_{min} + R_v) \; C \; \log_e \left(\frac{1}{1-\eta}\right) \qquad \ldots (1.13)$$

where $R_{min} + R_v$ = Charging path resistance

C = Capacitor

η = Intrinsic stand-off ratio

1.5 COMMUTATION METHODS

- SCR turn-OFF methods are called as commutation methods.
- The turn-OFF time T_{OFF} of the SCR may be defined as the minimum time interval between the instant the anode current becomes zero and the instant the device is capable of blocking the forward voltage. Turn-OFF time is a combination of the reverse recovery time (t_{rr}) and the gate recovery time (t_{gr}). Thyristor recovers the reverse blocking property during the reverse recovery time and forward blocking property during the gate recovery time. T_{off} for SCR BHt P61 is 150 µsec.
- The turn-OFF time provided by the turn-OFF circuit i.e. commutation circuit must be more than SCR turn-OFF time by a suitable margin, otherwise commutation failure occurs.
- Turn-OFF time depends on following factors :
  (1) Junction temperature.
  (2) Forward anode current.
  (3) Rate of decay of forward current.
  (4) Forward blocking voltage.
  (5) External gate impedance.
  (6) Positive gate bias voltage.
  (7) Peak reverse current.
  (8) Reverse voltage.
- The transition from ON to OFF state is called as turn-OFF or commutation. It can be achieved by
  1. Reducing the voltage applied to the thyristor making anode current fall below holding current.
  2. Reducing the current through thyristor below holding current value by increasing the load impedance.
  3. Applying a reverse voltage across anode and cathode of conducting thyristor and forcing the current to zero.

- The first method is called as natural commutation and is utilized for thyristor used in AC input circuits. No separate commutation circuit is required.
- The other two methods are forced commutation methods. These are used for thyristor operating on D.C. input system.

Types of Commutation Methods :

- Two main types of commutation methods are :
    - Natural commutation (Class F)
    - Forced commutation

Forced commutation method is further classified as

- Resonant commutation (Class A)
- Self commutation (Class B)
- Auxiliary commutation (Class C)
- Complementary commutation (Class D)
- External pulse commutation (Class E)

1.5.1 Class-A Commutation

- It is a current commutation method. Load resistance R_L and commutating components are as selected that their combination forms underdamped resonant circuit. It is suitable for high frequency operation i.e. above 1000 Hz. The d.c. excited voltage,

$$V = IR + L\frac{di}{dt} + \frac{1}{C}\int I\, dt \qquad \ldots (1.14)$$

- For series connection of load, L and C, the current reaches natural zero at $\omega_r t_0 = \pi$. So commutation of the thyristor takes place at $t = t_0$.

The ringing frequency, $\quad \omega_r = \dfrac{\pi}{\sqrt{\dfrac{1}{LC} - \dfrac{R^2}{4L^2}}}$

Class-A Commutation :

- This method of commutation is also called as resonant commutation. The commutation components L and C are connected in series with the load, thyristor and power supply. Fig. 1.22 shows the circuit for resonant commutation.

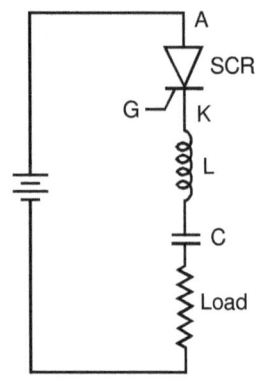
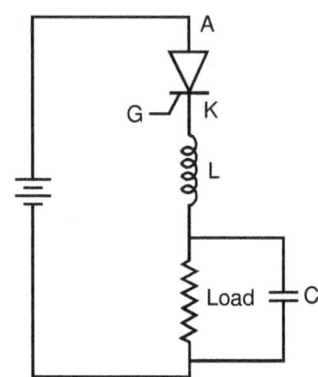

(a) Resonant commutation :
L and C connected in series with the load

(b) Resonant commutation :
C is connected in parallel with the load

Fig. 1.22

- In this method current through the SCR is reduced to natural zero due to L and C components.
- **Waveform :** Fig. 1.23 shows current waveform produced in class A commutation. When this current value is less than holding current, SCR commutates.

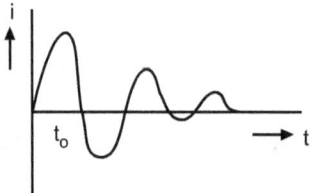
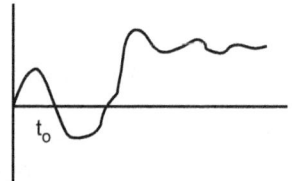

(a) Load in series with L and C   (b) Load in parallel with L and C

Fig. 1.23

1.5.2 Class-B Commutation

- This method of commutation is also called as self commutation. In this method also the thyristor is turned-OFF by the action of resonating LC circuit, but the commutation components L and C do not carry load current.

  Fig. 1.24 shows the circuit for self-commutation method. The time for which thyristor remains ON depends on L and C components.

- Initially the capacitor gets charged to the battery voltage with upper plate being positive. As soon as thyristor is turned ON, current flows through the SCR and load resistance R. Now capacitor starts discharging through the inductance and the thyristor.

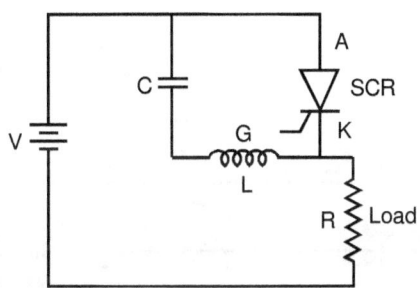

Fig. 1.24 : Class-B commutation

- After getting completely discharged, it starts getting charged in the opposite direction. The charging current reverses and this negative current opposes the load current. When the load current and the opposing capacitor current are equal, then thyristor is turned-OFF.
- In class-A commutation, commutation element carries load current, but that is not so in class-B commutation.
- The time for which thyristor remains ON depends on the value of L and C.

Capacitor current equation,

$$i_C = V\sqrt{\frac{C}{L}} \sin \frac{t}{\sqrt{LC}} \qquad \ldots (1.15)$$

Peak capacitor current,

$$i_{C_p} = V\sqrt{\frac{C}{L}} \qquad \ldots (1.16)$$

Capacitor voltage, $\quad V_C = V \cos \dfrac{t}{\sqrt{LC}} \qquad \ldots (1.17)$

$$t_{OFF} = \frac{\pi}{2}\sqrt{LC} \qquad \ldots (1.18)$$

- Fig. 1.25 shows current and voltage waveforms for the capacitor.

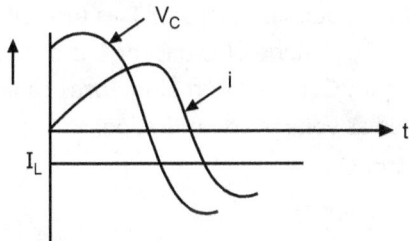

Fig. 1.25 : Capacitor current and voltage

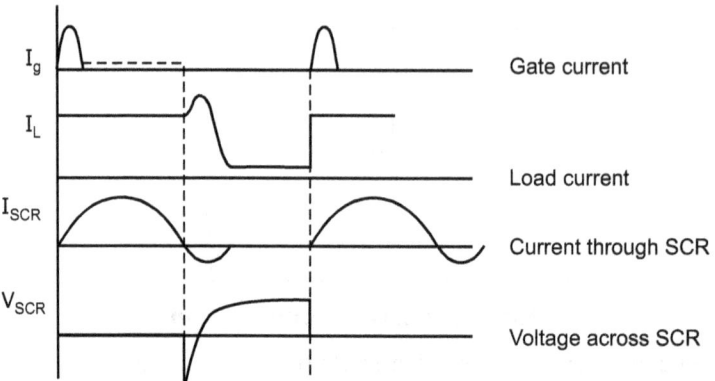

Fig. 1.26 : Class B commutation waveforms

1.5.3 Class-C Commutation

- This method of commutation is also called as auxiliary commutation. Commutation elements are inductor, capacitor and an auxiliary thyristor.

  Fig. 1.27 shows the circuit diagram for auxiliary commutation. In this circuit T_1 is main thyristor and T_2 is the auxiliary thyristor. It is a voltage commutation method.

- Initially when T_1 is ON, main current flows through T_1 and load capacitor gets charged due to current flowing through diode and inductor.

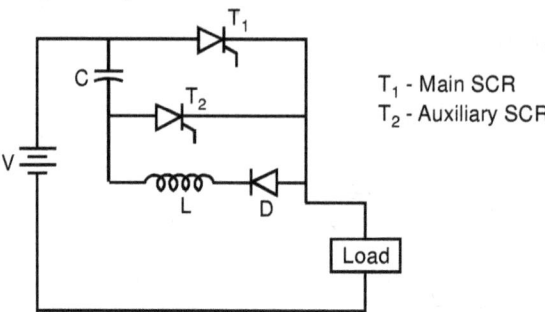

Fig. 1.27 : Auxiliary (voltage) commutation : Class-C commutation

- To turn-OFF main thyristor T_1, auxiliary thyristor T_2 is turn-ON by applying gate pulse. So capacitor C appears across T_1. Voltage of capacitor C is of opposite polarity. This reduces current though T_1 and T_1 turn OFF. As this method uses capacitor voltage to commutate the main SCR, so it is called as voltage commutation.

- Voltage across the capacitor C,

$$V_C = \frac{1}{C} \int_0^{t_{off}} I_L \, dt$$

$$C = \frac{I_L \, t_{off}}{V_C}$$

$$i_C = V\sqrt{\frac{C}{L}} \sin \frac{t}{\sqrt{LC}}$$

The peak capacitor current,

$$i_{C_p} = V\sqrt{\frac{C}{L}}$$

Also i_{C_p} should be less than maximum SCR current I_m,

$$V\sqrt{\frac{C}{L}} < I_m$$

$$L > \frac{V^2 C}{I_m^2} \qquad \ldots (1.19)$$

$$\therefore \quad C = \frac{I_L \, t_{off}}{V_C}$$

- Fig. 1.28 shows class-C commutation waveform at $gate_1$, $gate_2$ load current, SCR_1 voltage and capacitor current.

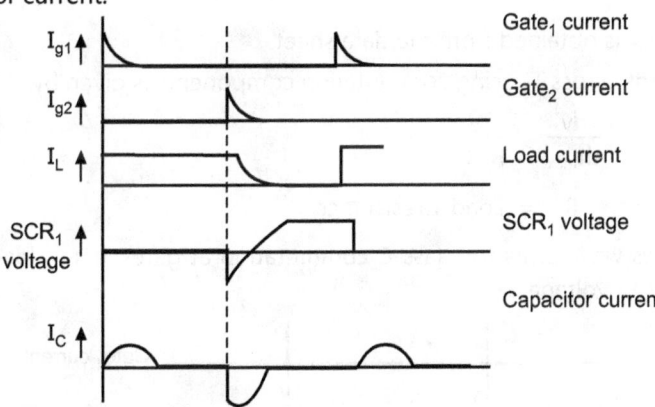

Fig. 1.28 : Class-C commutation waveforms

1.5.4 Class-D Commutation

- This method is also called as complementary commutation. The circuit consists of main thyristor T_1 and a complementary thyristor T_2 in parallel with T_1.
- Triggering of one thyristor turns-OFF other thyristor. Fig. 1.18 shows circuit diagram of complementary commutation method. When T_1 is turned-ON, current flows through load 1 and T_1.
- Also current flows through load 2, capacitor C and T_1. This current charges C with right side plate of the capacitor positive.

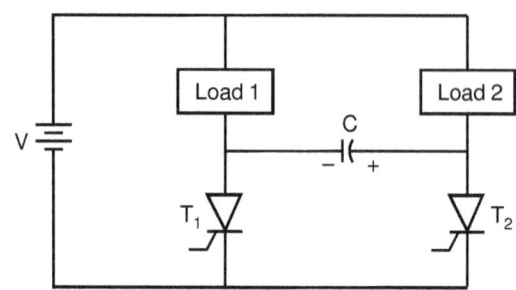

Fig. 1.29 : Class-D or Complementary Commutation

- When T_2 is turned-ON, the capacitor voltage appears as reverse bias across T_1 and turns it OFF. Now current flows through load 2 and T_2.
- In addition, current also flows from battery through load 1, capacitor and T_2. If T_1 is turned-ON by external gate pulse, then voltage across C appears in parallel with T_2 with opposite polarity. So T_2 turns-OFF. This method of commutation is used in the inverter.
- In this method, capacitor is selected using the formula,

$$C = 1.44 \frac{t_{off}}{R_{L_1}} \quad \ldots (1.20)$$

Main SCR T_1, t_{off} is obtained from the data sheet.

- Maximum dv/dt across T_1 using commutation components is given by,

$$\frac{dv}{dt_{max}} > \frac{2V}{R_{L_1}C} \quad \ldots (1.21)$$

where R_{L_1} = Load 1 resistance

- Fig. 1.30 shows waveforms for class-C commutation at $gate_1$, $gate_2$, $load_1$ current, SCR_1 current and SCR_1 voltage.

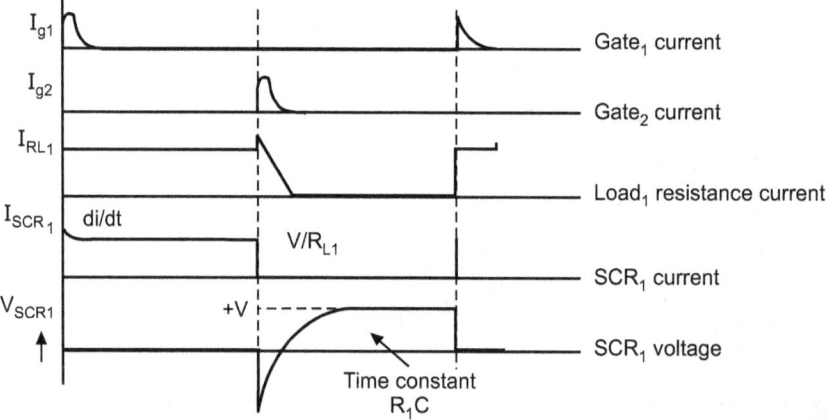

Fig. 1.30 : Class-D commutation waveforms

1.5.5 Class-E Commutation

- This method is also called as external pulse commutation.
- In this method, reverse voltage is applied to the current carrying thyristor from external pulse source.
- Pulse transformer is used to apply commutating pulse.
- Voltage at secondary of pulse transformer appears across thyristor T_1 as a reverse voltage and turns it OFF. Fig. 1.31 shows the circuit diagram for class-E commutation.

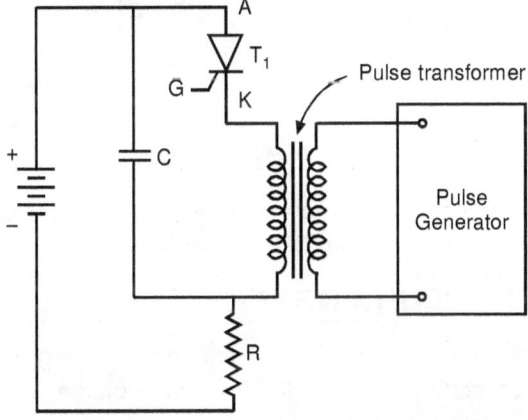

Fig. 1.31 : Class-E commutation method

- Pulse transformer provides tight coupling between primary and secondary. Pulse duration must be more than t_{off} rating of SCR. Applied pulse is of high frequency. For this method of commutation, efficiency is high as minimum energy is required.
- Fig. 1.32 shows the class-E commutation associated waveforms of SCR gate current, voltage across SCR, commutating pulse and SCR current.

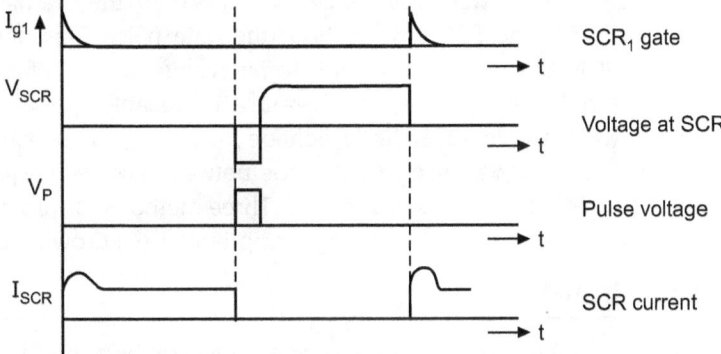

Fig. 1.32 : Class E-commutation waveforms

1.5.6 Class-F Commutation

- It is an A.C. line commutation method. If the supply is an alternating voltage, load current flows during the positive half cycle. During the negative half cycle, the SCR will turn-OFF. The duration of half cycle must be large as compared to turn-OFF time of SCR.

- Fig. 1.33 shows the circuit diagram of class-F commutation method. It is a natural commutation. It does not require any additional commutating element. This method is used in all controlled rectifier circuits.

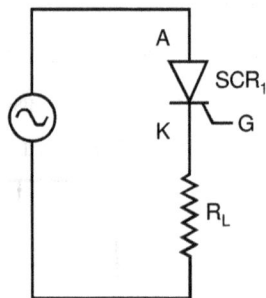

Fig. 1.33 : Class-F commutation

- Waveforms for this method of commutation are same as controlled rectifier waveform. Maximum frequency depends on turn OFF time of SCR.

1.6 PROTECTION CIRCUITS OF SCR

- In SCR circuit operation voltage over shunt may occur during turn OFF due to reverse recovery process of semiconductor devices, over-voltage also may occur due to inductive load. Over current may occur due to short circuit or mal operation in load of SCR circuit.

- For reliable operation of SCR circuits, suitable protection circuits are used with SCR against over voltage, over current, dv/dt, di/dt and thermal overshoot.

1.6.1 dv/dt Protection

- If the rate of application of forward voltage i.e. dv_{ak}/dt is high, the charging current i is large enough to turn ON the SCR even without the gate pulse. This phenomenon is called as dv/dt turn-ON. It is not desirable. It is to be avoided as it is a false turn ON of the SCR without controlling the gate signal. Therefore, for reliable operation of SCR, the rate of rise of forward anode to cathode voltage dv_{ak}/dt must be kept below the specified rated limit. Limiting values of dv/dt range between 20 – 500 V/μsec. To avoid false triggering due to dv/dt, R-C network is used. Three methods for protection against dv/dt are (i) Snubber circuit, (ii) Non-linear surge suppression, (iii) Crowbar protection.

1.6.2 Snubber Circuit

- Fig. 1.34 shows the snubber circuit. It consists of a series combination of resistor R and capacitor C placed in parallel with SCR.

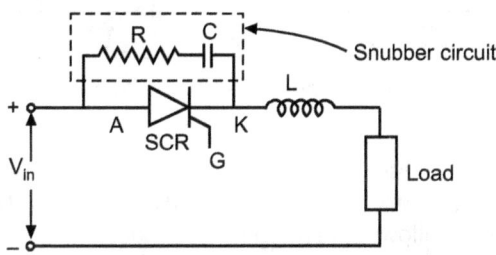

Fig. 1.34 : Snubber protection

- This snubber circuit protects SCR against turn ON dv/dt and reverse recovery transients. It also consists of inductor in series with SCR. It protects SCR against high di/dt. After sudden application of input voltage, voltage appears across SCR. Now, capacitor behaves like a short circuit and brings down the voltage across SCR to zero. Voltage across C increases slowly due to R. This rate of change of voltage is very less so avoids dv/dt turn ON.

- To limit the rate of change of discharging current of capacitor through SCR, a small value of resistance R is connected in series with capacitor and inductor L in series with SCR.

If R_L = Load resistance

$$R = 2\sqrt{\frac{L}{C}} - R_L \qquad \ldots (1.22)$$

$$L = \frac{V_{dc}}{(dt/dt)_{max}} \qquad \ldots (1.23)$$

For A.C. circuit,

$$R = 26\sqrt{\frac{L}{C}} \qquad \ldots (1.24)$$

$$C = \frac{1}{2L}\left(\frac{0.564\, V_{max}}{dv/dt}\right)^2 \qquad \ldots (1.25)$$

1.6.3 di/dt Protection

- The rate of rise of anode current at the time of turn ON is kept below the specified rating. When di/dt is very high the current may not spread uniformly and this will lead to the formation of local hot spots near gate-cathode junction due to high current density. This hot spot formation may damage the SCR. This di/dt protection is achieved by connecting a small inductor in series with the SCR. Typical value of di/dt ranges between 20-500 A/μsec.

1.7 SCR SPECIFICATIONS/RATINGS

- To get desirable, effective, reliable and efficient operation, SCR must be operated within specified rating.
- Thyristor rating denote voltage, current, power and temperature limit within which it can operate safely. It is the practice to select the device with rating higher than the required normal working values. It allows safe margin.
- Three types of rating are : continuous rating, repetitive rating and surge or non-repetitive rating.

1.7.1 Voltage Rating

- **Working Peak-OFF State Forward Voltage :** This is the maximum instantaneous value of the forward-OFF state voltage (V_{DWM}).
- **Repetitive Peak-OFF State Forward Voltage :** It is the peak transient voltage that a thyristor in the OFF state can block repeatedly in the forward direction (V_{DRM}).
- **Non-repetitive Peak-OFF State Forward Voltage :** This is the maximum instantaneous value of any non-repetitive transient-OFF state voltage that occurs across the thyristor (V_{DSM}). It is a surge rating.
- **Working Peak Reverse Voltage :** This is the maximum instantaneous value of the reverse voltage that occurs across the device excluding all repetitive and non-repetitive transient voltage (V_{RWM}).
- **Repetitive Peak Reverse Voltage :** This is the peak reverse transient voltage that may occur repeatedly in the reverse direction at the allowable maximum junction temperature. If this rating is exceeded, the SCR may be damaged (V_{RRM}).
- **Non-repetitive Peak Reverse Voltage :** This is the maximum transient reverse voltage which can be safely blocked by SCR. This rating can be increased by adding diode or another SCR in series (V_{RSM}). It is a surge rating.
- **ON State Voltage :** This is the voltage drop between anode and cathode with specified forward-ON state current and junction temperature. It is of the order of 1 V to 1.5 V (V_T).
- **Gate Trigger Voltage :** It is the minimum gate voltage required to produce the gate trigger current (V_{GT}).
- **Voltage Safety Factor :** The operating voltage and peak inverse voltage i.e. V_{RSM} values are related by voltage safety factor (V_j).

$$V_j = \frac{V_{RSM} \text{ (Peak reverse voltage)}}{\sqrt{2} \times \text{RMS value of input voltage}}$$

It is of the order of 2 to 2.5.

- $\dfrac{dv}{dt}$ **Rating :** The $\dfrac{dv}{dt}$ rating of SCR indicates the maximum rate of rise of anode voltage that will not trigger the SCR without any gate signal. If this rating exceeds, SCR switches to ON state from OFF state. Fig. 1.35 shows the voltage rating of SCR on the waveform.

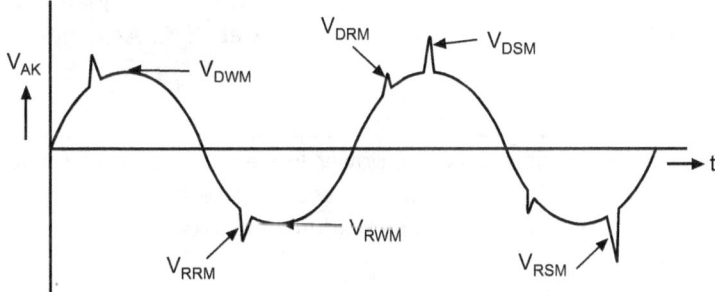

Fig. 1.35 : Voltage rating of SCR

[**Note :** The notation used for SCR rating has standard format. First letter may be V for voltage, I for current. Second letter D for forward blocking region with no gate current, T for ON state, R for reverse and F for forward. Third letter indicates W for working value, R for repetitive value, S for surge or non-repetitive value and T for trigger. The next letter M for maximum rating.]

1.7.2 Current Rating

- The various current ratings are

    (i) Average current rating, (ii) RMS current rating, (iii) Surge current rating.

    Average Current Rating : The average power loss varies with the average current of the SCR for different conduction angles.

    RMS Current Rating : The RMS current for different conduction angles remain same.

    Surge Current Rating : The surge current rating indicates the maximum possible non-repetitive or surge current, the device can withstand and this may occur due to non-repetitive faults, or short circuit during the life span of SCR.

    I²t Rating : I²t is the maximum allowable non-recurring value of the square of the instantaneous current integrated with respect to time.

    $\dfrac{di}{dt}$ **Rating :** The $\dfrac{di}{dt}$ rating of a SCR indicates the maximum rate of rise in anode to cathode current. The maximum rate of change of current that the device can withstand during its ON state is called its critical rate of rise of current.

Holding Current : The holding current may be defined as the minimum value of anode current below which the device stop conducting and returns to its 'OFF' state. For SCR BHt P61 holding corrent I_H = 150 mA at 25°C. Holding current value depends on operating temperature. As temperature increases, holding current value decreases.

Latching Current : The latching current of a device may be defined as the minimum ON state current required to keep the device in the ON state, after triggering pulse has been removed. For SCR BHt P61 latching current I_L = 1.0 A at 25°C. As temperature increases, latching current value decreases.

1.7.3 Power Rating

- During SCR operation various types of power losses occur such as forward conduction loss, turn-ON loss, turn-OFF loss, forward and reverse blocking loss and gate pulse triggering loss. For SCR BHt P61, maximum admissible gate power loss is 20 W.

1.7.4 Thermal Rating

- SCR is a semiconductor device. So thermal rating is essential to consider for reliable operation. Main thermal ratings are junction temperature and transient thermal resistance. For SCR BHt P61, maximum admissible continuous operating junction temperature is 140°C.

1.7.5 Heat Sink

- When current flows in a semiconductor junction, a small voltage drop occurs resulting in the conversion of some of the electrical energy into heat.
- Device failure occurs if this heat is not removed from the junction at a sufficient rate. For this purpose heat sink is used. The effectiveness of heat sink depends on following factors :
    1. Thermal conductivity of metals.
    2. Its surface area.
    3. Its surface condition.
    4. Thickness of the metal.
    5. Its orientation and situation.
    6. Attachment with case of device.
    7. Whether convection is free or forced.
- For high power SCR, liquid cooling and vapour phase cooling are used. Fig. 1.36 shows two types of heat sink.

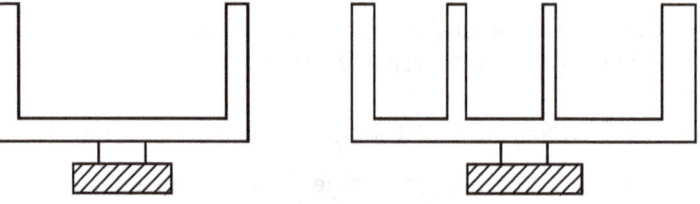

Fig. 1.36 : Types of heat sink

- At power frequency (50 Hz), the conduction or ON-state loss is usually the major component of power loss. Switching losses are small at power frequencies, but become large at high operating frequencies. These electrical losses produce thermal heat. This heat must be conducted away from the junction to prevent temperature rise. For normal operation, junction temperature is in the range of –25°C to 125°C for normal operation. The cooling of thyristor is essential. Heat sinks are usually provided with black anodized finish to enhance heat dissipation.
- The heat generated in a junction due to power loss takes the following path :

    Junction temperature → SCR case → Heat sink → Surrounding medium
- Mounting of SCR on heat sink depends on power rating of SCR. Five major mounting techniques are as follows :

    1. **Lead Mounting :** This technique is suitable upto 1 A current rating. This SCR does not require any additional cooling and heat sink. Its housing dissipates heat by radiation.
    2. **Stud Mounting :** It is suitable for small and medium size SCR. Copper or aluminium stud with machine thread is available with SCR. Stud size depends on current rating. It is used for providing mechanical, electrical and thermal contact to a heat sink.
    3. **Bolt Down Mounting :** It is also called as flat pack mounting. It is commonly used for small and medium rating SCR. The device has flanges or tabs which contain holes. Using bolt these SCRs are mounted on heat sink.
    4. **Press Fit Mounting :** It is used for large rating SCR. It is designed for normal insertion into a slightly larger heat sink.
    5. **Pressure Mounting :** The SCR is clamped under a very large external size heat sink. This mounting is used for very high current rating. These SCRs are also called as Huckey Puk SCRs because of their shape.

Table 1.3 : A typical specification sheet of SCR

• Type number	GE C38
• Rating	25 - 800 V
• Maximum RMS on-state current	35 A
• Maximum average on-state current at 180° conduction and case temperature 70°C	22.5 A
• Maximum peak non-repetitive one-cycle surge current	225 A
• Maximum I^2t for fusing for 5 - 8.3 msec.	100 A^2 sec
• Maximum rate of rise of on-state current	150 A/µsec
• Junction operating temperature range	– 65 to 125°C
• Minimum critical rate of rise of off-state voltage	20 V/µsec

1.8 SCR SELECTION FACTORS

Selection factors of heat sink for SCR are as follows :
1. SCR current rating.
2. SCR junction temperature rating.
3. Thermal conductivity of metals used for heat sink.
4. SCR casing (housing) structure.
5. Surface area of heat sink.
6. Surface condition of heat sink.
7. Thickness of metal used for heat sink.
8. Heat sink orientation and situation.
9. Attachment with case of SCR.
10. Whether heat convection is free or forced.

1.9 SCR TESTING

- A test of SCR function, or at least terminal identification, may be performed with an ohmmeter. Because the internal connection between gate and cathode is a single PN junction, a meter should indicate continuity between these terminals with the red test lead on the gate and the back test lead on the cathode as shown in Fig 1.37.

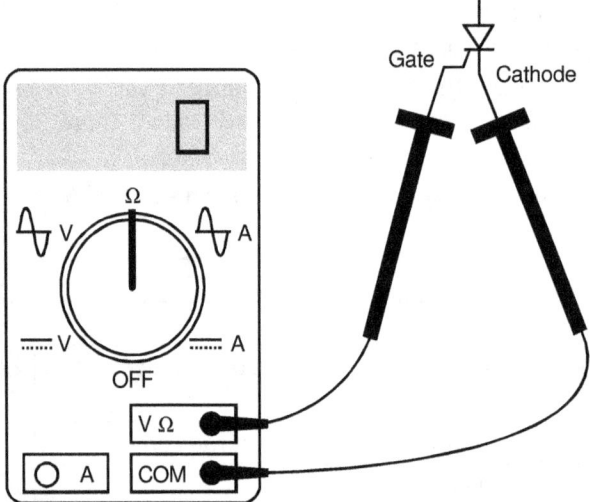

Fig. 1.37 : Testing of SCR using multimeter

- All other continuity measurements performed on an SCR will show "open" ("OL" on some digital multimeter displays).

- It must be understood that this test is very crude and does not constitute a comprehensive assessment of the SCR.

- It is possible for an SCR to give good ohmmeter indications and still be defective. Ultimately, the only way to test an SCR is to subject it to a load current.

- If you are using a multimeter with a "diode check" function, the gate-to-cathode junction voltage indication you get may or may not correspond to what is expected of a silicon P-N junction (approximately 0.7 volts).

- In some cases, we will read a much lower junction voltage, mere hundredths of a volt. This is due to an internal resistor connected between the gate and cathode incorporated within some SCRs. This resistor is added to make the SCR less susceptible to false triggering by spurious voltage spikes, from circuit "noise" or from static electric discharge. In other words, having a resistor connected across the gate-cathode junction requires that a strong triggering signal (substantial current) be applied to latch the SCR. This feature is often found in larger rating SCRs, not on small rating SCRs. Bear in mind that an SCR with an internal resistor connected between gate and cathode will indicate continuity in both directions between those two terminals.

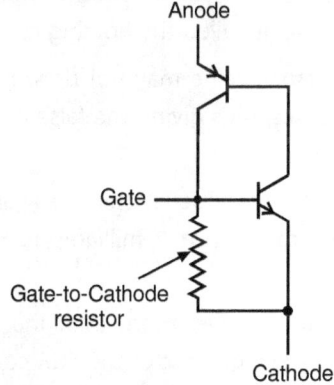

Fig. 1.38 : Gate-to-cathode resistor

- "Normal" SCRs, lacking this internal resistor, are sometimes referred to as sensitive gate SCRs due to their ability to be triggered by the small amplitude positive gate signal.

- The test circuit for an SCR is both practical as a diagnostic tool for checking suspected SCRs and also an excellent aid to understanding basic SCR operation.

- A D.C. voltage source is used for powering the circuit and two push-button switches are used to latch and unlatch the SCR, respectively.

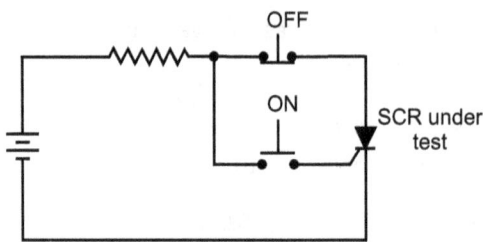

Fig. 1.39 : SCR testing circuit

- Actuating the normally-open "ON" push-button switch connects the gate to the anode, allowing current from the negative terminal of the battery, through the cathode-gate P-N junction, through the switch, through the load resistor, and back to the battery.

- This gate current should force the SCR to latch ON, allowing current to go directly from cathode to anode without further triggering through the gate.

- When the "ON" push-button is released, the load should remain energized.

- Pushing the normally-closed "OFF" push-button switch breaks the circuit, forcing current through the SCR to halt, thus forcing it to turn off (low-current dropout).

- If the SCR fails to latch, the problem may be with the load and not the SCR. There is a certain minimum amount of load current required to hold the SCR latched in the "ON" state. This minimum current level is called the holding current.

- A load with a too great resistance value may not draw enough current to keep an SCR latched when gate current ceases, thus giving the false impression of a bad (unlatchable) SCR in the test circuit.

- Holding current values for different SCRs should be available from the manufacturers. Typical holding current values range from 1 milliamp to 50 milliamps or more for larger units.

- For the test to be fully comprehensive, more than the triggering action needs to be tested. The forward breakover voltage limit of the SCR could be tested by increasing the DC voltage supply (with no push-buttons actuated) until the SCR latches all on its own.

- Beware that a breakover test may require very high voltage : many power SCRs have breakover voltage ratings of 600 volts or more. Also, if a pulse voltage generator is available, the critical rate of voltage rise for the SCR could be tested in the same way : subject it to pulsing supply voltages of different V/time rates with no push-button switches actuated and see when it latches.

- In this simple form, the SCR test circuit could work as a start/stop control circuit for a DC motor, lamp, or other practical load.

1.10 THYRISTOR FAMILY DEVICES

- Thyristor is a general name given to a family of power semiconductor switching devices. All these devices are of bistable switching action type. SCR is the most commonly used thyristor device.
- Two main types of thyristor devices are
- **Unidirectional Thyristor Devices :** These devices conduct only in one direction. Examples of unidirectional thyristors are SCR, LASCR, SCS (Silicon Controlled Switch), LASCS.
- **Bidirectional Thyristor Devices :** These type of thyristor devices conduct in both directions. Examples of bidirectional thyristor devices are DIAC, TRIAC, SBS (Silicon Bilateral Switch). Table 1.4 shows symbols and static V-I characteristics of various thyristor devices.

Table 1.4 : Power Electronic Devices

Device	Symbol	Static V-I characteristics
SCR (Silicon Controlled Rectifier)	(A, G, K symbol)	$V_G = V_2$, $V_G = V_1$, $V_G = 0V$; V_{Bo}, V_{Af}; $V_2 > V_1 > 0V$
DIAC	MT_1, MT_2	I vs +V characteristic
TRIAC	MT_1, Gate, MT_2	I_L vs $+V_{T_1T_2}$ characteristic

... Contd.

Device	Symbol	Characteristics
GTO	 A, G, K	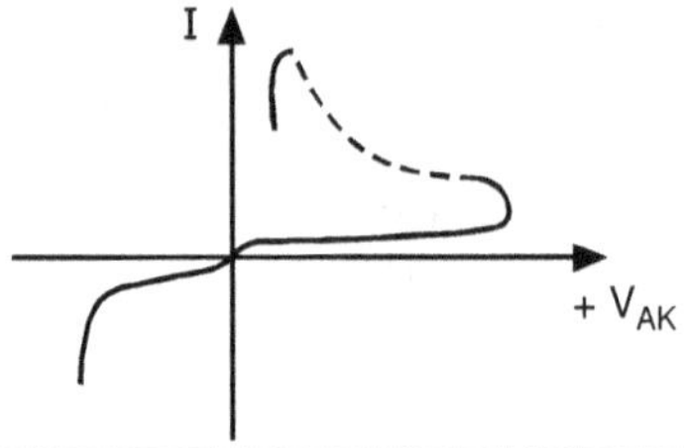 I vs $+V_{AK}$
IGBT (Insulated Gate Bipolar Transistor)	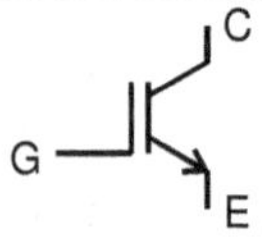 C, G, E	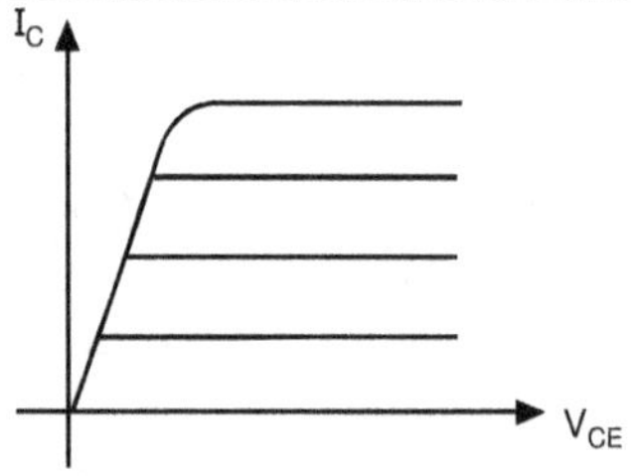 I_C vs V_{CE}
SUS (Silicon Unilateral Switch)	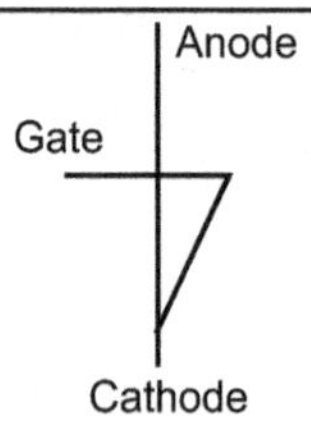 Anode, Gate, Cathode	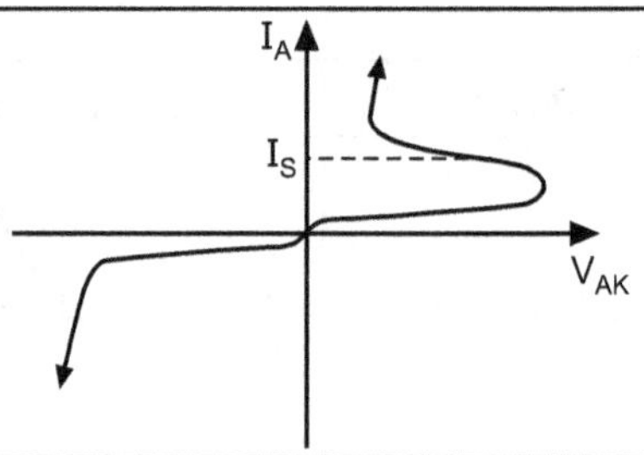 I_A, I_S vs V_{AK}
LASCR (Light Activated Silicon Controlled Rectifier)	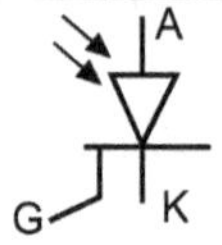 A, G, K	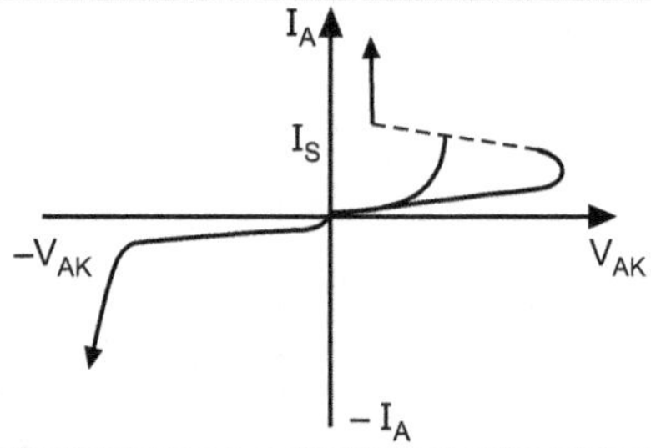 I_A, I_S vs V_{AK}, $-V_{AK}$, $-I_A$

- In addition to above thyristor devices, few more devices are thyristor family members, such as MCT (MOS controlled thyristor), Power MOSFET, Reverse conducting thyristor (RCT). Fig. 1.40 shows symbols for these thyristor devices.

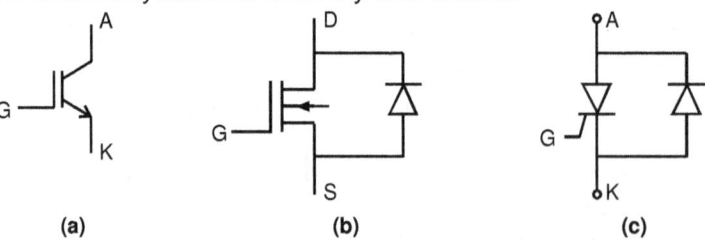

Fig. 1.40 : Symbol of (a) MCT, (b) Power MOSFET, (c) RCT

Table 1.5 shows maximum rating of presently available power electronic devices.

Table 1.5 : Maximum Rating of Power Electronic Devices

Device	Maximum voltage (V)	Maximum current (A)	Typical maximum frequency
1. Diode	5000 V	5000 A	1000 Hz
2. SCR	7000 V	5000 A	1000 Hz
3. TRIAC	1200 V	1000 A	500 Hz
4. LASCR	6000 V	3000 A	1000 Hz
5. RCT	2000 V	400 A	2000 Hz
6. GATT (Gate Assisted Turn-OFF Thyristor)	1500 V	200 A	3000 Hz
7. GTO	5000 V	3000 A	2000 Hz
8. Power Transistor	1400 V	400 A	10 kHz
9. MOSFET	500 V	30 A	1 MHz
10. Darlington BJT	500 V	500 A	5 kHz
11. IGBT	1000 V	50 A	50 kHz
12. JFET	600 V	60 A	10 kHz
13. MCT	1200 V	40 A	100 kHz

- Power transistor and SCR can be compared on various factors. Both transistor and SCR are semiconductor devices, but they differ in many ways as under.

Transistor	SCR (Thyristor)
1. Transistor is a three layer, two junction device.	1. SCR is a four layer, three junction device.
2. To keep transistor in the conduction state, a continuous base current is required.	2. Thyristor requires a pulse to make it conducting and thereafter it remains conducting.
3. When power BJT conducts, the forward voltage drop is of the order 0.3 V to 0.8 V.	3. The forward drop across the device is of the order of 1.2 V to 2 V.

... Contd.

4.	Lower voltage and current rating as compared to SCR.	4.	Thyristor with very high voltage and current rating are available.
5.	Power transistors have no surge rating and can withstand only a low rate of change of current.	5.	Thyristors have surge current rating and therefore can withstand high rate of change of current.
6.	Commutation circuit is not required.	6.	Commutation circuit is required.
7.	High frequency operation.	7.	Low frequency operation.
8.	Smaller size and less expensive.	8.	Larger size and more expensive.

APPLICATIONS OF VARIOUS THYRISTOR FAMILY DEVICES

SCR (Silicon Controlled Rectifier) :

1. Phase control
2. Power control
3. Inverter circuit
4. Chopper circuit
5. Temperature control
6. Motor speed control
7. Battery charger circuit
8. Relay control circuit

DIAC :

1. It is used for triggering of TRIAC.
2. It is used in light dimmer circuit.
3. It is used for heat control circuit.
4. It is used in fan speed regulator.

TRIAC :

1. It is used as static switch.
2. It is used for A.C. phase control.
3. It is used for light dimmer circuit.
4. It is used for heat control circuit.
5. It is used for fan speed regulator.
6. It is used in proximity detector.
7. Transformer tap charger.
8. Liquid level control.

IGBT (Insulated Gate Bipolar Transistor) :
1. DC and AC motor drives.
2. UPS.
3. Drives for solenoid, relays and contactors.

GTO (Gate Turn-Off Thyristor) :
1. UPS.
2. DC motor drive.

MCT (MOS Controlled Thyristor) :
1. Power switching device.
2. Medium and high rating motor control.

SUS (Silicon Unilateral Switch) :
1. Timing the logic circuit.
2. Trigger circuit.
3. Low rating trigger device.

PUT (Programmable Unijunction Transistor) :
1. Trigger circuit.
2. Sweep signal generation.

LASCR (Light Activated SCR) :
1. In HVDC transmission.
2. For isolation between trigger circuit and power circuit.
3. High rating power applications (4 kV with 1500 A).

SCS (Silicon Controlled Switch) :
1. Trigger circuit.
2. Pulse generation.
3. Voltage sensors.
4. Oscillators.

1.10.1 Insulated Gate Bipolar Transistor

- IGBT is a hybrid power switching device. It combines the fast acting feature and high power capability of the BJT with voltage control feature of the MOSFET gate. Collector-emitter characteristics of IGBT are similar to BJT but control features are those of the MOSFET. It is a voltage driven device with high input impedance. It does not show secondary breakdown phenomenon as that of MOSFET.

- Structure of IGBT consists of injection layer i.e. bipolar layer, buffer layer, drift layer, source layer.

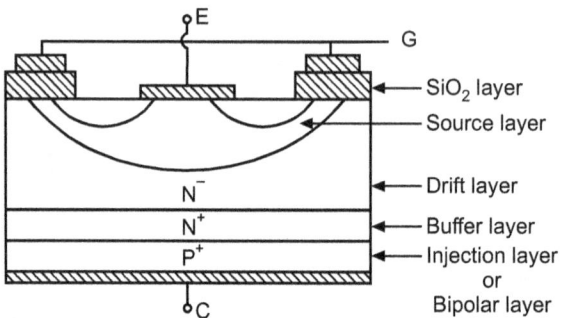

Fig. 1.41 : Structure of IGBT

- V-I characteristics of IGBT is a graph of V_{CC} and I_C. Fig. 1.42 shows V-I characteristics and transfer characteristics of IGBT.

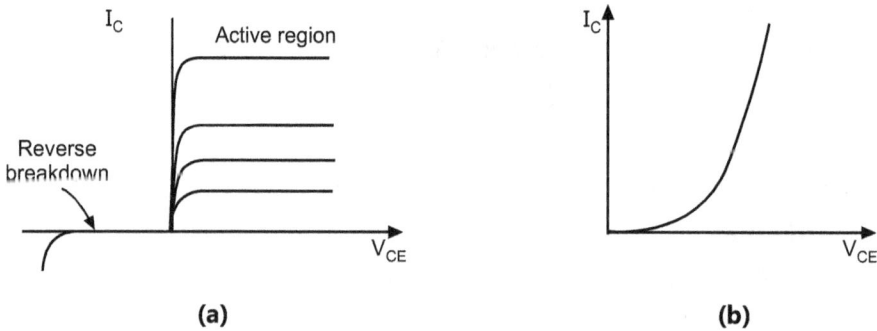

Fig. 1.42 : IGBT characteristics

1.10.2 Gate Turn OFF Thyristor (GTO)

- A GTO thyristor can be turned ON by a single pulse of positive gate current and it can be turned OFF by a pulse of negative gate current. Both ON-state and OFF-state operation of the device are controlled by the gate current. No extra commutation circuit is required. Latching current rating is higher than normal SCR. Switching losses are high. So GTO are restricted to operate below 1 kHz switching frequency. The power losses in gate drive circuit are also higher. But as no commutation circuit is essential, so overall efficiency is larger.

- Fig. 1.43 shows the structure of GTO. It consists of anode, cathode, gate with three junctions.

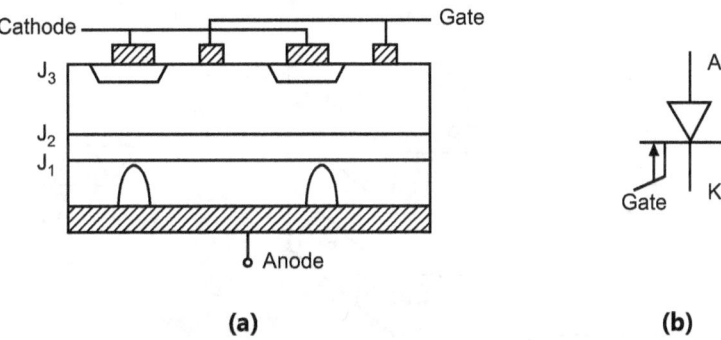

Fig. 1.43 : GTO structure and symbol

1.10.3 DIAC

- A DIAC is a five layer, four junction device. It has two electrodes MT_1 and MT_2. It can conduct in both directions. When applied voltage is more than breakover voltage, the device switches from high impedance state to low impedance state. The DIAC is used in the triggering circuit. It shows negative resistance region. It operates in relaxation mode over large frequency range. Fig. 1.44 shows the DIAC structure.

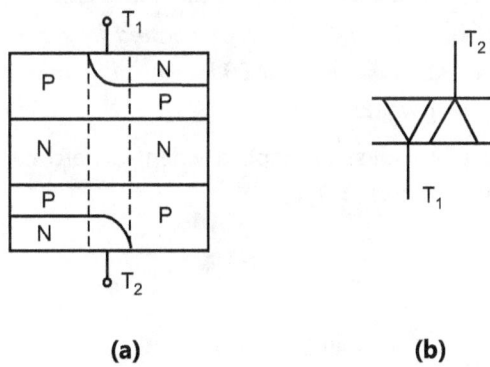

Fig. 1.44 : DIAC structure and symbol

1.10.4 TRIAC

- It is most widely used thyristor device. It is a bilateral device with three terminals MT_1, MT_2 and gate. TRIAC can be considered as antiparallel combination of SCR. Fig. 1.45 shows the cross-sectional view of TRIAC.

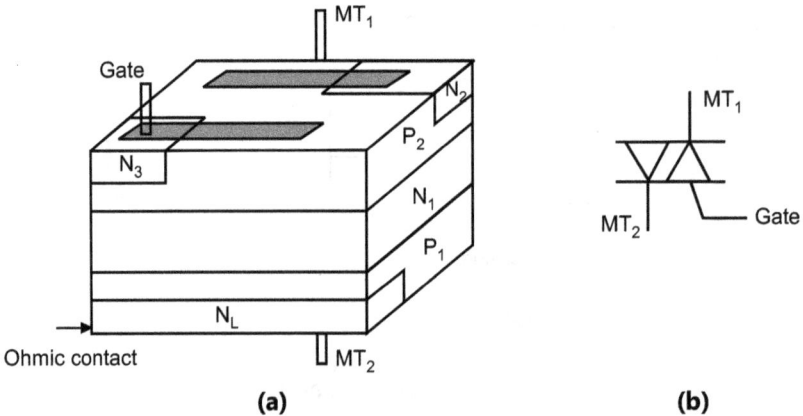

Fig. 1.45 : TRIAC structure and symbol

TRIAC shows four modes of operation :

Mode 1 : MT_2 positive w.r.t. MT_1, gate positive.

Mode 2 : MT_2 positive w.r.t. MT_1, gate negative.

Mode 3 : MT_2 negative w.r.t. MT_1, gate positive.

Mode 4 : MT_2 negative w.r.t. MT_1, gate negative.

SOLVED EXAMPLES

Example 1.1 : *If SCR is having I_L = 20 mA, operated in a phase control circuit having R = 10 Ω, L = 0.1 H, input voltage = 230 V at 50 Hz, calculate minimum gate pulse width for triggering of SCR. Assume firing angle α = 45°.*

Solution : The gate pulse must be applied when forward current of SCR reaches to I_L value i.e. 20 mA and pulse width $T_p > T_{ON}$.

Assume $\dfrac{di}{dt} = 0$

$\therefore \quad \dfrac{di}{dt} = \dfrac{\sqrt{2}\,V_s}{L} \sin \dfrac{\pi}{4}$ at t = 0

$\therefore \quad \Delta t = \dfrac{L\Delta I}{V_s} = \dfrac{0.1 \times 20 \times 10^{-3}}{230}$

$\quad\quad\quad = 8.6\ \mu sec$

Gate pulse width has to be greater than T_{ON} and 0.6 μsec.

Example 1.2 : *The voltage across the SCR is 1V when it is conducting. It has a holding current of 2 mA when I_G = 0. If the SCR is triggered ON by a pulse of gate current, calculate the value of V_s at which SCR turns OFF.*

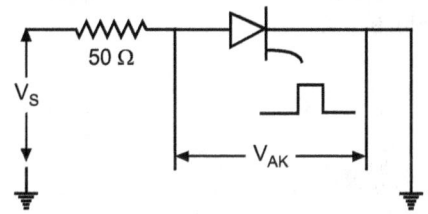

Fig. 1.46

Solution : According to KVL,

$$V_s - (I_{AK} \times 50) - V_{AK} = 0$$

$$\therefore \quad I_{AK} = \frac{V_s - 1}{50}$$

If I_{AK} falls below I_H the device turns OFF,

$$2 \times 10^{-3} = \frac{V_s - 1}{50}$$

$$\therefore \quad V_s = \mathbf{1.1\ V}$$

So when the input voltage is reduced below 1.1 V then SCR turns OFF.

Example 1.3 : *In a SCR circuit the initial rate of rise of current is 1000 A/sec. Calculate minimum duration of the gating pulse if I_L = 10 mA.*

Solution :

$$I_L = 10\ mA = 10 \times 10^{-3}$$

$$\frac{\Delta i}{\Delta t} = 1000\ A/sec$$

$$\left(\frac{\Delta i}{\Delta t}\right) t_p = I_L$$

$$\therefore \quad (1000\ A/sec)\ t_p = 10 \times 10^{-3}$$

$$\therefore \quad t_p = \frac{10 \times 10^{-3}}{1000} = \mathbf{10\ \mu sec}$$

$\therefore$ Gating pulse duration must be more than 10 μsec.

Example 1.4 : *The specification sheet for an SCR gives maximum RMS ON-state current as 50 A. If that SCR is used in a resistive circuit, calculation average ON state current rating for conduction angles 180°, 90° and 30° for sine wave half cycle.*

Solution : (i) For half cycle,

$$I_{av} = \frac{I_m}{2\pi}(1 + \cos\theta)$$

$$I_{rms} = \left[\frac{I_m^2}{2\pi}\left[\frac{\pi - \theta}{2} + \frac{1}{4}\sin 2\theta\right]\right]^{1/2}$$

(Chap. 1.49)

For 180° conduction angle, $\theta_1 = 0$.

$$\therefore \quad I_{av} = \frac{I_m}{\pi}$$

$$I_{rms} = \frac{I_m}{2}$$

$$\text{Form factor} = \frac{I_{rms}}{I_{av}} = \frac{I_m/2}{I_m/\pi} = \frac{\pi}{2}$$

$$I_{SCR} = \frac{I_{rms}}{PF} = \frac{50 \times 2}{\pi} = \mathbf{31.83 \ A}$$

(ii) For 90° conduction angle, $\theta = 90°$.

$$I_{av} = \frac{I_m}{2\pi}$$

$$I_{rms} = \frac{I_m}{2\sqrt{2}}$$

$$\text{Form factor} = \frac{I_{rms}}{I_{av}} = \frac{I_m/2\sqrt{2}}{I_m/2\pi} = \frac{\pi}{\sqrt{2}}$$

$$\therefore \quad I_{SCR} = \frac{I_{rms}}{PF} = \frac{50 \times \sqrt{2}}{\pi} = \mathbf{22.50 \ A}$$

(iii) For conduction angle of 30°, $\theta = 150°$.

$$I_{av} = \frac{I_m}{2\pi}[1 + (-0.866)] = 0.0213 \ I_m$$

$$I_{rms} = \left[\frac{I_m^2}{2\pi}\left\{\frac{\pi - (5\pi/6)}{2} + \frac{1}{4}(-0.866)\right\}\right]^{1/2} = 0.0849 \ I_m$$

$$\therefore \quad \text{Form factor} = \frac{0.0849 \ I_m}{0.0213 \ I_m} = 3.98$$

$$I_{SCR} = \frac{I_m}{3.98} = \frac{50}{3.98} = \mathbf{12.56 \ A}$$

Example 1.5 : *Design a UJT relaxation oscillator for triggering the SCR. The UJT has following parameters : $\eta = 0.72$, $I_p = 60 \ \mu A$, $V_v = 2.5 \ V$, $I_v = 4 \ mA$, $V = 15 \ V$, $R_{BA} = 5 \ k\Omega$, leakage current of 3 mA, triggering frequency is 1 kHz and $V_{q \ min} = 0.3 \ V$. Calculate $f_{i \ min}$ and $f_{i \ max}$.*

Solution : Assume C = 0.05 μF, Triggering frequency = 1 kHz.

∴ T = 1 msec, $T = \dfrac{1}{f}$.

∴ The value of R, $R = \dfrac{T}{C \ln\left(\dfrac{1}{1-\eta}\right)} = \dfrac{10^{-3}}{0.05 \times 10^{-6} \times \ln\left(\dfrac{1}{1-0.72}\right)}$

$= 15.71 \text{ k}\Omega$

Resistance in series base$_2$ i.e. R_2,

$$R_2 = \dfrac{10^4}{\eta V} = \dfrac{10^4}{0.72 \times 15} = 925.93 \text{ }\Omega$$

The minimum voltage across the gate when the UJT is OFF,

$$R_1 = \dfrac{V_{g\,(min)}}{\text{Leakage current}} = \dfrac{0.3}{3 \times 10^{-3}}$$

$= 100 \text{ }\Omega$

As $V_z = 0.6 \text{ V}$

$V_p = (0.72 \times 15) + 0.6 = 11.4 \text{ V}$

$R_{max} = \dfrac{15 - 11.4}{60 \times 10^{-6}} = 60 \text{ k}\Omega$

$R_{min} = \dfrac{15 - 2.5}{4 \times 10^{-3}} = 3.125 \text{ k}\Omega$

$f_{i\,max} = \dfrac{1}{T_{min}} = \dfrac{1}{R_{min} C \ln\left(\dfrac{1}{1-\eta}\right)}$

$= \dfrac{1}{3.125 \times 10^3 \times 0.05 \times 10^{-6} \ln\left(\dfrac{1}{1-0.72}\right)}$

$= \mathbf{5.03 \text{ kHz}}$

$f_{i\,min} = \dfrac{1}{T_{max}} = \dfrac{1}{R_{max} C \ln\left(\dfrac{1}{1-\eta}\right)}$

$= \dfrac{1}{60 \times 10^3 \times 0.05 \times 10^{-6} \ln\left(\dfrac{1}{1-0.72}\right)}$

$= \mathbf{261.86 \text{ Hz}}$

REVIEW QUESTIONS

1. Describe different modes of operation of a thyristor with the help of its static V-I characteristics.
2. Define the terms : Holding current, latching current and breakover voltage.
3. With the help of neat diagram, explain the two transistor analogy of an SCR.
4. Give the constructional details of SCR. Sketch its schematic diagram and its circuit symbol.
5. What is commutation ? List out types of commutation methods.
6. With neat circuit diagram explain :
   (a) Resonant commutation,
   (b) Self commutation,
   (c) Complementary commutation,
   (d) Auxiliary commutation,
   (e) External pulse commutation,
   (f) Natural commutation.
7. Compare forced commutation with natural commutation on the basis of input supply, circuit component requirement, applications.
8. Explain in brief various types of triggering methods of SCR. Which is the universal method ?
9. Sketch circuit diagram and explain synchronized UJT trigger circuit.
10. Draw the symbols of DIAC, SUS, PUT and IGBT. State one application of each.
11. Describe A.C. and D.C. gate control circuit of SCR.
12. List the factors required for selection of heat sink used for SCRs.
13. List any eight specifications of SCR.
14. Describe principle of forward voltage and light triggering methods of SCR.
15. Draw symbol and V-I characteristics of SCR and TRIAC.
16. Describe dv/dt and di/dt rating of SCR.
17. Describe the effect of gate current on forward breakover voltage of SCR.
18. List out various voltage and current ratings of SCR. State the meaning of working, repetitive and surge rating.
19. How to test SCR ?
20. Compare power transistors with thyristor.
21. Explain R, R-C triggering method for SCR.
22. Which type of protection circuits are required for SCR, hence explain them using circuit diagram ?
23. Explain constructional diagram of IGBT.

Chapter 2

LINE FREQUENCY CONTROLLED CONVERTER/RECTIFIER

Weightage of Marks = 16, Teaching Hours = 09

Contents

- Introduction
  - Necessity of converter
  - Principle of phase control
  - Concept of firing angle and conduction angle
  - Uncontrolled and controlled rectifier
  - Load types
  - Classification of converters
- Single-phase half controlled bridge rectifier
  - Resistive load
  - Resistive-inductive load
- Single-phase full controlled bridge rectifier
  - Resistive load
  - Resistive-inductive load
  - Comparison between half and full controlled bridge rectifier
- Three-phase half and full converter
  - Resistive load
  - Resistive-inductive load
- Effect of source inductance
  - Single-phase fully controlled rectifier
  - Three-phase fully controlled rectifier

Objectives

After learning this chapter, reader will be able to :
- State the necessity of converter.
- Know how phase control is done.
- Define and state significance of firing angle and conduction angle.
- Compare uncontrolled converter and controlled converter.
- Explain with waveform operation of 1φ half controlled bridge converter with resistive and R-L load.
- Explain with waveform operation of 1φ full controlled bridge converter with R and R-L load.
- Compare half controlled bridge converter with full controlled bridge converter.
- Explain with waveform 3φ half controlled converter with and RL load.
- Explain with waveform 3φ full controlled converter with R and RL load.
- State effect of source inductance in 1φ full controlled converter and in 3φ full controlled converter.

2.1 INTRODUCTION

Thyristors are commonly used for power conversion. A.C. to D.C. converters are also called as rectifiers or simply converters.

2.1.1 Necessity of Converter

- Converter takes A.C. supply as input and gives controllable D.C. voltage and power to D.C. load as output. Converter circuit has huge number of applications in industries, transportation, traction, power transmission and many more. A few important applications of converters are as follows :
  - Steel rolling mills
  - Electro-mechanical process
  - D.C. traction system
  - High voltage transmission
- The A.C. to D.C. converters are phase-controlled rectifiers. Basic features of converters are
  1. They use principle of phase control or phase angle control (PAC) to vary the output voltage.
  2. They are available in various circuit configurations.
  3. They operate from single-phase A.C. supply to three-phase A.C. supply.
  4. They use line commutation, so no need of separate commutation circuit.
  5. They use diode and SCRs.
  6. Trigger circuit provides trigger pulses at appropriate instant and control the operation of the converter.
  7. Converter circuit performance changes according to type of load and source impedance.

2.1.2 Principle of Phase Control

- Phase control is the process of rapid ON-OFF switching which connects A.C. supply to a load for a controlled function of each cycle. Phase control is done by power semiconductor device such as a thyristor.
- In input A.C. circuit, the SCR can be turned-ON by the gate at any angle with respect to the applied voltage. The firing angle is measured w.r.t. angle at which gate pulse is applied.
  Fig. 2.1 shows the circuit for half-wave uncontrolled, controlled rectifier and corresponding waveforms.
- Semiconductor diode conducts when anode-cathode voltage exceeds voltage (0.7 V for Si diode).
- If thyristor is used, conduction can be delayed by delaying the application of trigger pulse.
- For thyristor condition, anode to cathode voltage must be positive and trigger pulse must be present at gate.
- The application of trigger voltage at any desired instant during the period when thyristor is forward biased to control the magnitude of the D.C. output voltage is called phase control.

2.1.3 Concept of Firing Angle and Conduction Angle

- A firing angle is defined as the angle corresponding to the duration between the instant of triggering that gives the largest average voltage to the instant of triggering that gives any desired voltage.

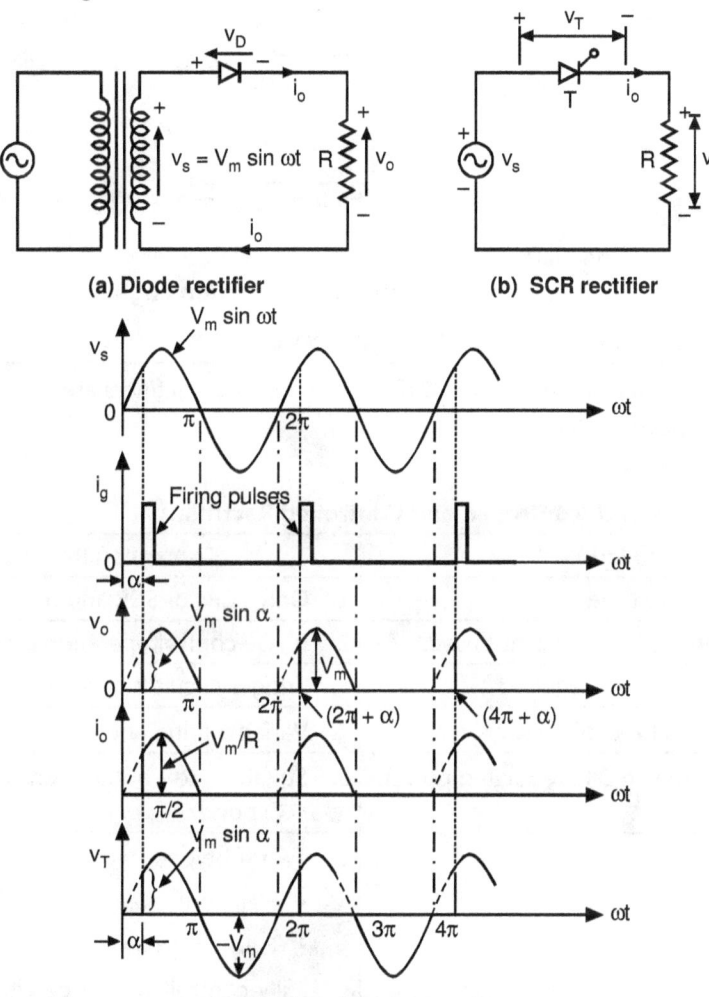

(a) Diode rectifier

(b) SCR rectifier

(c) Waveforms for SCR rectifier

Fig. 2.1 : Single-phase half-wave rectifier

- When thyristor is 'ON', load voltage is equal to supply voltage and load current equals to the supply current. Voltage across SCR becomes zero (ideal SCR).

- If firing angle is α, then current flows through the load for $\pi - \alpha$ angle. It is called as conduction angle.

- Conduction angle depends on firing angle and load angle. For resistive load, conduction angle is $\pi - \alpha$.

Fig. 2.2 indicates the firing angle α and conduction angle β for resistive load.

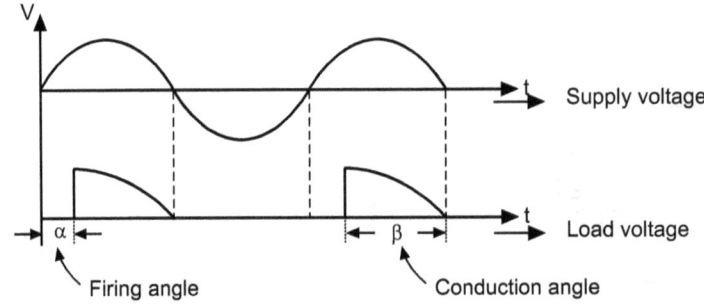

Fig. 2.2 : Firing angle and conduction angle

2.1.4 Uncontrolled and Controlled Rectifier

- Rectifier circuit converts A.C. into D.C. Two main types of rectifiers are :
  - Uncontrolled rectifier
  - Controlled rectifier

Comparison between Uncontrolled and Controlled Rectifier :

Uncontrolled Rectifier	Controlled Rectifier
1. Only diodes are used.	1. Only SCRs or SCR and diodes are used.
2. Phase control operation is not used.	2. Phase control operation is used.
3. Trigger circuit is not required.	3. Trigger circuit is required.
4. Firing angle is fixed and always zero.	4. Variable firing angle.
5. Suitable to obtain D.C. regulated power.	5. Suitable to obtain phase controlled D.C. power.
6. Two subtypes : • Half wave • Full wave	6. Two subtypes : • Half controlled • Fully controlled Fully controlled may be either half wave or full wave type.
7. It is used at low power rating.	7. It is used at medium and high power rating.
8. Filter circuit is used at the output.	8. Filter circuit is not used.
9. Application : D.C. power supply for constant D.C. supply requirement.	9. Applications : D.C. motor speed control, D.C. traction system, heating control.

2.1.5 Load Types

- Controlled rectifiers are used to drive or operate resistive, inductive and capacitive load.

Resistive Load :

- For resistive load, current and voltage are in phase. Load current and load voltage have same waveform.
- The load voltage will vary with the variation of firing angle and become maximum at $\alpha = 0$ (α = firing angle) and minimum when $\alpha = \pi$. The SCR and load average current are same. The r.m.s. current through the transformer secondary is the same as that of the load r.m.s. current.

Resistive-Inductive (RL) Load :

- For RL load, current and voltage are no longer in phase. Current waveform does not have same waveform as load voltage waveform.
- Average load voltage decreases as load power factor decreases.
- During inductive load, current increases gradually. Load voltage reverses, but SCR remains in conduction as current through the inductance cannot be reduced to zero.
- To overcome drawback due to inductive load, diode is connected across the load. It is called as free-wheel or fly-wheel or bypass diode. Two main functions of flywheel diode are :
  - It prevents reversal of load voltage.
  - It transfers the load current away from main rectifier, thereby allowing all of its thyristor to regain their blocking state.
- Due to this diode, load voltage never reverses. After 180° current will freewheel through the diode.
- Freewheel diode improves the input power factor.

Resistance-Inductance :

- E.m.f. load (RLE). In RLE load, E may be battery voltage or back e.m.f. of D.C. motor. Load current becomes pulsating due to presence of e.m.f. E.

2.1.6 Classification of Controlled Converters

(A) The phase controlled converters can be classified according to number of phases :
  1. Single phase converter
  2. Three phase converter : Converter circuit of output greater than a few kW are generally fed from three phase system.

Three phase system has following advantages :

- The three phase power supply is loaded uniformly.
- The harmonic content of the D.C. output of three phase converter is lower.

(B) Controlled converters can be classified based on the number of output voltage pulses per cycle.
   1. Single-pulse converter
   2. Two pulse converter
   3. Three pulse converter
   4. Six pulse converter
(C) Controlled converters can also be classified based on circuit configuration :
   1. Mid-point type converter
      (a) Single phase [Fig. 2.3 (a)]
      (b) Three phase [Fig. 2.3 (b)]
   2. Bridge type converter
      (a) Single phase [Fig. 2.3 (c)]
      (b) Three phase [Fig. 2.3 (d)]

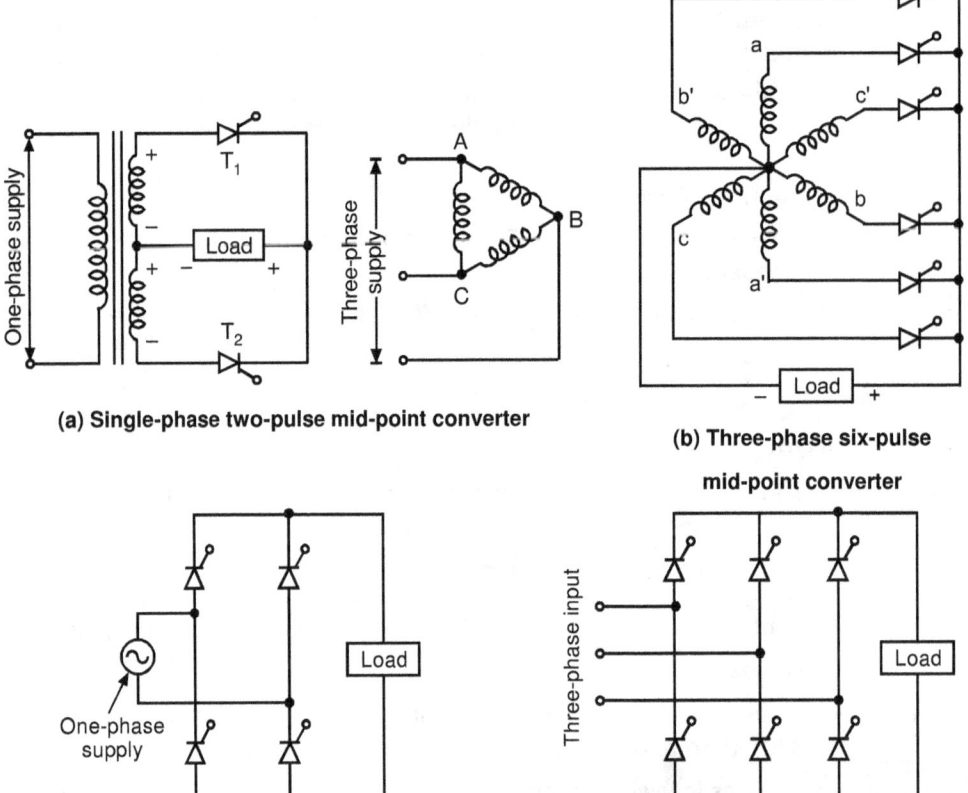

(a) Single-phase two-pulse mid-point converter

(b) Three-phase six-pulse mid-point converter

(c) Single-phase two-pulse bridge converter

(d) Three-phase six-pulse bridge converter

Fig. 2.3 : Converters

(D) Converters are also classified based on the mode of operation :

    (a) **Single quadrant operation** : Output voltage cannot be made negative with a given polarity of the output current.

    [**Note** : Quadrant operation of converter relates to output voltage either positive or negative with a given polarity of output current.]

    (b) **Two quadrant converter** : If the output voltage can be made either positive or negative with a given polarity of the output current, converter system is known as a two quadrant converter.

    (c) **Four quadrant converter** : Both output voltage and output current can be either positive or negative.

Table 2.1 shows circuits and quadrant operation of all types of single-phase converters.

Table 2.1 : Single-phase thyristor phase controlled converter circuits

Circuit	Type	Typical kW	Ripple frequency	Quadrant operation
(Half wave circuit with T_1, D_f, V_{dc}, Vf_s)	Half wave	Below 500 W	f_s	(First quadrant V_{dc} vs i_{dc})
(Semi-converter circuit with T_1, T_3, D_4, D_2, D_f)	Semi-converter full wave	Upto 15 kW (75 kW in traction systems)	$2f_s$	(First quadrant V_{dc} vs i_{dc})
(Centre tap circuit with T_1, T_2, V, f_s, LOAD)	Centre tap (two pulse mid point) full wave	Upto 15 kW	$2f_s$	(First quadrant V_{dc} vs i_{dc})

... Contd.

Circuit	Type	Typical kW	Ripple frequency	Quadrant operation
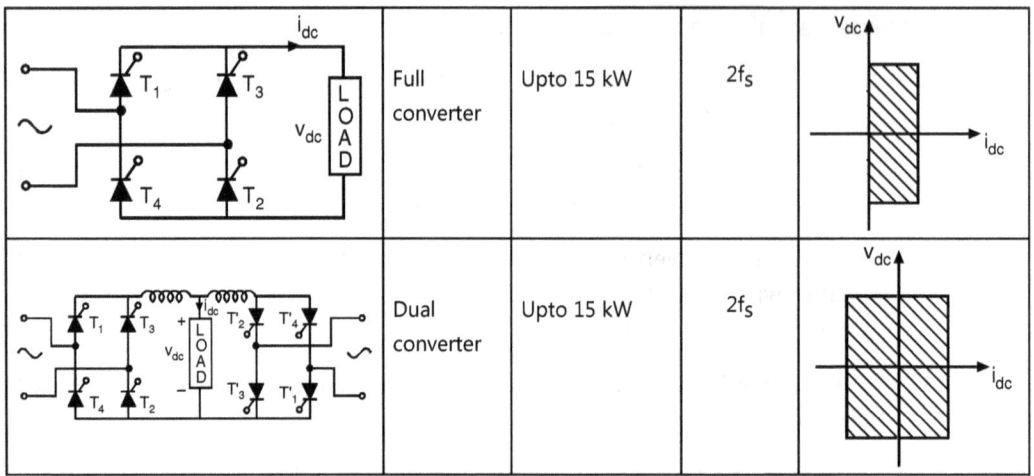	Full converter	Upto 15 kW	$2f_S$	
	Dual converter	Upto 15 kW	$2f_S$	

(E) Based on the control over output voltage, converters are classified as :
    1. Half-wave controlled rectifier
    2. Full-wave controlled rectifier

(F) Converters can also be classified as
    1. Semi converter : Half of the devices in bridge configuration are diodes.
    2. Full converter
    3. Dual converter

Table 2.2 shows circuits and quadrant operation of all types of three phase converters.

Table 2.2 : Three-phase thyristor phase controlled converter circuits

Circuit	Type	Typical kW	Ripple frequency	Quadrant operation
	Half wave	7.5 – 35 kW	$3f_S$	
	Semi-converter	Upto 120 kW	$3f_S$	

... Contd.

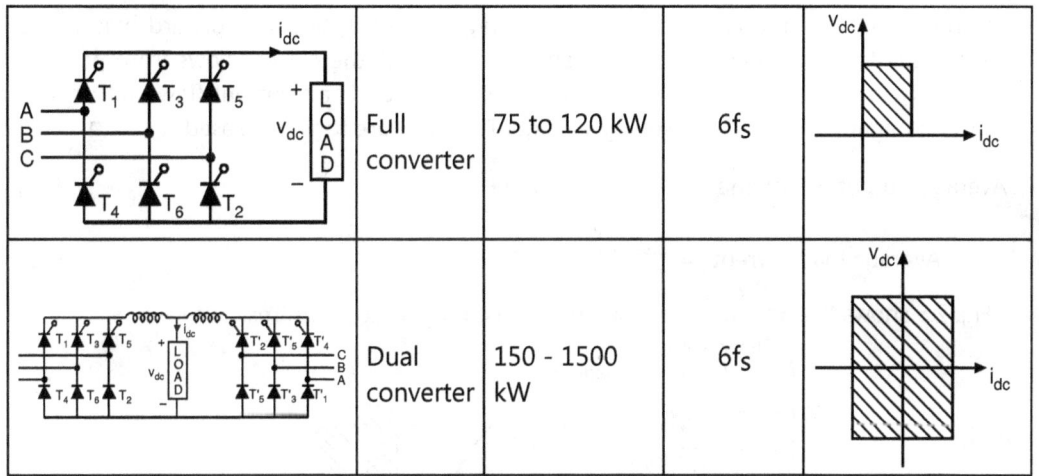

Full converter	75 to 120 kW	6f$_s$	
Dual converter	150 - 1500 kW	6f$_s$	

- A full converter permits power flow from A.C. to D.C. and from D.C. to A.C. i.e. it can work as rectifier as well as inverter. Semi-converter permits power flow from A.C. to D.C. as a rectifier.

- Dual converters are back to back connection of full converters. These are used in high power variable speed drive.

2.2 SINGLE-PHASE HALF CONTROLLED BRIDGE RECTIFIER

- In bridge converter if two SCRs are replaced by two diodes then the circuit becomes half controlled bridge converter. This circuit shows only one quadrant operation.

- Two possible configurations for half controlled bridge converter are (a) symmetrical configuration, (b) asymmetrical configuration. Fig. 2.4 shows the circuit diagram of symmetrical half controlled bridge converter. In this circuit, cathodes of two SCRs are at same potential. Hence in both SCRs, gate pulse can be fed from one trigger circuit. The SCR which is forward biased at the instant of firing will turn ON.

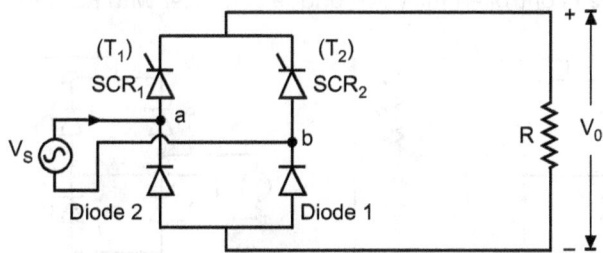

Fig. 2.4 : Symmetrical configuration of half controlled bridge converter with resistive load

- During positive half cycle of supply voltage (V_s), T_1 and D_1 become forward biased and are in the forward blocking state. When T_1 is triggered, the current flows from point 'a' to T_1, T_1 to load R then through diode D_1 to point 'b'. Load current flows till $\omega t = \pi$. During negative half cycle of supply voltage, T_2 and D_2 are forward biased.

$$\text{Average output dc voltage} = \frac{V_m}{\pi}(1 + \cos\alpha) \qquad \ldots (2.1)$$

$$\text{Average load current} = \frac{V_m}{\pi R}(1 + \cos\alpha) \qquad \ldots (2.2)$$

Fig. 2.5 shows the waveforms for symmetrical configuration with resistive load.

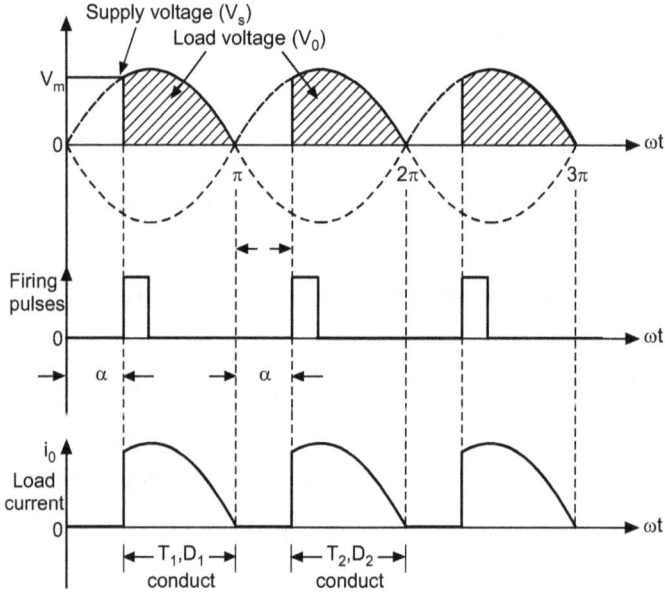

Fig. 2.5

- In asymmetrical configuration, separate trigger circuits are used for SCRs.

Fig. 2.6 shows half controlled full wave bridge converter with RL load.

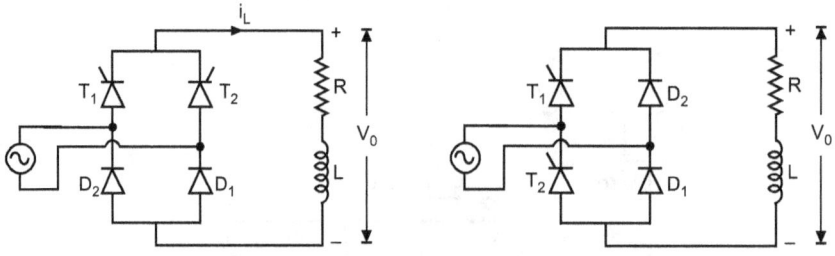

(a) Symmetrical configuration   (b) Asymmetrical configuration

Fig. 2.6 : Half controlled full wave bridge converter

- With RL load, if value of L is large then it gives continuous load current. In both these circuits line commutation occurs. Waveforms are similar to that of fully controlled converter with RL load. For circuit of Fig. 2.6 (a), conduction period of thyristors and diode is equal, so this circuit is called as symmetrical configuration.
- Fig. 2.6 (b) shows asymmetrical configuration. During positive half cycle of the supply, T_1 and D_1 are forward biased. SCR T_1 is triggered at angle α. During negative half cycle, T_2 and T_2 conduct from $\pi + \alpha$ to 2π. The free wheeling action is provided by D_1 and D_2 from 0 to α and π to $\pi + \alpha$. As the conduction period of the SCRs and diodes are unequal, the converter is called as asymmetrical converter.

Advantages of Half controlled Full wave converter : • Improved power factor.
- Cost is reduced as 2 SCRs are replaced by two diodes.
- More output power.

Disadvantages : • It can be operated only in rectification mode.
- Energy feedback from load to source is not possible.

Fig. 2.7 shows the waveforms for RL load operated by (a) symmetrical configuration, (b) asymmetrical configuration.

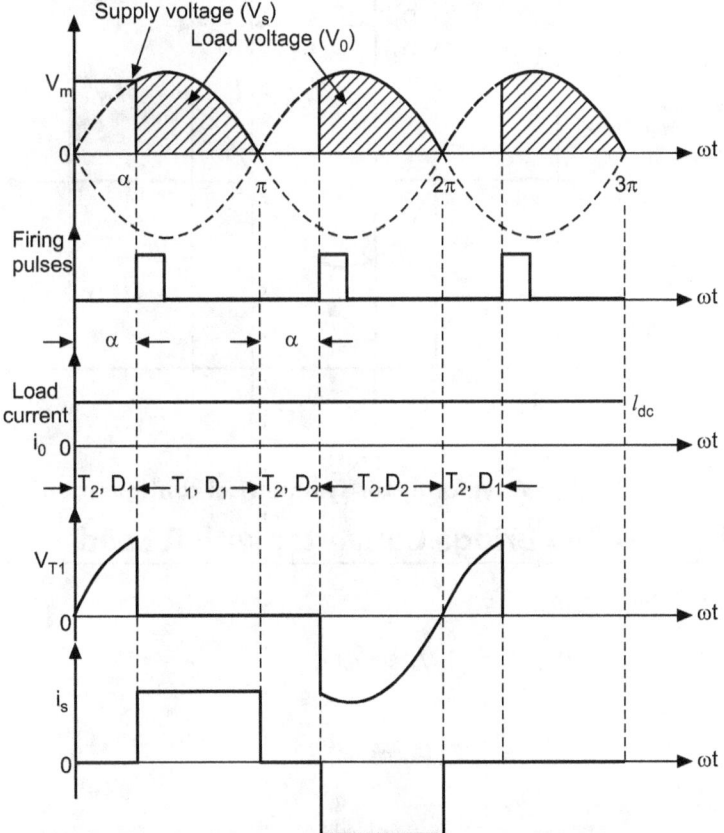

Fig. 2.7 (a) : Waveforms for symmetrical configuration

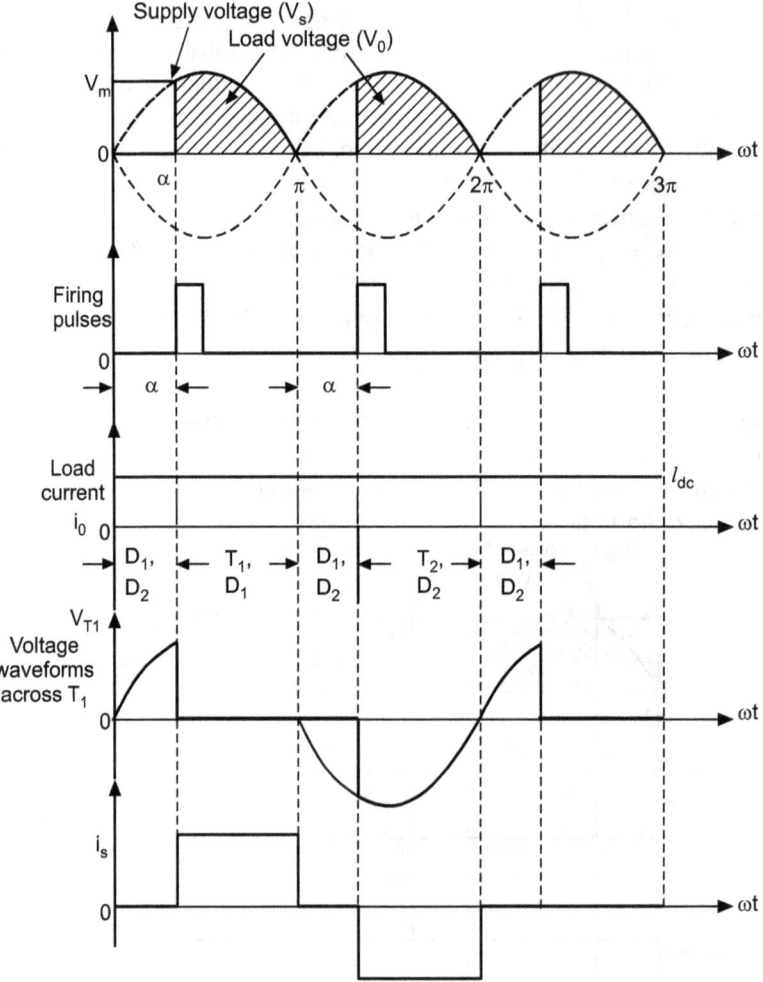

Fig. 2.7 (b) : Waveforms for symmetrical configuration

2.2.1 Half Controlled Bridge Converter with R Load

- Average d.c. load voltage,

$$V_{dc} = \frac{1}{\pi} \int_0^\pi V_m \sin \omega t \, d(\omega t)$$

$$= \frac{1}{\pi} V_m [-\cos \omega t]_0^\pi$$

$$= \frac{V_m}{\pi} [1 + \cos \alpha] \qquad \ldots (2.3)$$

- Average load current,

$$I_{dc} = \frac{V_m}{\pi \cdot R}[1 + \cos \alpha] \qquad \ldots (2.4)$$

- RMS load voltage

For firing angle α,

$$V_{rms} = \left[\frac{V_{dc}^2}{\pi} \int_0^\pi \sin^2(\omega t)\, d(\omega t)\right]^{1/2}$$

$$= V_m \left[\frac{1}{\pi} \int_0^\pi \left(\frac{1 - \cos 2\omega t}{2}\right) d(\omega t)\right]^{1/2}$$

$$= V_m \left[\frac{1}{2\pi}\left(\omega t - \frac{\sin 2\omega t}{2}\right)\right]_0^{\pi\;1/2}$$

$$= V_m \left[\frac{\pi - \alpha}{2\pi} - \frac{\sin 2\alpha}{4\pi}\right]^{1/2} \qquad \ldots (2.5)$$

- Input signal consists of fundamental components along with superimposed harmonic components. Therefore depending on the load current waveform, phase difference between input voltage and current may be introduced by the controlled rectifier. So it changes the power factor.

- **Active power input (P_i)**: Only the fundamental component in series of input current contributes to the mean a.c. input power and the mean power as the harmonic component of current is zero.

The mean A.C. input power is given by,

$$P_i = \text{RMS line voltage} \times \text{RMS fundamental component of current} \times \text{Displacement factor}$$

$$= V_{rms} \times I_i \times \cos \alpha$$

$$= V_{rms} \times \frac{2\sqrt{2}\, I_d}{\pi} \cos \alpha$$

$$= \frac{2V_m}{\pi} I_d \cos \alpha \qquad \ldots (2.6)$$

- Reactive power input (Q_i),

$$Q_i = V_{rms} \cdot I_f \sin \alpha = \frac{2V_m}{\pi} I_d \sin \alpha \qquad \ldots (2.7)$$

- **Current distortion factor :** The distortion factor of the current in a given input line is defined as the ratio of the RMS amplitude of the fundamental component to the total RMS amplitude.

Therefore, input current distortion factor $= \dfrac{I_i}{I_{rms}} = \dfrac{2\sqrt{2}\, I_d}{\pi\, I_d} = \dfrac{2\sqrt{2}}{\pi}$ ... (2.8)

- **Displacement angle (ϕ_1) :** It is defined as the angular displacement between fundamental component of A.C. line current and the associated line to the neutral voltage. In controlled rectifier the fundamental component is either in phase or lags behind the voltage by an angle depending on the firing angle.

Input displacement factor is the cosine of input displacement angle.

$$\text{DSF} = \cos\alpha \qquad \qquad \ldots (2.9)$$

- **Input power factor :** It is defined as the ratio of the total mean input power to the total RMS input VA (apparent) power.

$$PF = \dfrac{V_i\, I_i \cos\phi_i}{V_{rms}\, I_{rms}} = \dfrac{I_i}{I_{rms}} \cos\phi_i$$

where
- $V_i = V_{rms} =$ Phase voltage
- $I_i =$ Fundamental component of the supply current
- $\phi_i =$ Input displacement angle
- $I_{rms} =$ Supply RMS current

For controlled converter

Input power factor (PF),

$$PF = \left(\dfrac{I_i}{I_{rms}}\right) \cos\phi$$

$$= \left[\dfrac{\dfrac{2\sqrt{2}\, I_d}{\pi}}{I_d}\right] \cos\alpha$$

$$= \dfrac{2\sqrt{2}}{\pi} \cos\alpha \qquad \qquad \ldots (2.10)$$

- **Ripple factor :** Two different ripple factors are voltage ripple factor and current ripple factor.
- **Voltage ripple factor :** It is a ratio of the net harmonic content of the output voltage to the average output voltage,

$$K_v = \dfrac{\sqrt{V_{dc\,rms}^2 - V_{dc}^2}}{V_{dc}}$$

(Chap. 2.14)

For controlled converter,

$$K_v = \frac{\left[\frac{V_m^2}{2} - \left(\frac{2V_m}{\pi}\cos\alpha\right)^2\right]^{1/2}}{\frac{2V_m}{\pi}\cos\alpha}$$

$$= \frac{V_m\left[\frac{1}{2} - \frac{4}{\pi}\cos^2\alpha\right]^{1/2}}{2V_m\cos\frac{\alpha}{\pi}}$$

$$= \frac{\pi\left[\frac{1}{2} - \frac{4}{\pi}\cos^2\alpha\right]^{1/2}}{2\cos\alpha}$$

$$= \frac{\pi\left[\frac{\pi^2 - 8\cos^2\alpha}{2\pi^2}\right]^{1/2}}{2\cos\alpha}$$

$$= \left[\frac{\pi^2 - 8\cos^2\alpha}{2\cos^2\alpha}\right]^{1/2}$$

$$\therefore \quad K_v = \left[\frac{\pi^2}{8\cos^2\alpha} - 1\right]^{1/2} \quad \ldots (2.11)$$

- **Current ripple factor (K_i)** : It is defined as the ratio of the net harmonic content of the output voltage to the average output current.

$$K_i = \frac{\sqrt{I_{d\,rms}^2 - I_d^2}}{I_d}$$

where I_d = Average value of output current

$I_{d\,rms}$ = RMS value of output current

K_i can be defined in terms of form factor,

$$K_i = \frac{\text{rms value of output ripple current}}{\text{dc output current}}$$

$$= \sqrt{FF_i^2 - 1} = \frac{\sqrt{I^2R - I_d^2}}{I_d} \times 100\%$$

where FF_i = Form factor of output current

I_R = RMS value of output current

I_d = Average value of output current

Ideal value of K_i = 0

- **Form factor :** This is a measure of the shape of output voltage waveform and defined as

$$FF = \frac{V_R}{V_0}$$

Ideal value of FF = 1 i.e. output voltage as pure dc.

- **Efficiency :** It is the ratio of dc output power to ac output volt-ampere.

$$\eta = \frac{dc\ output\ power}{ac\ output\ VA} = \frac{P_{dc}}{P_{ac}}$$

$$= \frac{V_0 I_0}{V_R I_R}$$

V_0, I_0 are average values.

V_R, I_R are RMS values.

- **TUF (Transformer Utilization Factor) :** It is the ratio of dc output power to the input V.A.

$$TUF = \frac{dc\ output\ power}{Input\ volt\ ampere}$$

$$= \frac{P_{DC}}{V_S \cdot I_S} \times 100\%$$

V_S and I_S are the RMS voltage and current of the secondary of the transformer which is connected to the input terminals of the converter.

- **Harmonic factor :** It is also known as total harmonic distortion. It is the measure of distortion of waveform.

$$HF = \frac{\sqrt{I^2 - I_i^2}}{I_i}$$

$$= \sqrt{\left(\frac{I}{I_i}\right)^2 - 1}$$

where, I = RMS value of total current

I_i = RMS value of the fundamental component of i

- **Crest factor :** It is the measure of the peak input current I_p as compared to its RMS value I. This is required to specify the peak current rating of the devices and components used in the circuit.

$$CF = \frac{I_p}{I}$$

Controlled converter parameters are not constant but depends on the firing angle α.

2.2.2 Half Controlled Converter with RL Load

- In practice all load consists of finite value of inductance with resistance R. The actual value of R and L decides the amount of stored energy by the load and time required to release that energy in the process of freewheeling. So operation of half controlled converter can be divided into two categories.

    (1) Continuous current mode.

    (2) Discontinuous current mode.

- In continuous current conduction mode, the load current increases and decreases gradually and has a finite ripple but due to the higher value of inductance of load, load current does not go to zero. The conduction angle for the devices in symmetrical configuration will remain π radian. During freewheeling interval, load current decreases from I_{max} to I_{min}. This mode is more suitable for motor application.

- In discontinuous conduction mode the load current decreases to zero in the freewheeling interval even before the next SCR is turned ON. In this mode, load current ripples are more. This mode is not suitable for motor applications.

- For half controlled converter with RL load

    Performance factors are as follows :

    Average output voltage,
    $$V_{dc} = \frac{2V_m}{\pi} \cos \alpha \qquad \ldots (2.12)$$

    Supply RMS current $= I_d$

    Supply fundamental RMS current $= \frac{2\sqrt{2}}{\pi} I_d$.

    Power factor or displacement factor $= \cos \alpha$.

    Voltage ripple factor, $\quad K_v = \left[\frac{\pi^2}{8 \cos^2 \alpha} - 1 \right]^{1/2}$

2.3 SINGLE-PHASE FULL CONTROLLED BRIDGE RECTIFIER

- Single-phase full-wave bridge converter is equivalent to single-phase full-wave mid-point converter. For both the converters, the output voltage and current waves are same if same supply voltage, firing angle and load parameters are given. Bridge converter is also called as B-4 connection.

- For bridge converter, input transformer is not essential, as mid-point converter requires centre tapped transformer.

- Mid-point converter connection requires thyristor of double rating as those used for bridge converter for same output voltage and current.
- Two types of bridge converters are half controlled bridge converter and fully controlled converter.
- Half controlled bridge converter consists of two SCRs and two diodes. It is a one quadrant converter. This type of bridge converter is also called as B-2 connection.
- Fully controlled bridge converter consists of all four SCRs. It is a two-quadrant converter.

Single-phase Fully Controlled Bridge Converter with Resistive Load

- The circuit and the associated waveform of the single-phase bridge converter connected to resistive load are shown in Fig. 2.8.

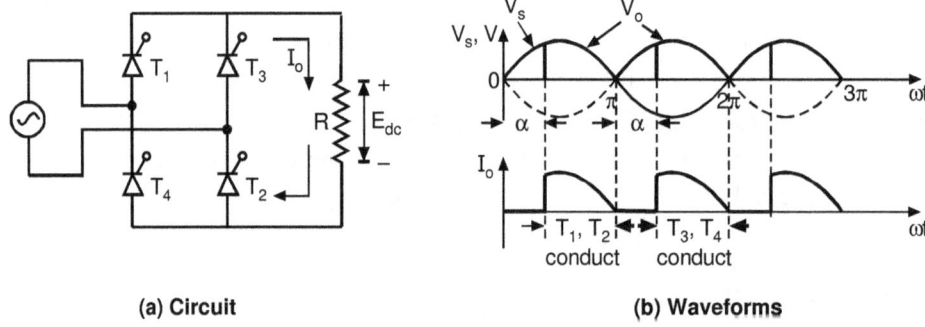

(a) Circuit (b) Waveforms

Fig. 2.8 : Single-phase bridge rectifier with R load

- T_1 and T_2 are fired simultaneously at an angle α in the positive half cycle. T_3 and T_4 are fired at angle $\pi + \alpha$ during negative half cycle. As load is resistive, current becomes zero at π, 2π, ... The current flow is discontinuous. The average value of the output voltage is simply twice the output voltage of the half-wave controlled rectifier.

Output voltage, $\quad V_{dc} = \dfrac{V_m}{\pi}(1 + \cos\alpha)$ ... (2.13)

Output current, $\quad I_{dc} = \dfrac{V_{dc}}{R}$ ... (2.14)

- In the bridge circuit, diagonal opposite pairs of thyristor are made to conduct and are commutated simultaneously.

Single-phase Fully Controlled Bridge Converter with RL Load

- The circuit and the associated waveforms of the single-phase fully controlled bridge converter connected to RL load are shown in Fig. 2.9.
- The output waveforms for the circuit depend on the values of the inductance L and firing angle α. If inductance value is large, then output current is continuous. Diagonal SCRs conduct till other diagonal SCRs are fired. Load current shifts from one pair of SCRs to

other pair. Due to large value of load inductance, output current is constant and ripple free. Thyristors T_1 and T_2 conduct from α to $\pi + \alpha$ and other SCRs T_3 and T_4 conduct from $\pi + \alpha$ to $2\pi + \alpha$. Each pair conducts for angle π.

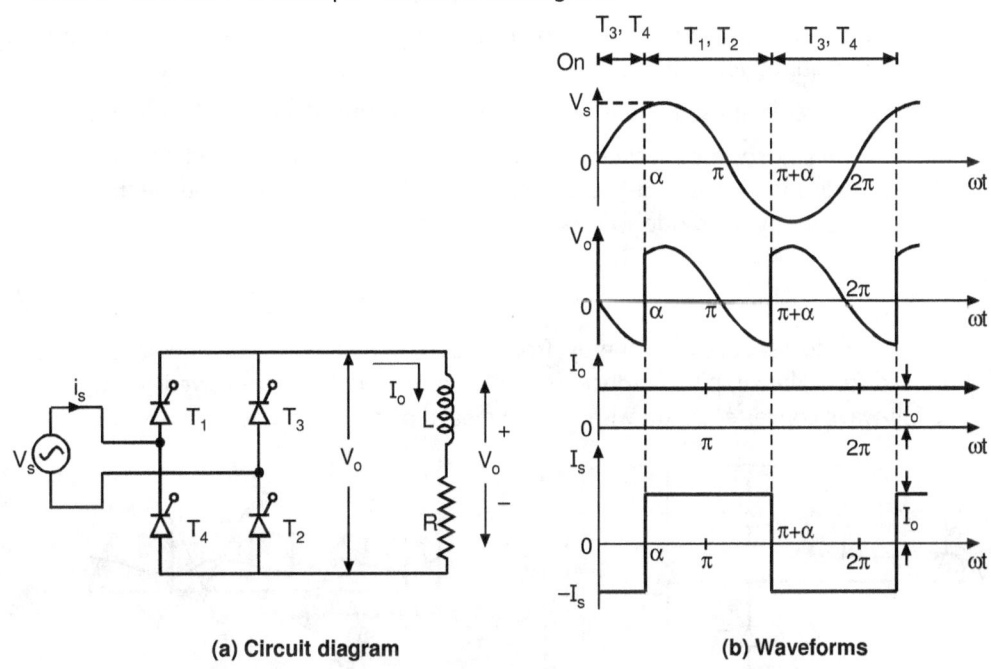

(a) Circuit diagram   (b) Waveforms

Fig. 2.9 : Single-phase bridge rectifier with RL load

- The D.C. output voltage V_o is given by

$$V_o = \frac{2V_m}{\pi} \cos \alpha \qquad \ldots (2.15)$$

- To fire two SCRs simultaneously, same firing circuit is used. When T_1 and T_2 are fired, current flows from supply T_1 SCR, L, R, T_2 SCR and to the supply.

- Similarly when T_3 and T_4 are fired, current flows from supply T_3 SCR, L, R, T_4 SCR and to the supply.

- By controlling the phase angle of firing pulses applied to the gates of SCRs in the range 0° to 180°, the average value of D.C. voltage can be varied from positive maximum to negative maximum.

- Current flows in D.C. terminal in unidirectional, the power flow in the converter can be in either direction. Two modes of operation are rectifying mode and inverting mode. For inverting mode with load a D.C. source is connected in series. Such operation is used in the regenerative breaking mode of D.C. drive and HVDC transmission.

Advantages of Bridge Converter :

- Low rating SCRs are also suitable for bridge converter as compared to SCRs of mid-point converter for same output voltage and current rating.
- For mid-point converter, transformer rating must be double that of load rating. This is not required for bridge converter.

- Bridge converter is not suitable when D.C. load one terminal has to be grounded.
- The circuit and associated waveforms of single-phase fully controlled bridge converter with RL load and flywheel diode are shown in Fig. 2.10. The output voltage will be clamped to zero by the diode. The average value of the output voltage,

$$V_o = \frac{V_m}{\pi}(1 + \cos \alpha) \qquad \ldots (2.16)$$

- As there is no feedback of energy from the load to the supply, the reactive power received from the supply is reduced by 50% compared to that received for the case of the full-wave converter circuit without fly-wheel diode.

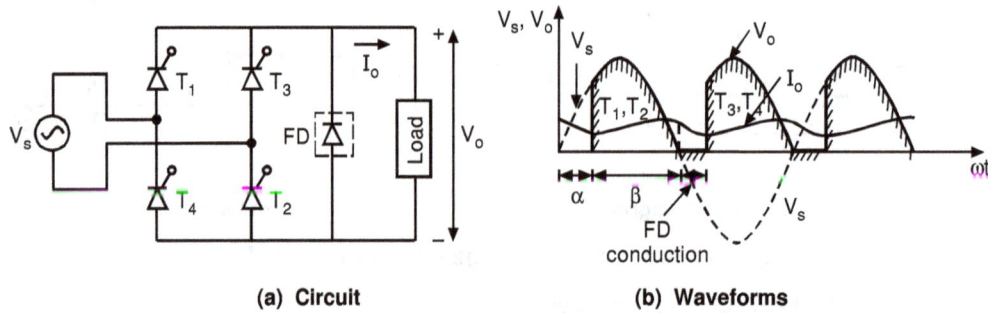

(a) Circuit (b) Waveforms

Fig. 2.10 : Single-phase bridge rectifier RL load with free-wheeling diode

Comparison between 1φ half controlled and 1φ fully controlled converter

1φ Half Controlled Converter	1φ Fully Controlled Converter
1. This type of converter consists of two SCRs and two diodes.	1. This type of converter consists of four SCRs in bridge connection and two SCRs in M-2 connection.
2. This type is available only in bridge connection.	2. This type is available in both M-2 connection as well as in bridge connection.
3. It is a one quadrant converter.	3. It is a two quadrant converter.
4. Suitable for low rating applications.	4. Suitable for high rating applications.

... Contd.

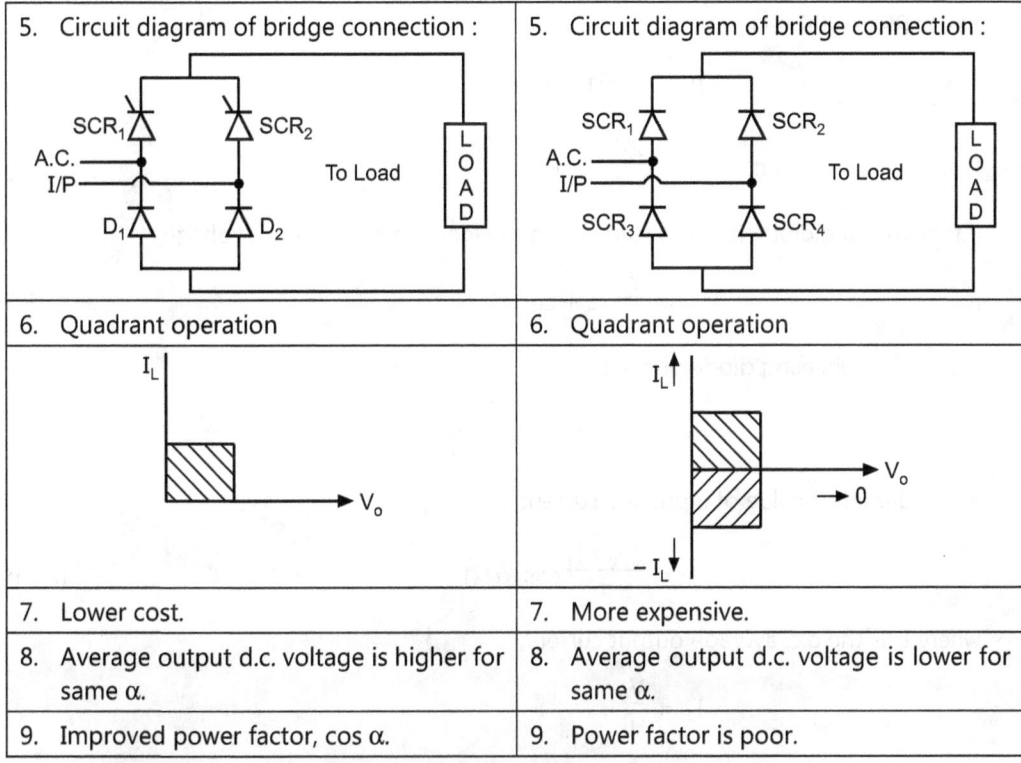

5. Circuit diagram of bridge connection	5. Circuit diagram of bridge connection
6. Quadrant operation	6. Quadrant operation
7. Lower cost.	7. More expensive.
8. Average output d.c. voltage is higher for same α.	8. Average output d.c. voltage is lower for same α.
9. Improved power factor, cos α.	9. Power factor is poor.

2.3.1 Full Controlled Bridge Converter with R Load

- Bridge converters are also called as B-2 connection.

Average dc voltage, $V_{dc} = \dfrac{V_m}{\pi}(1 + \cos\alpha)$ ... (2.17)

Average load current, $I_{dc} = \dfrac{V_m}{\pi R}(1 + \cos\alpha)$ ... (2.18)

RMS load voltage, $V_{rms} = V_m\left[\dfrac{\pi - \alpha}{2\pi} + \dfrac{\sin 2\alpha}{4\pi}\right]^{1/2}$ ... (2.19)

2.3.2 Full Controlled Bridge Converter with R-L Load

- Average dc output voltage,

$$V_{dc} = \dfrac{1}{\pi}\int_{\alpha}^{\pi + \alpha} V_m \sin\omega t \, d(\omega t)$$

$$= \dfrac{V_m}{\pi}[\cos\alpha - \cos(\pi + \alpha)]$$

$\therefore \quad V_{dc} = \dfrac{2V_m}{\pi}\cos\alpha$ ... (2.20)

- Active power input P_i,

$$P_i = \frac{2V_m}{\pi} I_d \cos \alpha \qquad (2.21)$$

- Reactive power input, $\quad Q_i = \frac{2V_m}{\pi} I_d \sin \alpha \qquad \ldots (2.22)$

- If freewheeling diode is connected across the load then the output voltage,

$$V_{dc} = \frac{V_m}{\pi} (1 + \cos \alpha) \qquad \ldots (2.23)$$

Due to freewheeling diode phase angle ϕ,

$$\phi = \frac{\alpha}{2}$$

So fundamental value of input line current,

$$I_i = \frac{2\sqrt{2} I_d}{\pi} \cos (\alpha/2) \qquad \ldots (2.24)$$

where I_d is the d.c. average output current,

$$I_d = \frac{V_{dc}}{R}$$

Now the active power input (P_i),

$$P_i = V_{rms} \times I_i \times \cos (\alpha/2) \qquad \ldots (2.25)$$

and reactive power input,

$$Q_i = \frac{V_{rms} \sqrt{2}}{\pi} I_d \sin \alpha \qquad \ldots (2.26)$$

For full converter

$$\text{RMS load voltage, } V_{rms} = \frac{V_m}{\sqrt{2}} \qquad \ldots (2.27)$$

$$\text{Form factor} = \frac{\pi}{2\sqrt{2} \cos \alpha} \qquad \ldots (2.28)$$

$$\text{Ripple factor} = \left[\frac{\pi^2}{8 \cos^2 \alpha} - 1 \right]^{1/2} \qquad \ldots (2.29)$$

$$\text{Rectification efficiency, } \eta = \frac{8 \cos^2 \alpha}{\pi^2}$$

- Full controlled bridge converter shows two quadrant operation i.e. rectification and inversion.

  Fundamental power factor = cos α

  Input power factor = $\dfrac{2\sqrt{2}}{\pi} \cos \alpha$

  Harmonic factor, HF = $\left[\dfrac{\pi^2}{8} - 1\right]^{1/2}$

- In bridge converter of full controlled type, supply current is square wave with only odd harmonics and bidirectional.
- Reactive power input to half converter is half of the reactive power input to the full converter.

2.4 THREE PHASE CONTROLLED CONVERTER

- Three phase AC to DC converters are preferred for high power DC loads. These converters are also phase controlled. The various types of three phase converters are :
  (1) Three phase half-wave converter (three pulse converter).
  (2) Three phase full wave mid point converter (six pulse or M-6 converter).
  (3) Three phase fully controlled bridge converter.
  (4) Three phase half controlled bridge converter.
- Three phase half wave converters are rarely used in industries because they introduce DC component in the supply circuit. Six pulse connections are widely used for industrial applications whereas for transmission lines 12-pulse connections are preferred.
- The six-pulse i.e. full converter of 3φ has following advantages :
  (1) Easy commutation.
  (2) AC side distortions are reduced.
  (3) Less requirement of inductance.
- Full wave three phase converters may be
  (1) Simple six pulse converter.
  (2) Six-pulse mid-point converter with interphase transformers.
  (3) Six pulse bridge converter.

2.4.1 Three Phase Half Controlled Converter

- A three phase semi-converter i.e. half controlled converter can be obtained by connecting a freewheeling diode across the RL load of the three phase full converter. It can also be obtained by replacing top three or bottom three SCRs of the full converter by diodes. SCRs are triggered at an interval of 120° in a proper sequence. A three phase semi converter or half controlled converter voltage and current waveforms are as shown in Fig. 2.11 (a) with circuit diagram.

- It works as a six pulse converter for $\alpha < 60°$ and as a three pulse converter for $\alpha \geq 60°$. Fig. 2.11 (b) shows output waveform and conduction of SCR and diode for $\alpha = 0°$, $\alpha = 15°$, $\alpha = 60°$, $\alpha = 90°$ and $\alpha = 120°$.

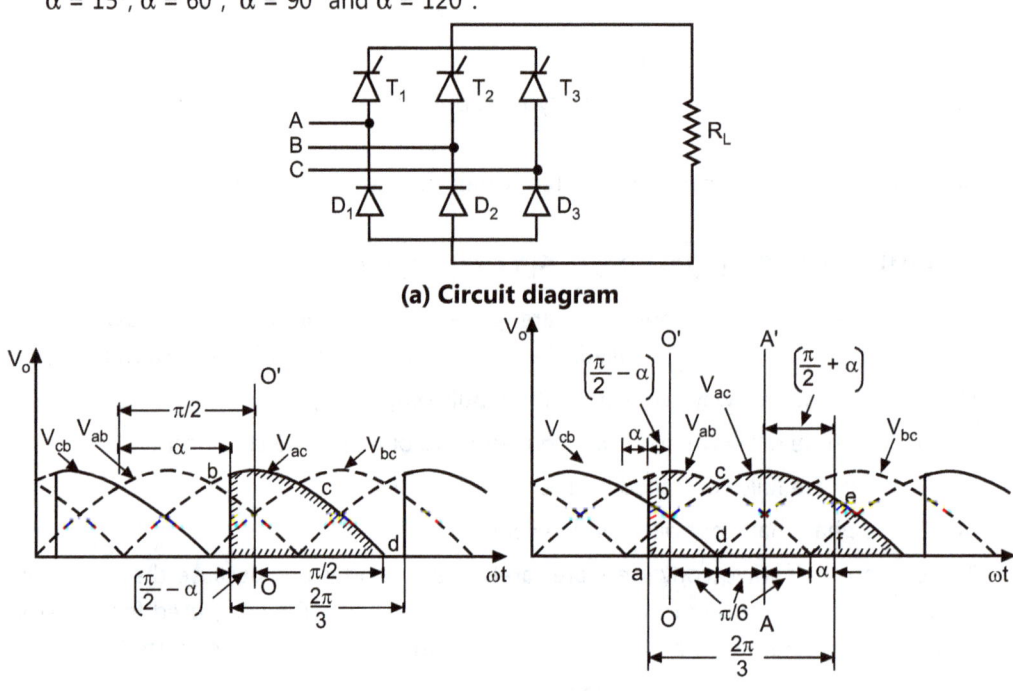

(a) Circuit diagram

(b) Waveforms

Fig. 2.11 : Three phase half controlled converter

- Diode conducts as soon as they are forward biased line.

For $\alpha < 60°$, output voltage average,

$$V_{dc} = \frac{3\sqrt{3}\, V_m}{2\pi}(1 + \cos\alpha) \qquad \ldots (2.30)$$

RMS output voltage for $\alpha < 60°$,

$$V_{rms} = \frac{3}{2} V_m \left[\frac{2}{3} + \frac{\sqrt{3}}{2\pi}(1 + \cos 2\alpha)\right]^{1/2} \qquad \ldots (2.31)$$

For $\alpha > 60°$,

$$V_{rms} = \frac{3V_m}{2}\left[\frac{\pi - \alpha + \frac{1}{2}\sin 2\alpha}{\pi}\right]^{1/2} \qquad \ldots (2.32)$$

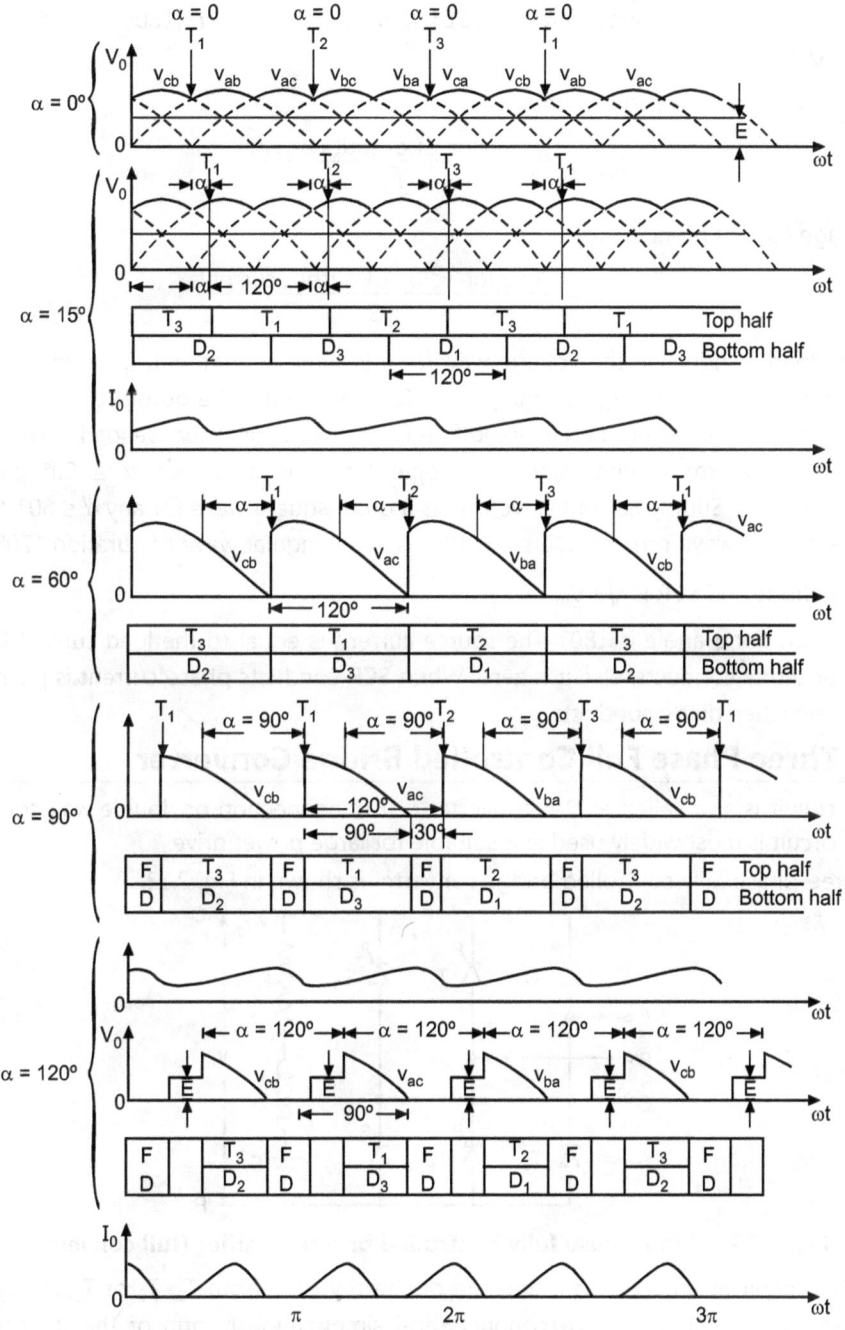

Fig. 2.12 : Three phase converter output waveforms
for α = 0°, α = 15°, α = 60°, α = 90°, α = 120°

(Chap. 2.25)

- SCR and diodes conduct only for 120° if α ≤ 60° and for (180° − α) for α ≥ 60° when α ≤ 60°.

  SCR and diode RMS current rating,

  $$I_{rms} = \frac{\text{rms value of output current}}{\sqrt{3}}$$

  Average current rating,

  $$I_D = \frac{\text{Average value of output current}}{3}$$

- When load is inductive the voltage waveform is same as that with (R) load. So average and rms values of the output voltage waveform are same. The output current waveform is continuous for α < 60° and is ripple free for α = 30°. For inductive load, form factor of current waveform is unity and the ripple factor is zero. For α ≥ 60° current is discontinuous. Supply current waveform is a quasi square wave for any α ≤ 60°. SCR and diode current waveform for α, 0 ≤ α ≤ 180° is a rectangular wave of duration 120°.

  PIV of diode and SCR is $\sqrt{3}\, V_m$.

- Maximum firing angle is 180°. The source current is equal to the load current I_{dc} when SCR or diode conducts, else it is zero. When SCR conducts phase current is positive and negative when diode conducts.

2.4.2 Three Phase Full Controlled Bridge Converter

- This circuit is also called as B-6 converter or B-6 connection or double way connection. This circuit is most widely used and suitable for large power drive.
- A three-phase fully controlled bridge converter is shown in Fig. 2.13.

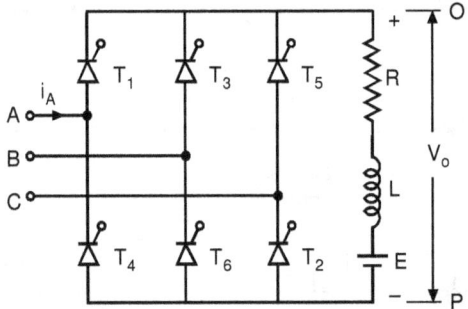

Fig. 2.13 : Three-phase fully controlled bridge rectifier (full converter)

- In this circuit at any given instant one of the thyristor from T_1, T_3 or T_5 whose anode voltage is maximum positive conducts and simultaneously one of the thyristor from T_2, T_4 or T_6 whose cathode is maximum negative conducts. T_1, T_3 and T_5 form the positive group, while T_2, T_4 and T_6 form negative group of SCRs.

- In this circuit, line commutation is used. The firing frequency is six times the line frequency.
- Thyristors are triggered at 60° intervals. For every cycle, there are six pulses at the output, each at 60° duration. Therefore, it is called as six pulse converter.
- Firing angle is measured for positive group thyristor from the instant when anode voltage becomes maximum positive.
- Firing angle is measured for negative group thyristor from the instant when cathode voltage become maximum negative.

Circuit Operation :

- At instant K, thyristor T_1 is triggered with firing angle α. When T_1 is conducting, the voltage between line A and C reverse biases T_5. So T_5 turns OFF. Voltage across A and B appears across output OP through thyristors T_1 and T_6. Current flows from A, T_1, O, L, R, P, T_6 to B. This current flows till T_2 SCR is turned ON.
- When T_2 is turned ON, voltage across B reverses and turn OFF T_6 SCR. Now voltage across A and C appears across O and P. The conduction pattern of SCRs is expressed through six modes. Each mode is for 60°. Table 2.3 shows six modes along with firing sequence.

Table 2.3 : Six conduction modes with firing sequence

Mode	Conducting SCR	Incoming SCR	Outgoing SCR
1	5, 6	1	5
2	6, 1	2	6
3	1, 2	3	1
4	2, 3	4	2
5	3, 4	5	3
6	4, 5	6	4

- At any given time two thyristors, one from each group (T, T_3, T_5 and T_4, T_6, T_2) conduct to deliver line voltage to load as output voltage.
- Each thyristor conducts for a period of 120°. Fig. 2.14 shows waveform of this circuit operation. Voltage corresponding to V_{ab}, V_{ac}, V_{bc}, V_{ba}, V_{ca} and V_{cb} appear in succession at output.
- Output voltage V_o is given by

$$V_o = \frac{3V_m}{\pi} \cos \alpha \qquad \ldots (2.33)$$

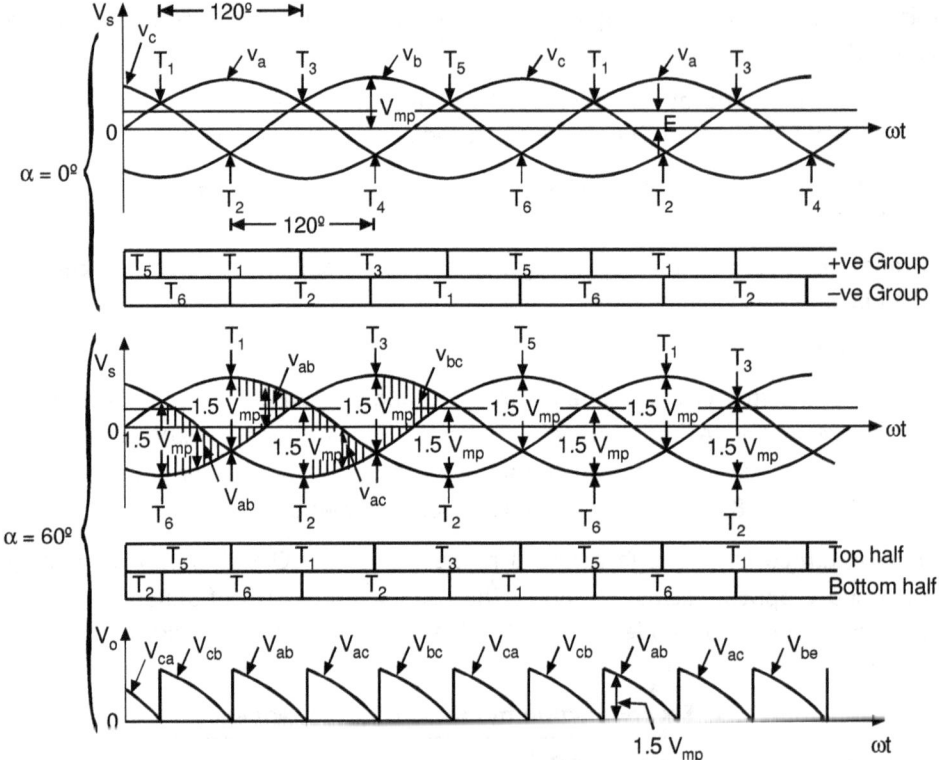

Fig. 2.14 : Waveforms and thyristor conduction periods (phase voltages)

- This converter is most widely used for industrial application upto 120 kW where two quadrant operation is required. Each SCR can conduct for 120°. The phase shift between the triggering of two adjacent SCRs is 60°. At any instant two SCRs can conduct and there are such six pairs. Each SCR conducts in two pairs and each pair conducts for 60°.

For continuous conduction mode ($\alpha < 60°$)

$$V_{dc} = \frac{3\sqrt{3}}{\pi} V_m \cos \alpha \qquad \ldots (2.34)$$

$$I_d = \frac{3\sqrt{3}}{\pi} \frac{V_m}{R} \cos \alpha \qquad \ldots (2.35)$$

For discontinuous conduction mode ($\alpha > 60°$),

$$V_{dc} = \frac{3\sqrt{3}}{\pi} V_m [1 + \cos (\alpha + \pi/3)] \qquad \ldots (2.36)$$

$$I_d = \frac{3\sqrt{3}}{\pi R} V_m [1 + \cos (\alpha + \pi/3)] \qquad \ldots (2.37)$$

- For inductive load waveforms are similar with R load for α = 0°, α = 30° and α = 60°. For α > 60° waveforms are different. The voltage goes negative due to inductive nature of the load. For α = 90° area under positive and negative cycles are same, so average voltage is zero. The maximum value of α = 180°. The output is always six pulse i.e. ripple frequency is 300 Hz.

$$V_{dc} = \frac{3\sqrt{3}\,V_m}{\pi} \cos \alpha \quad \text{for } 0 \leq \alpha \leq 180°, \qquad \ldots (2.38)$$

$$V_{rms} = \frac{3V_m}{2}\left[\frac{2}{3} + \frac{\sqrt{3}}{\pi}\cos 2\alpha\right]^{1/2}$$

- As the firing angle changes from 0° to 90° the voltage also changes from maximum to zero and the converter is said to be in rectification mode. For α in the range 90° to 180°, the voltage varies from 0 to negative maximum and converter is in inversion mode. It can transfer power from D.C. side to A.C. side.

2.4.3 Comparison of Three-Phase and Single-Phase Converters

	Single-phase converters		Three-phase converters
1.	These are mainly used for low power D.C. loads.	1.	Three-phase A.C. to D.C. converters are preferred for high power D.C. load.
2.	Filtering requirement for smoothing out load current is more.	2.	Due to presence of large ripple frequency, filtering requirement for smoothing out the load current is reduced.
3.	D.C. motor performance is not better if fed from single-phase converter.	3.	As the load current is continuous, D.C. motor performance is superior as compared to single-phase converter fed.
4.	Non-uniform loading occurs if used for high power D.C. drives.	4.	Uniform loading occurs if used for high power D.C. drives.
5.	Less number of thyristors are required.	5.	More number of thyristors are required.
6.	Suitable for low current rating applications.	6.	Suitable for high current applications.
7.	Mid-point converter requires two SCRs and bridge converter requires four SCRs.	7.	Mid-point converter requires six SCRs and bridge converter also requires six SCRs.
8.	Single-phase converter is less expensive.	8.	Three-phase converter is more expensive.
9.	It requires simple triggering circuit.	9.	It requires complex triggering circuit.
10.	Construction of circuit and mounting is easy.	10.	Construction of circuit and mounting is complex.

2.5 EFFECT OF SOURCE INDUCTANCE ON CONVERTER OPERATION

- In single-phase or three-phase converter, current is transferred from outgoing SCR to incoming SCR instantaneously if source has no internal impedance.

- If source impedance is resistive then output voltage reduces. If source impedance is inductive, then it causes outgoing and incoming SCRs to conduct together.

- During commutation period, all SCRs conduct. This period is known as overlap period and the angle is known as overlap angle.

- For single-phase converter, during overlap period, output voltage is zero. Commutation overlap occurs twice per cycle. The commutation overlap is more in full converter than semi or half converter.

- In three-phase converter when positive group SCRs are undergoing commutation, two SCRs from the positive group and one SCR from negative group conduct.

- After the commutation of positive group is completed, only two SCRs conduct one from positive group and one from negative group.

- Similar operation occurs with negative group SCRs. This results in lower average D.C. output voltage.

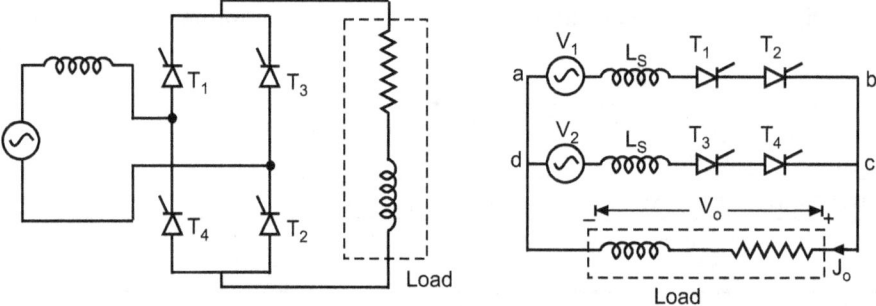

Fig. 2.15 : Fully controlled converter with source inductance and equivalent circuit

- In overlap angle for single phase converter the load voltage will be zero and for a three phase converter the load voltage is $(V_a + V_b)/2$ i.e. average value of the conducting phases a and b. Fig. 2.16 shows waveforms for single phase converter with source inductance.

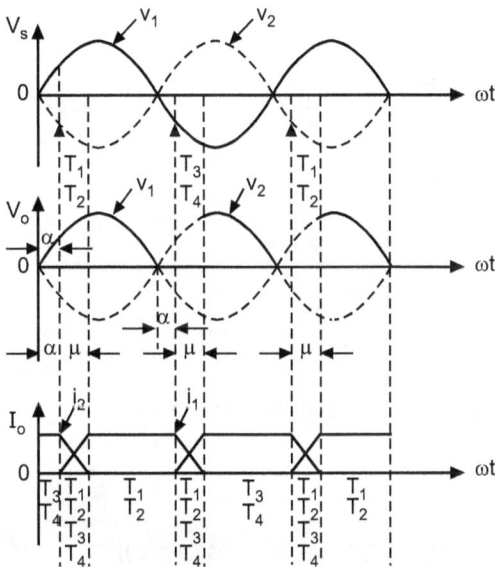

Fig. 2.16 : Waveforms for effect of source inductance on single phase converter

- The output voltage is zero during overlap angle. Commutation overlap occurs twice per cycle. These commutation overlaps cause reduction in the output voltage. During the commutation of (T_1, T_2) and (T_3, T_4) i.e. during overlap angle, Kirchhoff's voltage law for the loop abcd of equivalent circuit gives

$$V_1 - L_s \frac{di_1}{dt} = V_2 - L_s \frac{di_2}{dt}$$

$$V_1 - V_2 = L_s \left(\frac{di_1}{dt} - \frac{di_2}{dt} \right)$$

If
$$V_1 = V_m \sin \omega t$$

and
$$V_2 = -V_m \sin \omega t$$

$$L_s \left(\frac{di_1}{dt} - \frac{di_2}{dt} \right) = 2V_m \sin \omega t$$

As load current is constant, $i_1 + i_2 = i_0$.

∴ By differentiating,

$$\frac{di_1}{dt} + \frac{di_2}{dt} = 0 \qquad \ldots (2.39)$$

$$\frac{di_1}{dt} - \frac{di_2}{dt} = \frac{2V_m}{L_s} \sin \omega t \qquad \ldots (2.40)$$

By adding equations (2.39) and (2.40),

$$2\frac{di_1}{dt} = 2\frac{V_m}{L_s}\sin\omega t$$

$$\therefore \frac{di_1}{dt} = \frac{V_m}{L_s}\sin\omega t$$

$$\int_0^{i_1} di_1 = \frac{V_m}{L_s}\int_{\alpha,\omega}^{(\alpha+\mu)\omega}\sin\omega t\, dt$$

$$\therefore I_0 = \frac{V_m}{\omega L_s}[\cos\alpha - \cos(\alpha+\mu)]$$

V_0 is zero from α to $\alpha + \mu$.

$$\therefore \text{Average voltage, } V_0 = \frac{V_m}{\pi}[\cos\alpha + \cos(\alpha+\mu)]$$

$$\cos(\alpha+\mu) = \cos\alpha - \frac{\omega L_s}{V_m}I_0$$

$$\therefore V_0 = \frac{2V_m}{\pi}\cos\alpha - \frac{\omega L_s}{\pi}I_0$$

$$\cos\alpha = \frac{\omega L_s}{V_m}I_0 + \cos(\alpha+\mu)$$

$$\therefore V_0 = \frac{2V_m}{\pi}\cos(\alpha+\mu) + \frac{\omega L_s}{\pi}I_0$$

- **Effect of source inductance on three phase full controlled bridge converter**

Fig. 2.17 shows bridge converter with source inductance L_s.

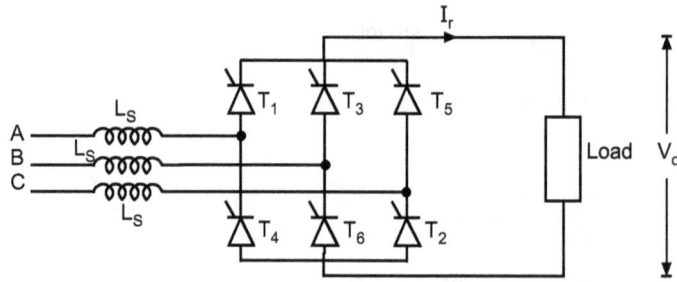

Fig. 2.17 : Bridge converter with source inductance

- Source inductance reduces output voltage, load current is constant and ripple free. Fig. 2.18 shows waveforms.

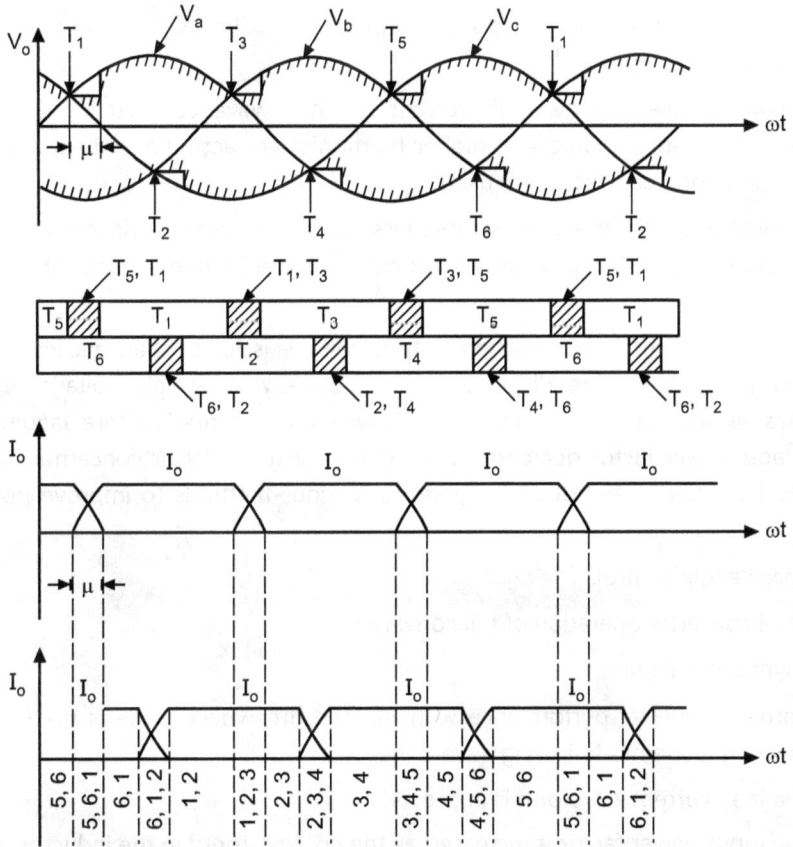

Fig. 2.18 : Three phase full converter with source inductance waveforms

- The current in the thyristor rise and decay in an exponential manner due to source inductance. The number of SCRs involved in overlap are three if overlap angle μ is less than 60°.

Output voltage, $\quad V_0 = \dfrac{3V_m}{\pi} \cos(\alpha + \mu) + \dfrac{3\omega L_s}{\pi} i_0$

- In this three phase converter six commutation in each cycle of the supply voltage.

2.6 SELECTION OF CONVERTER

- Following factors are considered while selecting converter for any application :
  (1) Higher pulse numbers are desirable. It reduces magnitude of ripple voltage and current in the load circuit.
  (2) Fully controlled circuits are capable for inversion, second quadrant operation, so regeneration occurs. This regeneration does not occur in half controlled converter.

(3) Bridge converter requires lower rating SCR as compared to half wave converter. So bridge converters are used most widely.

(4) Bridge converter requires double number of SCRs as compared to half wave converter.

- In general for low voltage, high current use half wave converters are used. When regeneration is not required and higher harmonics are acceptable then half controlled three pulse bridge converters are used.

- Phase controlled converters are simple, less expensive, reliable and do not require any commutation circuit. In these converters class-F commutation i.e. natural commutation occurs.

- Supply power factor is lower when output voltage is lower than maximum i.e. when firing angle is large. The displacement angle between supply voltage and current increases as the firing angle increases. Now converter draws more lagging reactive power and power factor decreases. Poor power factor is major concern in high power drive and variable speed drive applications. Various methods to improve power factor are :

    (1) Phase angle control.
    (2) Semi converter operation of full converter.
    (3) Asymmetrical firing.

- To improve converter performance with RL load, freewheel diode is used. The use of freewheeling diode has following advantages :

    (1) The load current waveform is improved.
    (2) The input power factor is increased as the energy stored in the inductor is delivered to the load instead of going back to the supply.
    (3) The gate is permitted to have control over the thyristor.
    (4) Proper commutation of thyristor is done.
    (5) It prevents reversal of load voltage.

SOLVED EXAMPLES

Example 2.1 : *The SCR shown in circuit diagram is triggered by a dc signal applied to the gate. The supply voltage is v = 220 sin 314 t. Calculate :*

(i) The average value of the current.

(ii) Power loss in the resistor.

(iii) Power supplied to the load.

(iv) Power factor.

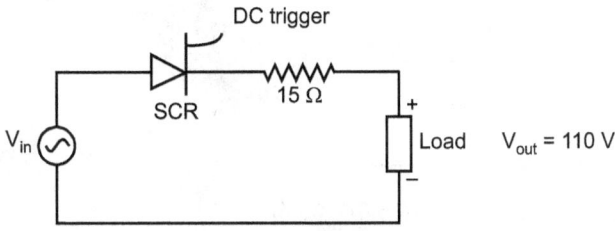

Fig. 2.19

Solution : The input voltage is $v = V_m \sin \omega t$.

∴ $V_m = 220$ V and $\omega = 314$ rad/sec.

SCR turns ON when it is forward biased.

$$\omega t = \alpha$$

∴ $$V_m \sin \alpha = V_{out}$$

∴ $$\alpha = \sin^{-1}\left(\frac{V_{out}}{V_{in}}\right)$$

$$= \sin^{-1}\left(\frac{110}{220}\right) = 30° = \frac{\pi}{6} \text{ rad}$$

$$\text{Load current, } i = \frac{V_m \sin \omega t - V_{out}}{R}$$

$$= \frac{V_m}{R}(\sin \alpha - m)$$

where, $$m = \frac{V_{out}}{V_m} = \frac{110}{220} = 0.5$$

$$\beta = \pi - \alpha$$

β angle at which SCR turns OFF.

(i) The average value of i is given by,

$$i_{av} = \frac{1}{2\pi} \int_{\alpha}^{\pi - \alpha} i \, d(\omega t)$$

$$= \frac{V_m}{R} \cdot \frac{1}{2\pi} \int_{\alpha}^{\pi - \alpha} (\sin \omega t - m) \, d(\omega t)$$

$$= \frac{V_m}{R} \cdot \frac{1}{2\pi} [2 \cos \alpha - m (\pi - 2\alpha)]$$

$$= \frac{220}{2\pi \times 15}\left[2 \cos \frac{\pi}{6} - 0.5 \left(\pi - \frac{2\pi}{6}\right)\right]$$

$$= 1.6 \text{ A}$$

(ii) The RMS value of current,

$$i_{rms} = \sqrt{\frac{1}{2\pi} \int_{\alpha}^{\pi-\alpha} i^2 \, d(\omega t)}$$

$$= \frac{V_m}{R} \sqrt{\frac{1}{2\pi} \int_{\alpha}^{\pi-\alpha} \sin(\omega t - m)^2 \, d(\omega t)}$$

$$= \frac{V_m}{R} \sqrt{\frac{1}{2\pi} \left[\left(\frac{1}{2} + m^2\right)(\pi - 2\alpha) - 4m \cos\alpha + \frac{\cos 2\alpha + \sin 2\alpha}{4} \right]}$$

$$= \frac{220}{15} \sqrt{\frac{1}{2\pi} \left[\left(\frac{1}{2} + 0.5^2\right)\left(\pi - \frac{2\pi}{6}\right) - 4 \times 0.5 \cos\frac{\pi}{6} + \cos\frac{2\pi}{6} + \frac{\sin 2\pi/6}{4} \right]}$$

$$= 5.985 \text{ A}$$

Power loss in the resistor,

$$P_R = I_R^2 R = (5.985)^2 \times 15 = 537.3 \text{ watt}$$

(iii) Power supplied to the load,

$$P_L = I_{out} \times V_{out} = 1.6 \times 110 = \textbf{176 watt}$$

(iv) Power factor $= \dfrac{\text{Total output power}}{\text{Input VA}} = \dfrac{537.3 + 176}{(220\sqrt{2}) \times 5.985}$

$$= \textbf{0.766 (lagging)}$$

Example 2.2 : *A single phase full converter operating from a single phase 230 V, 50 Hz supply has a purely resistive load of R = 15 Ω. If the average load current is 11.78 A, calculate :*

(i) The delay angle α, (ii) The RMS values of output voltage and current, (iii) Average and RMS values of SCR current.

Solution : (i) Load is purely resistive, the full converter output voltage waveform is similar to that of semi-converter.

$$\therefore \quad V_o = I_o R = 11.78 \times 15 = 176.7 \text{ V}$$

$$V_o = \frac{230\sqrt{2}}{\pi}(1 - \cos\alpha)$$

$$\therefore \quad 176.7 = \frac{230\sqrt{2}}{\pi}(1 - \cos\alpha)$$

$$\therefore \quad \alpha = \textbf{45°}$$

(ii) The RMS value of the output voltage,

$$V_R = 230 \sqrt{\frac{1}{\pi}\left(\pi - \frac{\pi}{4} + \frac{\sin\frac{2\pi}{4}}{2}\right)}$$

$$= 219.3 \text{ V}$$

RMS value of the output current,

$$i_R = \frac{V_R}{R} = \frac{219.3}{15} = \textbf{14.62 A}$$

(iii) RMS value of SCR the current,

$$I_{SCR\,(RMS)} = \frac{I_R}{\sqrt{2}} = \frac{14.62}{\sqrt{2}} = \textbf{10.34 A}$$

Average value of SCR current,

$$I_{SCR\,(av)} = \frac{I_o}{2} = \frac{11.78}{2} = \textbf{5.89 A}$$

Example 2.3 : *A single-phase full converter with R-L load is operating from 230 V, 50 Hz supply. The load inductance L is very large. If R = 6 Ω and output voltage = 40 V, find the value of average load current for a delay angle of π/3. Find SCR average current.*

Solution : Total output voltage,

$$V_{oT} = V_R + V_o$$
$$= I_o R + V_o$$

where I_o is the average value of load current.

$$V_{oT} = \frac{2 \times 230\sqrt{2}}{\pi} \cos\frac{\pi}{3} = 103.54 \text{ V}$$

∴
$$i_o = \frac{V_{oT} - V_o}{R} = \frac{103.54 - 40}{6} = \textbf{10.59 A}$$

Average SCR current,

$$I_{SCR\,(av)} = \frac{I_o}{2} = \frac{10.59}{2} = \textbf{5.3 A}$$

Example 2.4 : *A single phase full converter operating from 230 V, 50 Hz supply provides an average load current of 6 A at a delay angle α = 45°. If the ripple content of the load current is negligible, determine :*

(i) The dc load voltage and dc output power.

(ii) dc load voltage and power with freewheel diode.

Solution : (a) Average output current $I_o = 6$ A.

$$\therefore \quad V_o = \frac{2V_m}{\pi} \cos\alpha = \frac{2 \times 230\sqrt{2}}{\pi} \cos 45°$$

Average output voltage = 146.42 V

The dc output power,

$$P_o = V_o I_o = 146.42 \times 6 = \mathbf{878.54\ V}$$

(b) The load resistance is,

$$R = \frac{V_o}{I_o} = \frac{146.42}{6} = 24.4\ \Omega$$

When a freewheel diode is connected across the output, the converter behaves as a semi-converter.

$$\therefore \quad V_o = \frac{V_m(1+\cos\alpha)}{\pi} = \frac{230\sqrt{2}(1+\cos 45)}{\pi}$$

$$= \mathbf{176.75\ A}$$

So dc output power, $\quad P_o = \frac{V_o^2}{12} = \frac{(176.75)^2}{24.4} = \mathbf{1280.4\ watt}$

Example 2.5 : *Input voltage to a fully controlled SCR converter is 230 V at 50 Hz. A resistance of 50 Ω with a large inductance from load. If α = 30°, calculate :*

(i) *Average voltage across 30 Ω.*

(ii) *RMS value of current through SCR.*

Solution : (i) Average voltage,

$$V_o = \frac{R}{2\pi} \int_{\alpha}^{\pi+\alpha} V_m \sin\omega t\ d(\omega t)$$

$$= \frac{2V_m}{\pi} \cos\alpha$$

$$= \frac{2 \times 230\sqrt{2} \cos 30°}{\pi}$$

$$= 179.29\ V$$

Average current, $I_o = \dfrac{V_o}{R} = \dfrac{179.29}{50} = \mathbf{3.58\ A}$

(ii) RMS value of SCR current $= \dfrac{I_o}{\sqrt{2}} = \mathbf{2.5318\ A}$ ... **Ans.**

Example 2.6 : *A single-phase fully controlled SCR converter is connected to a load having R = 2 Ω and L = 0.3 H. The supply voltage is 230 V/50 Hz. Find average load voltage, average load current, input power factor. α = 30°.*

Solution : Average load voltage $= \dfrac{2V_m}{\pi} \cos \alpha = \dfrac{2 \times 230\sqrt{2}}{\pi} \cos 30° =$ **179.3 V**

Average load current, $I_o = \dfrac{V_o}{R} = \dfrac{179.3}{2} =$ **89.65 A**

RMS value of the input current,

$$I_s = I_o$$

$$I_s = \dfrac{4I_o/\pi}{\sqrt{2}}$$

$$= \dfrac{2\sqrt{2}}{\pi} \times 89.65$$

$$= 80.71 \text{ A}$$

$$PF = \dfrac{\text{Average power}}{\text{Apparent power}} = \dfrac{V_o I_o}{V_s I_s} = \dfrac{179.3}{230}$$

$$= 0.77$$

REVIEW QUESTIONS

1. What is a converter ? State basic features of converter.
2. List out applications of converter.
3. With neat waveform explain principle of phase control.
4. Compare uncontrolled and controlled rectifier.
5. State the effect of inductive reactance load on the performance of controlled rectifier. How to eliminate this effect ?
6. State the detail classification of controlled converters.
7. Define following terms :
   (a) Firing angle (b) Conduction angle (c) Extension angle
   (d) One quadrant converter
8. What is semiconverter, full converter and dual converter ?
9. With neat circuit diagram and waveform explain the operation of single-phase half-wave controlled rectifier with RL load. Why free-wheel diode is connected across the load ?
10. What is a flywheel diode ? State its advantages.

11. Sketch circuit diagram of M-2 connection with resistive load, indicate current direction.
12. Compare mid-point converter with bridge converter.
13. With neat circuit diagram and waveforms explain bridge converter.
14. State advantages and limitations of bridge converter.
15. List out types of three-phase converter. State applications of three-phase converter.
16. Explain with circuit diagram three-phase fully controlled bridge converter with RL load. State firing sequence. Sketch waveform for $\alpha = 60°$.
17. Compare single-phase and three-phase converter.
18. Illustrate the effect of source impedance on converter operation.
19. Sketch fully controlled bridge rectifier with source inductance and sketch its equivalent circuit.
20. Define and state equation for ripple factor, current ripple factor, form factor, TUF.
21. Explain three phase full controlled converter.

Chapter 3
DC-DC CONVERTER

Weightage of Marks = 16, Teaching Hours = 07

Contents

- Introduction
- Chopper working principle
- Control strategies
- Classification of choppers
  - Class A
  - Class B
  - Class C
  - Class D
  - Class E
- Commutation methods for chopper
  - Voltage commutation
  - Current commutation
  - Load commutation
- Step down chopper
  - Continuous conduction mode
  - Discontinuous conduction mode
- Step-up chopper
- Full bridge chopper
- SMPS

Objectives

After learning this chapter reader will be able to :

- State the need of chopper.
- Explain basic operation of chopper.
- State importance and applications of chopper.
- Classify chopper in terms of quadrant operation.
- State and explain basic strategies for chopper control.
- Explain various commutation techniques such as voltage, current, load commutation.
- Explain continuous conduction mode and discontinuous conduction mode.
- Explain full bridge DC-DC converter.
- Explain with block diagram SMPS.

3.1 INTRODUCTION

- A D.C. chopper converts a fixed voltage D.C. supply into a variable voltage D.C. supply using the principle of ON-OFF control.
- The D.C. to D.C. converter can be considered as a D.C. equivalent to an A.C. transformer with a continuously variable turns ratio. Like transformer, a chopper can be used to step down or step up the input D.C. voltage.
- A step-down chopper produces an output voltage, which is variable and less than the input voltage.
- A step-up chopper provides an output voltage which is variable, but higher than the input voltage.
- D.C. choppers are single-stage converters, so they are more efficient.
- Inverter-rectifier is called as A.C. link chopper. In A.C. link chopper, the D.C. is first converted to A.C. by an inverter.
- The obtained A.C. is then stepped up or down by a transformer, and then rectified back to D.C. by a rectifier. It is a two-stage process.
- It is more expensive and less efficient technique. Transformer provides isolation between load and source.
- A D.C. chopper is a static switch. It is also called as time ratio controller (TRC).

Major Features :

- Solid state converter.
- Fast response.
- Power saving.
- High efficiency.
- Smaller size.
- Smooth control.

Applications of chopper :

1. Trolley cars.
2. Battery operated vehicles.
3. Traction motor control.
4. Control of large number of D.C. motors using common D.C. source.
5. Control of induction motor.
6. Marine hoists.
7. Forklift trucks.
8. Mine haulars.

9. Chopper stabilized power supply.
10. D.C. drive.
11. SMPS (Switch Mode Power Supply).
12. Degenerative braking in D.C. drive.
13. D.C. current source.
14. Battery charging circuit.
15. Time ratio controller.

For chopper circuit, switching power BJT, GTO, MOSFET, IGBT or SCR are used.

3.1.1 Chopper Principle

- The fixed voltage of a D.C. source can be converted to a variable, average voltage on a load by placing a high speed switch between the D.C. source and the load.
- This high speed static switch is called as chopper.
- A chopper is a thyristor based ON/OFF switch that connects load to and disconnect it from the supply and produces a chopped load voltage from a constant input supply voltage.
- A basic chopper circuit and its associated waveforms are shown in Fig. 3.1.

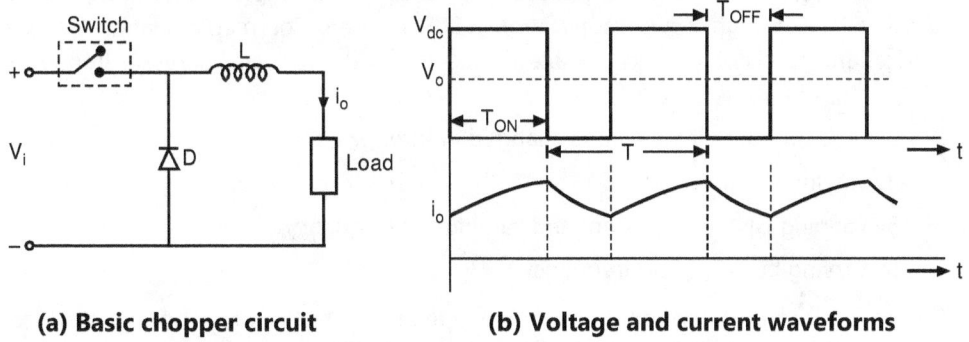

(a) Basic chopper circuit   (b) Voltage and current waveforms

Fig. 3.1

In Fig. 3.1, switch may be any switching device such as SCR, BJT, MOSFET, GTO, IGBT. D is a freewheeling diode. It conducts only when switch is in OFF state. L is a filter inductance. V_i is input fixed D.C. voltage. V_o is a chopped output voltage, i_o is a current flowing through the load.

- The chopper periodically switches ON and OFF the supply voltage V_i to and from the load, at any desired frequency. During ON period, the chopper switch is closed and the load voltage is equal to source voltage V_i. Some negligible voltage drop occurs across the switching device.

- During OFF period, chopper switch is open. But load current flows through free wheeling diode. So the load voltage reduces to zero. Alternate turn-ON and turn-OFF of the chopper in a periodic manner produces a chopped D.C. voltage. It appears like a pulse train across the load.

- Average load voltage, $V_o = \dfrac{T_{ON}}{T_{ON} + T_{OFF}} \times V_{in}$ ... (3.1)

$$= K \cdot V_{in}$$

$$K = \text{Duty cycle} = \dfrac{T_{ON}}{T_{ON} + T_{OFF}}$$

$$T_{ON} = \text{ON time}$$

$$T_{OFF} = \text{OFF time}$$

If f = Chopping frequency

then $V_o = f\, T_{ON}\, V_{in}$ ... (3.2)

- Load voltage is independent of load current. Load voltage can be controlled by varying the duty cycle K. For K < 1, output voltage $V_o < V_{in}$.

- As switch is SCR, so it requires commutation circuit to turn it OFF and firing circuit to turn it ON. For high power applications, SCR is used. For medium and low power application, transistor is most suitable device. For SCR chopper, operating frequency is low.

- The average output voltage can be changed in three ways :
  1. By varying ON time,
  2. By keeping ON time constant and varying the frequency,
  3. By varying both T_{ON} and frequency.

- The filter plays an important role in the operation of chopper. The inductor stores energy during ON period and delivers it during the OFF period.

- The type of load is an important factor for selection of frequency.

- For motor load frequency is 100 Hz to 500 Hz. From chopper circuit operation point of view for a particular application, working at a low chopper frequency is preferred for two reasons :
  1. Increase in the range of load voltage particularly when forced commutation devices are used as a switch.
  2. Reduction in the electrical power dissipation in the circuit.

- Working at a high chopper frequency reduces the voltage and current ripples.

3.1.2 Control Techniques

- The output voltage V_o can be controlled by periodic opening and closing of the switch. There are two schemes by which the duty cycle can be varied leading to the variation in the output voltage. These methods are

  1. Constant frequency system,
  2. Variable frequency system.

- In both the methods, the ratio of T_{ON}/T is varied by varying the value of T_{ON} or T. Therefore, they are called as Time Ratio Control (TRC).

Constant Frequency System :

- In this method, only the ON time T_{ON} is varied keeping the chopping period T constant. Variation of T_{ON} means adjustment of pulse width.

- This method is also called as pulse width modulation (PWM). Duty cycle can be varied from 0 to 1 changing the output voltage from 0 to V_{in}.

  Fig. 3.2 shows output voltage waves for two different duty cycles.

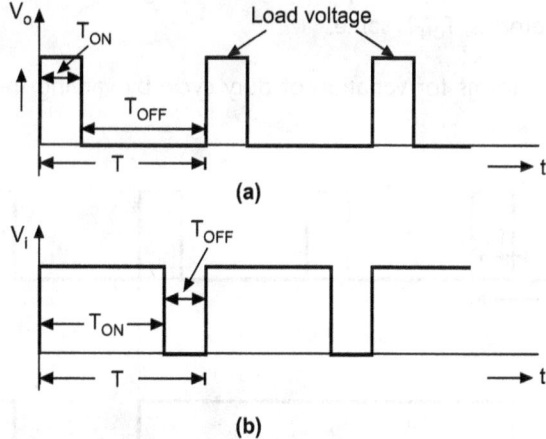

Fig. 3.2 : Constant frequency method for variation of duty cycle

In Fig. 3.2, waveform (a) has lower duty cycle as compared to duty cycle of waveform (b). This method is most widely used.

- The use of constant chopper frequency permits the use of tuned filters and simpler control circuits.

Variable Frequency System :

- In this type of control method, the chopping frequency f is varied and either (i) ON time T_{ON} is kept constant, (ii) OFF time T_{OFF} is kept constant.

- This method is called as frequency modulation control.

Fig. 3.3 shows the variation of duty cycle by varying total T and keeping T_{ON} constant.

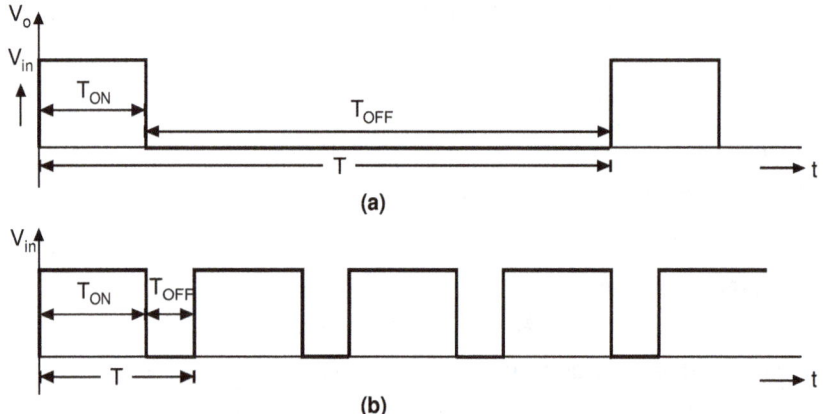

Fig. 3.3 : Duty cycle variation by varying T and keeping T_{ON} constant

In Fig. 3.3 (a), T is very large, so frequency is low. In Fig. 3.3 (b), T is small, so frequency is large. In both waveforms, T_{ON} is same.

Fig. 3.4 shows waveforms for variation of duty cycle by varying frequency and keeping T_{OFF} constant.

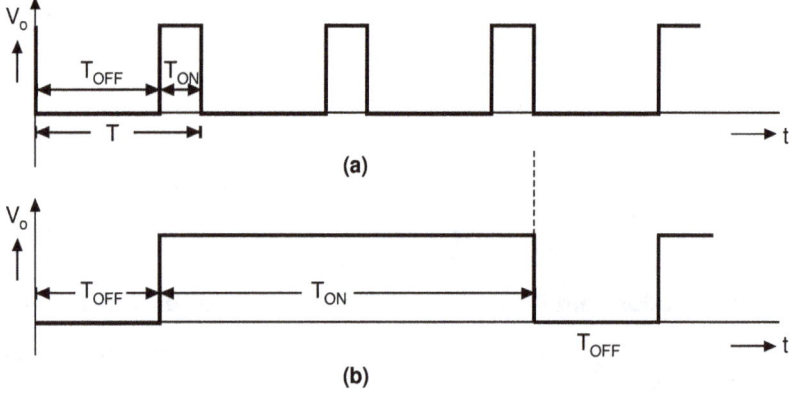

Fig. 3.4 : Duty cycle variation by varying T and keeping T_{OFF} constant

In Fig. 3.4, for duty cycle variation, frequency variation is shown. In Fig. 3.4 (a), waveform is having high frequency, whereas in Fig. 3.4 (b), waveform has low frequency. In both these waveforms, T_{OFF} is maintained constant.

- Frequency modulation control method has following drawbacks as compared to pulse width modulation control :

  (a) As chopping frequency has to be varied over a wide range, so filter design is difficult.

  (b) More possibility of interference with signaling and telephone lines signal.

  (c) Load may be subjected to no current condition which is not desirable.

- PWM method is better than variable frequency scheme. In PWM, low range of duty cycle is not possible.

3.1.3 Chopper Classification

- Choppers are classified on various basis. According to output voltage level compared with input voltage level, choppers are classified as :

  (a) Step-up choppers,

  (b) Step-down choppers.

- In step-up chopper, chopping element is connected in parallel with load and source. So it is also called as parallel chopper. For step-down chopper, chopping element is in series, therefore, it is called as series chopper.

- Choppers are also classified according to type of method used for controlling the output voltage. The types of chopper are :

  (a) PWM choppers,

  (b) FM choppers.

- Choppers are also classified according to the type of commutation used for SCR turn-OFF. Three types of choppers are :

  (a) Voltage commutation choppers,

  (b) Current commutation choppers,

  (c) Load commutation choppers.

- Choppers can be classified according to the output current and output voltage polarity. It is also known as quadrant operation. According to quadrant operation, three main types of choppers are :

  (a) One quadrant chopper :

  Two subtypes are

    (i) Type-A first quadrant chopper,

    (ii) Type-B second quadrant chopper.

(b) Two quadrant choppers :

   Two subtypes are :

   (i) Type-C first and second quadrant operation of chopper,

   (ii) Type-D first and fourth quadrant operation of chopper.

(c) Four quadrant choppers or Type E.

- Choppers are also classified according to the number of chopping elements connected. The types of choppers are :

   (a) Single-phase choppers : One chopping element is used.

   (b) Multiphase choppers : Two SCRs (Chopping Elements) are connected in parallel.

- In the following section, quadrant choppers are explained.

Type-A Chopper :

- It is a first quadrant chopper. When chopper is ON, the load is connected to the supply. So $V_o = V_{in}$ and load current I_o flows in one direction. When chopper element (SCR) is OFF, the load current continues to flow in the same direction. This current flows due to conduction of free-wheel diode.

- Average values of V_o and I_o are positive, hence it is first quadrant chopper. In this chopper, power flow is always from supply to the load.

- It is also called as step-down chopper, because average output voltage V_o is always less than input voltage V_{in}.

Fig. 3.5 shows the circuit diagram and output voltage and current polarities.

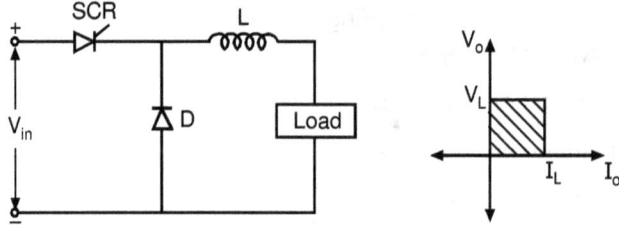

Fig. 3.5 : Type-A chopper

- This operation is used for motoring operation of D.C. motor load. Type-A chopper is also called as motoring chopper.

Type-B Chopper :

- It is a second quadrant chopper. Output voltage and output current are in second quadrant. It is a step-up chopper. In type-B chopper, output voltage is more than input voltage V_i.

- The load contains D.C. source E which may be a battery or representing back e.m.f. of a D.C. motor. I_o is negative. V_o is positive. Hence it is a second quadrant chopper.

  Fig. 3.6 shows the circuit diagram for type-B chopper and output voltage and output current polarities.

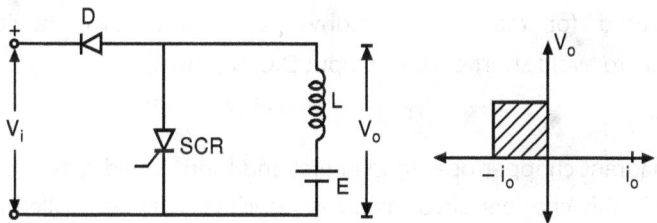

Fig. 3.6 : Type-B chopper

- Load may be D.C. motor. The chopper element is turned ON and OFF during regular interval. When chopper is ON, $V_o = 0$ and when the chopper is OFF, the load current has the opposite direction.
- Now, $V_o = E$ or back e.m.f. This action is known as regenerative breaking of D.C. motors. It is commonly used in traction. SCR is commutated externally.

Type-C Chopper :

- It is a two quadrant chopper. It is a parallel combination of type-A and type-B chopper. Output voltage is positive. Output current is positive or negative.
- It is possible to have either first or second quadrant operation at any given period. This chopper is also called as two quadrant type-A chopper.
- It consists of two SCRs and two diodes D_1 and D_2. Diode D_1 is a free-wheel diode.

  Fig. 3.7 shows the circuit connection of type-C chopper and output voltage and output current relation.

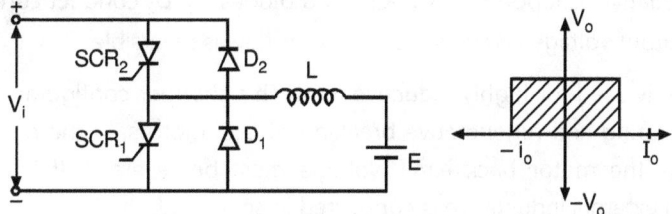

Fig. 3.7 : Type-C chopper

- The output voltage V_o is always positive, because of diode D_1. Free-wheeling diode is connected across the load. When SCR_1 is ON or when D_1 conducts, then output voltage $V_o = 0$. When SCR_2 is ON or diode D_2 conducts, output voltage $V_o = V_{in}$. The load current can flow in reverse direction.

- When SCR_2 or D_1 conducts, then load current is positive. Power flow may be from source to load or from load to source. This type of chopper is used for motoring and regenerative breaking of D.C. motor.

- When SCR_1, SCR_2 and D_1, D_2 are OFF, then load is isolated from source. This type of chopper is used for machine tool drive. SCR_1 and SCR_2 should not be 'ON' simultaneously to avoid short circuit of input D.C. supply.

Type-D Chopper :

- It is a two quadrant chopper operating in first and fourth quadrants. The direction of the load current in this chopper circuit is always positive. It is also called as two quadrant type-B copper. Fig. 3.8 shows circuit connection of type-D chopper and output voltage-current relation.

- Output load voltage can be either positive or negative. When SCR_1 and SCR_2 both are 'ON', output voltage is positive. Output voltage is negative when both SCR_1 and SCR_2 are 'OFF'.

- When SCR_1 and SCR_2 are OFF, diodes D_1 and D_2 conduct.

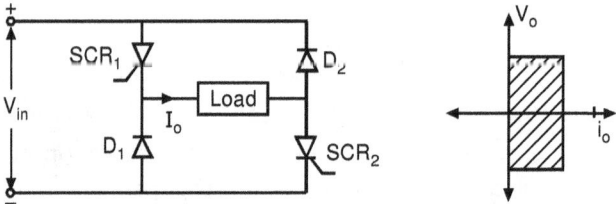

Fig. 3.8 : Type-D chopper

- When $T_{ON} > T_{OFF}$, then average output voltage is positive. When $T_{ON} < T_{OFF}$, then output voltage is negative. Choppers SCR_1, SCR_2 and diodes D_1, D_2 conduct current only in one direction. Output voltage is reversible, so power flow is reversible.

- This chopper is used for highly inductive load. This chopper configuration may be used for both motoring and regenerative breaking of D.C. motors. In the regenerative mode of operation, the motor back e.m.f. voltage must be reversed. If load inductance is smaller, then external inductance is connected in series with the load.

Type-E Chopper :

- It is a four quadrant chopper, four quadrant chopper system can be considered as the parallel combination of two type-C choppers. The circuit consists of four SCRs and four diodes. Fig. 3.9 shows the circuit connection and output voltage current relation.

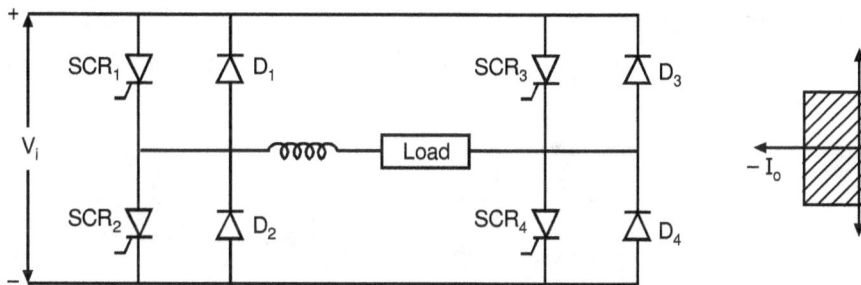

Fig. 3.9 : Type-E chopper

- Using this chopper, polarity of output voltage (V_O) as well as the direction of the output current (I_O) can be reversed. In this chopper configuration with motor load, the direction of rotation can be reversed without reversing the polarity of excitation. In this circuit, SCR_1, SCR_4, D_2 and D_3 form one chopper of type C. SCR_2, SCR_3, D_1 and D_4 form another chopper of type C.
- When SCR_4 is 'ON', SCR_3 must be OFF. Now the circuit operates in first and second quadrant with output voltage positive and output current positive and negative.
- When SCR_2 is ON, SCR_1 must be OFF. Now, if SCR_3 is ON or D_4 conducts, then both load voltage V_O and load current I_O are negative. If SCR_4 is 'ON' or D_3 conducts then V_O is negative, but I_O is positive. It shows fourth quadrant operation. This four quadrant chopper configuration can be used for a reversible regenerative D.C. drive.
- This four quadrant chopper circuit consists of two bridges, forward bridge and reverse bridge. Chopper bridge SCR_1 to SCR_4 is the forward bridge. It permits power flow from source to load. Diode bridge D_1 to D_4 is the reverse bridge which permits the power flow from load to source.

3.1.4 Chopper Commutation

- Chopper circuit consists of switching element. If switching element is SCR, then it requires external turn-ON circuit (firing circuit) and turn-OFF circuit (commutation circuit). Commutation circuit reduces anode circuit current to zero and apply a reverse voltage for sufficient time to enable the SCR to switch to blocking state. The commutation circuits can be broadly classified as
    1. **Forced Commutation :** In this type of commutation, current through the SCR is forced to become zero to turn it OFF. Forced commutation circuit consists of L and C. Forced commutation is done in two ways :
       (a) Voltage Commutation, (b) Current Commutation.
    2. **Load Commutation :** In this type of commutation, the load current flowing through the SCR is transferred to another device.
- **Auxiliary commutation :** Chopper circuit consists of auxiliary SCR along with power SCR. Voltage commutation method and current commutation method consist of auxiliary SCR, so these are also called as auxiliary commutated chopper circuits.

Voltage Commutated Chopper :
- It is a one type of auxiliary commutated chopper. Fig. 3.10 shows the circuit diagram of voltage commutated chopper.

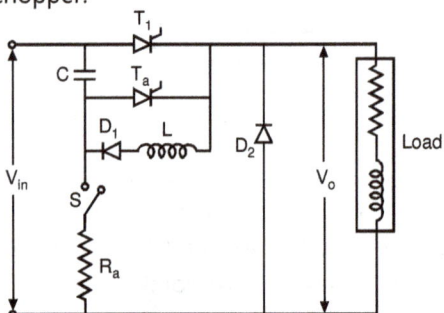

Fig. 3.10 : Voltage commutated chopper

- Commutation circuit consists of C, diode D_1, inductor L and auxiliary SCR T_a. It is a series step-down chopper of type A. In this circuit, SCR_1 is a main SCR. The commutation of main SCR T_1 is done by applying reverse voltage across it. This reverse voltage is obtained from the charge stored in the capacitor C and firing of auxiliary SCR T_a. Diode D_2 is a free-wheel diode.
- Initially capacitor C is charged. This charging is done by switching 'ON', switch S or by triggering auxiliary SCR T_a. In first method, capacitor C voltages due to current flowing from V_{in}, capacitor, switch S and resistor R_a. When voltage across the capacitor C is $V_c \approx V_{in}$, then 'S' is turned OFF.
- In second method, SCR T_a is fired, so current flows from V_{in}, capacitor C, SCR T_a to load. When capacitor charges fully, charging current through the capacitor C decays and it reaches to zero. Then SCR T_a is turned OFF. This chopper operation is described in following four modes.

Mode I : When main SCR T_1 is fired, it carries both load current and capacitor current. If SCR T_1 is triggered at t = 0, then from t = 0 to t = t_1 period, capacitor voltage changes from $V_c = V_{in}$ to $V_c = -V_{in}$.

Mode II : This mode exists from period t = t_1 to t = t_2. During this period, only load current i_o flows.

Mode III : This mode is from t_2 to t_3. In this mode, commutation of main SCR T_1 is done with the help of auxiliary SCR T_a. When T_a is fired, voltage across the capacitor ($-V_{in}$) appears across T_1 to reverse bias it. This turns OFF the main SCR T_1. Now current of main SCR becomes zero. Load current flows from capacitor, auxiliary SCR to load. Load voltage $V_o = V_{in} + V_c$.

Mode IV : This mode starts after T_3. Now diode D_2 conducts and turns-OFF auxiliary SCR T_a.

- It is a simple circuit and used extensively.

Demerits :
- A starting circuit is required.
- Load voltage jumps to twice the supply voltage when commutation is initiated.
- Turn-OFF time is load dependent.
- Circuit does not work at no-load condition.
- Main SCR T_1 has to carry load current and commutation current.

Fig. 3.11 shows related voltage and current waveforms of voltage commutated chopper.

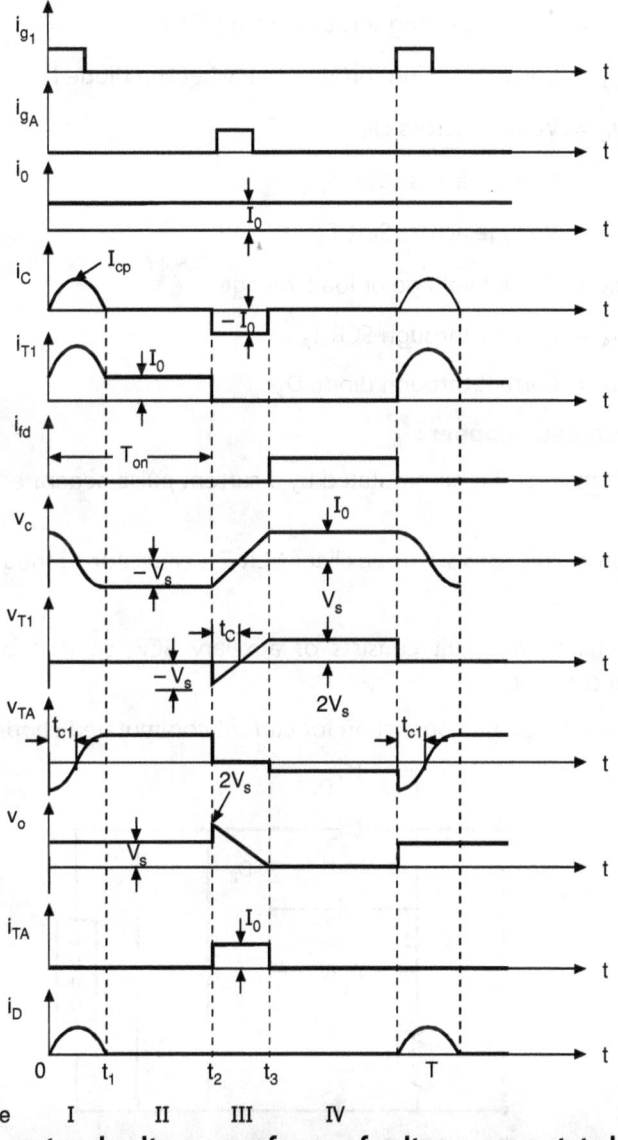

Fig. 3.11 : Current and voltage waveforms of voltage commutated chopper
(Chap. 3.13)

In Fig. 3.11,

i_{g1} = Gate current pulse for SCR T_1

i_{ga} = Gate current pulse for SCR T_a

i_o = Output current i.e. load current

i_c = Capacitor C current

i_{T1} = Current flowing through main SCR T_1

i_{fd} = Current flowing through free wheeling diode D_2

V_c = Voltage across capacitor C

V_{T1} = Voltage across SCR T_1

V_{in} = Voltage across SCR T_A

V_o = Output voltage or load voltage

i_{TA} = Current through SCR T_A

i_D = Current through diode D_1

Current Commutation Chopper :

- In this circuit, main SCR is commutated by a current pulse generated in the commutation circuit.
- Commutation circuit consists of auxiliary SCR T_a, capacitor C, inductor L, diode D_1 and diode D_2.
- As the commutation circuit consists of auxiliary SCR, so it is one type of auxiliary commutated chopper.

Fig. 3.12 shows the circuit connection for current commutated chopper.

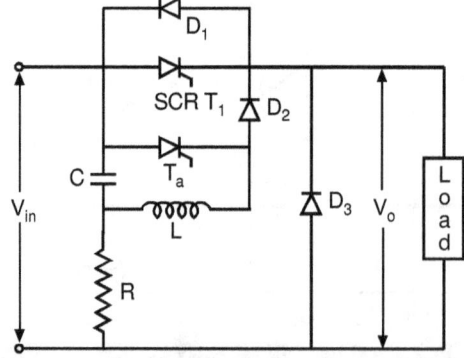

Fig. 3.12 : Current commutated chopper

- Diode D_3 is a free-wheel diode. Resistor R is the charging resistor. Capacitor C is charged to V_{in} level, so it can provide energy for commutating SCR T_1. The charging current flows from V_{in}, capacitor C and through resistor R.

- At t = 0, SCR T_1 (main SCR) is fired, so $V_o = V_{in}$ and load current I_o flows. To commutate the main SCR T_1, auxiliary SCR T_a is triggered.

This commutation operation is explained in following five modes.

Mode I : This mode begins with SCR T_A if turned ON. Till this instant main SCR T_1 conducts. If T_a is turned ON at t_1, then SCR T_1 conducts from t = t_0.

From $t = t_1$ as SCR T_a conducts, so auxiliary current set up in the circuit. It flows through C, T_a and L. This current increases to peak value and then decreases to zero. It decreases to zero at time t = t_2. At t_2 this current reverses in auxiliary SCR T_a and commutate it. At t_2, the reversal of capacitor voltage is complete, so voltage across it $V_c = - V_{in}$. In this mode, $V_o = V_{in}$ and load current = I_o.

Mode II : During this mode, SCR T_1 is turned OFF with the help of auxiliary current. As at t_2, SCR T_a commutates, auxiliary current i_c flows through C, L, D_2 and T_1. This is due to discharging of capacitor C. This current flows through T_1 and not through D_1. Now current through T_1 is a difference between main current and auxiliary current i_c.

$$I_{T1} = I_o - i_c$$

At t = t_3, $i_c = I_o$ and I_{T1} = 0. So SCR T_1 (main SCR) commutates. As due to current i_c commutation occurs, so it is called as current commutated chopper.

Mode III : SCR T_1 is turned OFF at t_3. After t_3, i_c supplies load current I_o and excess current $I_{D1} = i_c - I_o$ conducts through D_1. If voltage across the capacitor V_c is more than V_{in} then diode D_3 conducts at t = t_4.

Mode IV : At t_4, i_c reduces to I_o, so I_{D1} = 0 and diode D_1 is turned OFF. (Diode is a current operating device.) After t_4, constant current I_o flows through V_{in}, C, L, D_2 and load. So capacitor charges to V_{in} at t_5.

$\therefore$ $t_5 - t_4$ period $I_o = i_c$

Now load voltage decreases and capacitor voltage increases.

Mode V : Now $V_c > V_{in}$, diode D_3 starts conducting, i_c decreases and turned OFF diode D_2. Again cycle restarts.

Merits of current commutated chopper :

- Commutation is reliable as long as load current is less than peak commutating current.
- Capacitor is always charged with correct polarity.
- Auxiliary SCR T_a is naturally commutated.

Fig. 3.13 shows related voltage and current waveforms of current commutated chopper.

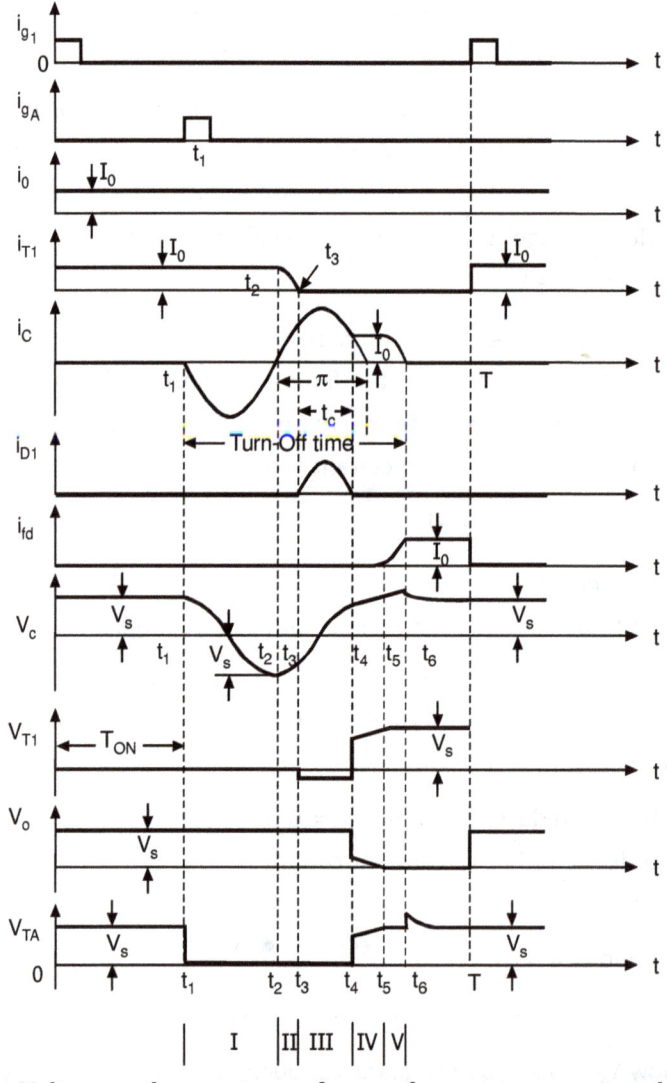

Fig. 3.13 : Voltage and current waveforms of current commutated chopper

In Fig. 3.13,

i_{g1} = Gate current pulse for SCR T_1

i_{gA} = Gate current pulse for SCR T_A (auxiliary SCR)

i_o = Current through load (output current)

i_{T1} = Current through SCR T_1 (main SCR)

i_c = Current flowing through capacitor

i_{D1} = Current flowing through diode D_1

i_{fd} = Current flowing through diode D_3 (free-wheeling diode)

V_c = Voltage across capacitor

V_{T1} = Voltage across SCR T_1

V_o = Voltage across load (output voltage)

V_{TA} = Voltage across auxiliary SCR T_a

Load Commutated Chopper :

- It consists of four chopper elements SCR T_1, SCR T_2, SCR T_3 and SCR T_4. Fig. 3.14 shows the circuit diagram of load commutated chopper.

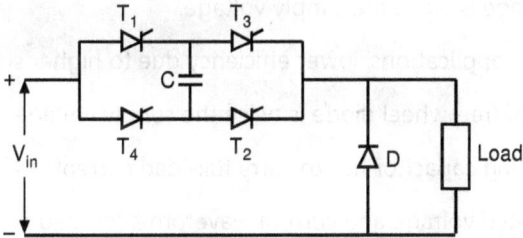

Fig. 3.14 : Load commutated chopper

- In this circuit, C is a commutating capacitor and diode D is a free-wheel diode. T_1, T_2 and T_3, T_4 conduct alternately to load current. When T_1 and T_2 are turned ON, T_3 and T_4 act as commutating components. Similarly, when T_3 and T_4 are conducting, T_1 and T_2 form the commutation circuit. The current through the load is constant. The working of this chopper is explained in following four modes.

Mode I : Initially capacitor is charged to V_{in} with upper plate negative and lower plate positive. At t = 0, T_1 and T_2 are triggered. Load voltage rises to $V_o = V_{in} + V_c = 2V_{in}$. Load current flows through V_{in}, T_1, C, T_2, load. Due to this load current, capacitor charges to $-V_{in}$ level with upper plate positive. At t_1, $V_c = -V_{in}$, so load voltage $V_o = 0$. Due to V_c, T_3 and T_4 are forward biased.

Mode II : At t = t_1, capacitor is slightly over-charged, so free-wheeling diode gets forward biased and load current flows through diode D.

During $t_2 - t_1$, $V_c = -V_{in}$ and $V_o = 0$ V, $IT_1 = IT_2 = 0$.

Mode III : At t = t_2, SCR T_3 and SCR T_4 are triggered and load voltage $V_o = V_{in} + V_c = 2V_{in}$ as $V_c = V_{in}$. SCR$_1$ and SCR$_2$ are reverse biased and turned OFF at t = t_2. Now load current flows through V_{in}, T_4, C, T_3 and load. This current charges capacitor in opposite direction to $-V_{in}$. So $V_o = 0$ at t = t_3. At t = t_3, SCR T_1 and SCR T_2 get forward biased.

At t_3 capacitor C is somewhat overcharged and D gets forward biased after t_3 load current flows through free-wheeling diode. Again if SCR T_1 and SCR T_2 are fired, mode I repeats.

Merits :

- It is capable of commutating any amount of load current.
- No commutating inductor is required.
- It can work at kHz frequencies. So filter becomes simple.

Demerits :

- Peak load voltage is twice the supply voltage.
- For high power applications, lower efficiency due to higher switching losses.
- Required PIV of free-wheel diode is twice the supply voltage.
- The commutating capacitor has to carry full-load current.

Fig. 3.15 shows related voltage and current waveforms for load commutated chopper.

In Fig. 3.15,

I_o = Output current

V_c = Voltage across capacitor

V_o = Output voltage

i_c = Current through capacitor C

i_{fd} = Current flowing through free-wheeling diode D_1

i_{T1}, i_{T2} = Current flowing through SCR T_1 and SCR T_2

i_{T3}, i_{T4} = Current flowing through SCR T_3 and SCR T_4

V_{T1}, V_{T2} = Voltage across SCR T_1 and SCR T_2

V_{T3}, V_{T4} = Voltage across SCR T_3 and SCR T_4

(Chap. 3.18)

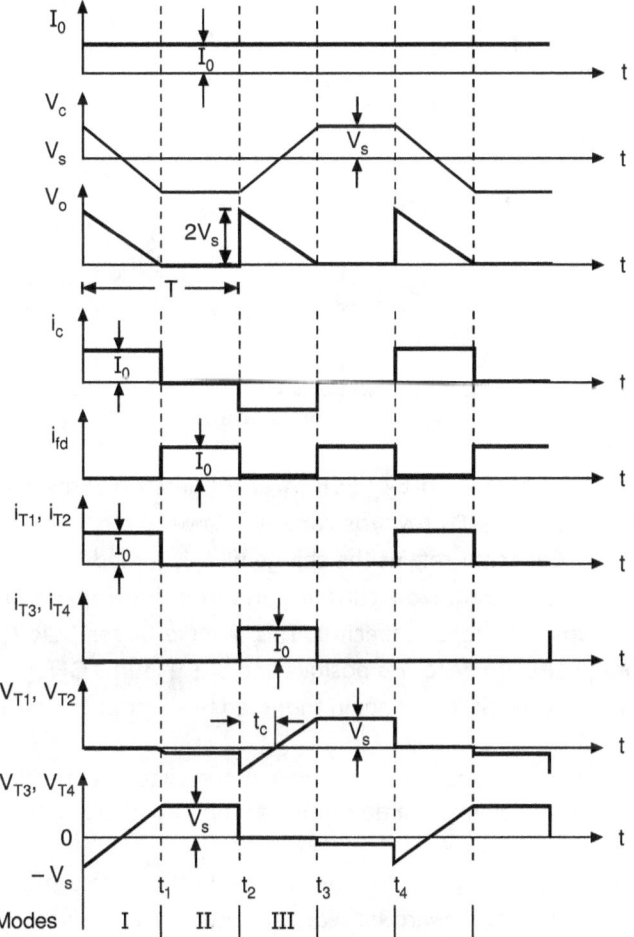

Fig. 3.15 : Voltage and current waveforms of load commutated chopper

3.1.5 Jones Chopper

- In this chopper, class-D commutation is used. Commutating circuit consists of SCR T_2, capacitor C, diode D_2 and auto-transformer. SCR T_1 is a main SCR and diode D_1 is a free-wheeling diode. Fig. 3.16 shows the circuit diagram of Jones chopper.

- L_1 and L_2 of tapped transformer are closely coupled so that capacitor sets sufficient energy to turn OFF the main SCR T_1.

- When T_1 is turned ON for long time, then motor will rotate with maximum speed. When T_1 is turned OFF, motor will not rotate. If T_1 is ON-OFF periodically, then motor rotates at desired speed.

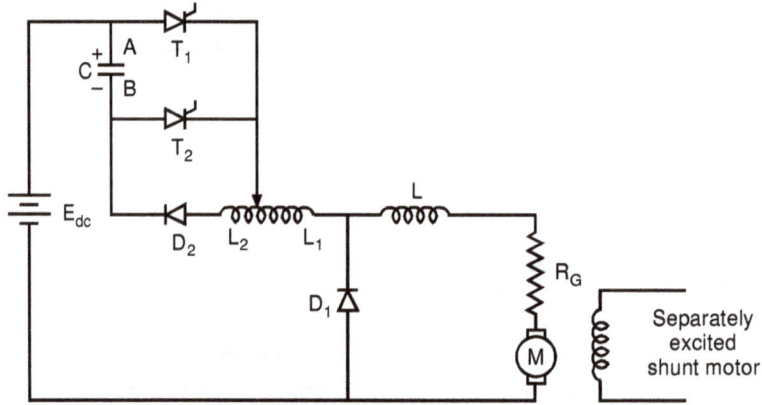

Fig. 3.16 : Jones chopper

Circuit operation :
- Initially capacitor is charged to E_{dc}. SCR T_1 is triggered at time $t = t_1$. Current flows through capacitor C, T_1, L_2, D_2 towards capacitor lower plate. Now capacitor charges in opposite direction. Capacitor retains the charge till t_2 is turned ON.
- At $t = t_3$, SCR T_2 is triggered. Now current flows from lower plate of capacitor, SCR T_2, SCR T_1 towards upper plate of capacitor. This reverse biases SCR T_1 and turns it OFF. Now capacitor upper plate becomes positive and SCR T_2 turns OFF.
- This cycle repeates when SCR T_1 is again triggered. Auto-transformer improves reliability of circuit.
- The main advantage of Jones chopper over other circuit is that it allows the use of higher voltage and lower microfarad commutating capacitor. More flexible control on T_{ON} and T_{OFF} is possible.
- Capacitor starts charging from t_3 to t_5. At t_5, the bottom plate of capacitor reaches to peak value. Diode D_1 gets forward biased. Capacitor C starts discharging to a value less than E_{dc}. Fig. 3.17 shows voltage and current waveforms.

In Fig. 3.17,

I_{g1} = Gate of SCR T_1 trigger pulse

I_{g2} = Trigger pulse for SCR T_2

E_{T1} = Voltage across SCR T_1

E_{T2} = Voltage across SCR T_2

i_{T1} = Current flowing through SCR T_1

i_{T2} = Current flowing through SCR T_2

V_C = Voltage across capacitor

E_O = Load voltage

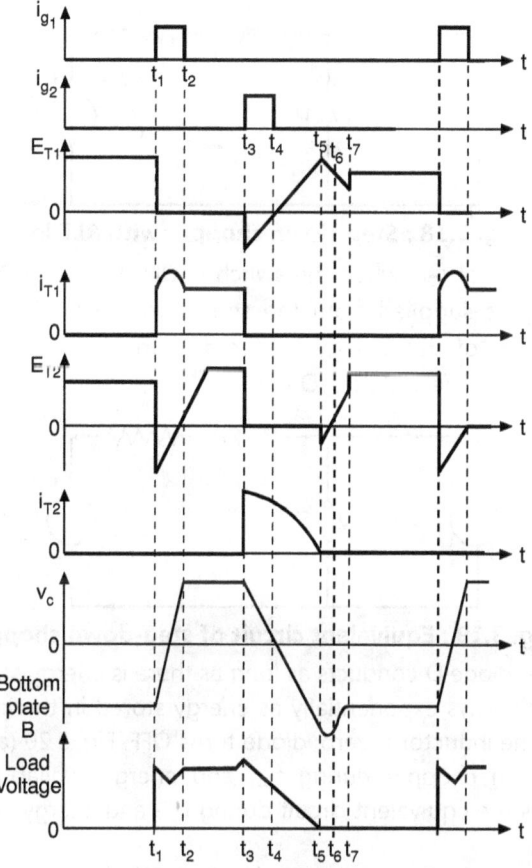

Fig. 3.17 : Jones chopper voltages and current waveforms

3.2 STEP DOWN DC-DC CHOPPER

- DC motor control is one of the most important applications of chopper. DC motor armature circuit has some resistance (R), inductance (L) and also a back emf (E_b). This type of load is known as RLE load. Typically the supply voltage V is greater than the back emf E_b. A diode is connected across such loads. It provides path for the load current when the switching device is OFF. This diode reduces the load current ripple and also prevents impulse voltage appearing across the switching device when it turns OFF. Fig. 3.18 shows the basic circuit of setp down chopper with RLE load.

- V is dc input source, S is a switching device, may be SCR, MOSFET, BJT, GTO or IGBT. E_b is the back emf.

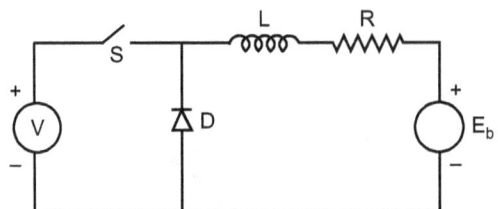

Fig. 3.18 : Step-down chopper with RLE load

- During the time interval t_{ON}, when the switch is ON the diode D is OFF as it is reverse biased and energy is supplied from the source to the load. So load current i_0 rises exponentially. A part of this energy is stored in the inductance. Fig. 3.19 shows the equivalent circuit when the switch is 'ON'.

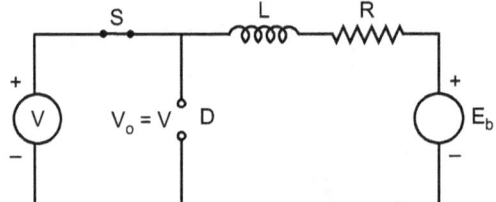

Fig. 3.19 : Equivalent circuit of step-down chopper

- When S is OFF, the diode D conducts as long as there is energy stored in the inductance. Now load current decays exponentially as energy stored in the inductor is spent. When energy stored in the inductor is zero, diode turns OFF. Fig. 3.20 (a) shows the equivalent circuit of step-down chopper during t_{OFF} and energy available in the inductor and Fig. 3.20 (b) shows the equivalent circuit during t_{OFF} and energy stored in the inductor is zero.

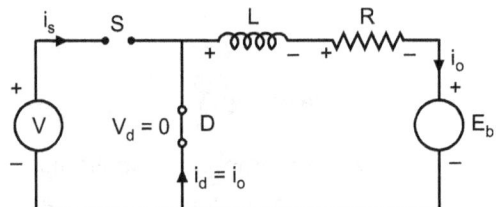

(a) When energy is available in the inductor

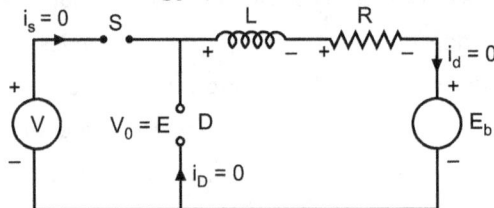

(b) When zero energy is available in the inductor

Fig. 3.20 : Equivalent circuit of step-down chopper

- Under steady-state condition, if the inductance has sufficient stored energy at the beginning of time interval t_{OFF}, the chopper operates in continuous current mode and load current varies between I_{max} and I_{min}. If the stored energy in the inductance is not sufficient the load current falls to zero at t_S within the time interval t_{OFF}. This is known as discontinuous current mode. For any chopper application it is essential to know that either chopper output current is continuous or discontinuous.

3.2.1 Continuous Current Mode

- Fig. 3.21 shows the waveform for continuous mode operation.
- To find load current and voltage apply KVL for the loop formed by load and diode.

$$V_0 - V_L - V_R - E_b = 0 \qquad \ldots (3.1)$$

from which we get,

$$V_L + V_R = V_0 - E_b$$

$$L\frac{di_0}{dt} + Ri_0 = V_0 - E_b$$

Dividing by L,

$$\frac{di_0}{dt} + \frac{R}{L}i_0 = \frac{V_0 - E_b}{L} \qquad \ldots (3.2)$$

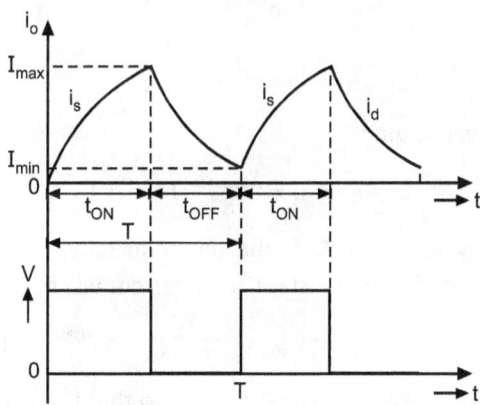

Fig. 3.21 : Waveforms for continuous operating mode chopper

- When switching device is 'ON' at $t = 0$, then during t_{ON}, $V_0 = V$ as the diode is reverse biased.

$$\therefore \qquad \frac{di_0}{dt} + \frac{R_0}{L}i_0 = \frac{V - E_b}{L} \qquad 0 \leq t \leq t_{ON}$$

- This is the first order linear differential equation. Its characteristic equation is,

$$S + \left(\frac{R}{L}\right) = 0$$

Its root is,
$$S = -\frac{R}{L}$$

So the natural component of solution is given by,
$$i_{ON} = K\,e^{-(R/L)t}$$

K is a arbitrary constant. It can be found by initial condition. As the forcing function is on right hand side and is a constant, assuming constant $i_{OFF} = A$, A = constant.

$$\therefore \quad \frac{R}{L}A = \frac{V - E_b}{L}$$

$$\therefore \quad A = \frac{V - E_b}{R}$$

Applying these two equations,
$$i_{ON} + i_{OFF} = K\,e^{-(R/L)t} + \frac{V - E_b}{R}$$

$$i_0 = I_{min} \text{ at } t = 0+$$

Substituting this initial condition,
$$I_{min} = \frac{V - E_b}{R} + K$$

$$\therefore \quad K = I_{min} - \frac{V - E}{R}$$

Substituting and by rearranging,
$$i_0 = i_s = \frac{V - E_b}{R}(1 - e^{-t/T}) + I_{min}\,e^{-t/T} \qquad 0 \le t \le t_{ON} = \delta T$$

where δ is the duty cycle, $T = (L/R)$ is the time constant of the load circuit. At $t = t_{ON}$ switching device is opened at that instant, load current will be

$$i_{0\,t=t_{ON}} = I_{max} = \frac{V - E_b}{R}(1 - e^{-t_{ON}/T}) + I_{min}\,e^{-t_{ON}/T}$$

A new time variable $t = t'$ which is zero at $t = t_{ON}$, so that $t' = t = t_{ON}$.

At $t = t_{ON}$ when the switching device is opened the diode starts conducting due to the energy stored in the inductor of load. Assume that load current is continuous due to large amount of stored energy in the inductor. So the equivalent circuit shown in Fig. 3.20 is applicable for the entire time interval t_{OFF}. When diode D is conducting, $V_0 = 0$.

Substituting this in the equation,
$$\frac{di_o}{dt} + \frac{R}{L}i_o = -\frac{E_b}{L} \qquad 0 \le t' < (T = t_{ON})$$

Power Electronics (NMU) — DC-DC Converter

This is also a first order linear differential equation. Its initial condition is $i_0{}_{(t'=0)} = I_{max}$. Solving equation with this initial condition,

$$i_o = i_D = -\frac{E}{R}(1 - e^{-t'/T}) + I_{max}\, e^{-t'/T} \qquad 0 \leq t' < t_{ON}$$

At $t' = T - t_{ON}$ or $t = T$.

The load current $i_o = I_{min}$. So, from equation,

$$I_{min} = -\frac{E_b}{R}(1 - e^{(-T=-tON)/T}) + I_{max}\, e^{(-T-tON)/T}$$

Solving these equations for I_{max} and I_{min},

$$I_{max} = \frac{V(1 - e^{-tON/T})}{R(1 - e^{-T/t})} - \frac{E_b}{R}$$

$$I_{min} = \frac{V(e^{-(T-tON)/T} - e^{-T/T})}{R(1 - e^{-T/E})} - \frac{E_b}{R}$$

$$= \frac{V}{R}\frac{(e^{tON/T} - 1)}{(e^{T/T} - 1)} - \frac{E_b}{R}$$

Average output voltage, $\qquad V_0 = \delta V$

Average output current, $\qquad I_0 = \dfrac{V_0 - E_b}{R}$

$$= \frac{I_{max} + I_{min}}{2}$$

The rms output voltage, $\qquad V_R = \sqrt{\delta}\, V$

The rms output current, $\qquad I_R = \sqrt{\dfrac{1}{T}\displaystyle\int_0^T i_o^2\, dt}$

Output voltage V_0 can be represented by Fourier series,

$$v_0 = V_0 + \sum_{n=1}^{\infty}(a_n \cos n\omega t + b_0 \sin n\omega t)$$

$$= V_0 + \sum_{n=1}^{\infty}[n \sin(n\omega t + \theta_n)]$$

$$\omega = 2\pi f = \frac{2\pi}{T}$$

(Chap. 3.25)

$$\therefore \quad b_n = \frac{2}{T} \int_0^T v_o \sin n\omega t \, dt$$

$$= \frac{2}{T} \int_0^{t_{ON}} V \sin\left(\frac{2\pi\omega}{T}\right) dt$$

$$= \frac{V}{n\pi} [1 - \cos n\omega \, t_{ON}]$$

$$\therefore \quad a_n = \frac{2}{T} \int_0^T v_0 \cos n\omega t \, dt$$

$$= \frac{2}{T} \int_0^{t_{OFF}} V \cos\left(\frac{2\pi\omega}{T}\right) dt$$

$$= \frac{V}{n\pi} [1 - \sin n\omega \, t_{OFF}]$$

$$c_n = \sqrt{a_n^2 + b_n^2}$$

$$\theta_n = \tan^{-1}\left(\frac{a_n}{b_n}\right)$$

The RMS value of the load current,

$$i_R = \sqrt{I_0^2 + \sum_{n=1}^{\infty} I_{nR}^2}$$

$$= \sqrt{I_0^2 + \sum_{n=1}^{\infty} \left(\frac{V_{nR}}{|Z_n|}\right)^2}$$

$$= \sqrt{I_0^2 + \sum_{n=1}^{\infty} \left(\frac{c_n}{|Z_n|\sqrt{2}}\right)^2}$$

where I_{nR} is the RMS value of nth harmonic content.

V_{nR} = RMS value of nth harmonic voltage

$|Z_n| = \sqrt{R^2 + (n\omega L)^2}$

= Impedance offered to the nth harmonic current

The peak-to-peak output current ripple in the load,

$$\Delta I = I_{max} - I_{min}$$

$$= \frac{V}{R} \frac{1}{(1 - e^{-T/t})} [1 + e^{-T/t}) - (e^{-\delta T/t} + e^{-(1 - \delta T/t)})]$$

Maximum absolute value of the peak-to-peak ripple current occurs at 50% duty cycle.

$$\Delta I_{max} = \frac{V}{R} \tanh\left(\frac{R}{4fL}\right)$$

By approximation,
$$\Delta I_{max} \approx \frac{V}{R} \cdot \frac{R}{4fL}$$

$$\approx \frac{V}{4fL}$$

3.2.2 Discontinuous Current Mode

- When the load current is discontinuous then i_o starts rising from zero in each cycle when switching devices are ON. Then putting $I_{min} = 0$ in the equation

$$i_{0\, t = t_{ON}} = I_{max} = \frac{V - E_b}{R}(1 - e^{-t_{ON}/\tau}) + I_{min}\, e^{-t_{ON}/\tau}$$

$$\therefore \quad I_{max} = \frac{V - E_b}{R}(1 - e^{-t_{ON}/\tau})$$

$$\therefore \quad I_o = I_D = -\frac{E_b}{R}(1 - e^{-t'/\tau}) + \frac{V - E_b}{R}(1 - e^{-t_{ON}/\tau})\, e^{-t/\tau}$$

- Fig. 3.22 shows the waveform for discontinuous operating mode.

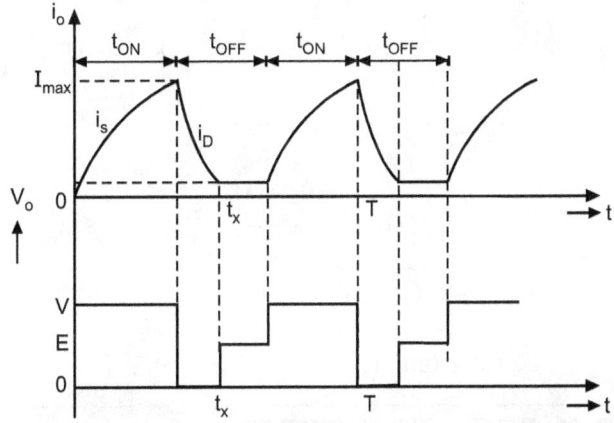

Fig. 3.22 : Discontinuous operating mode current and voltage waveforms at load

The current $i_o = 0$ at $t = t_x$ or when $t' = t_x - t_{ON}$.

- By substituting this condition and by rearranging the terms after taking natural log,

$$t_x = \tau \ln\left\{e^{n\omega/\tau}\left[1 + \left(\frac{V - E_b}{E_b}\right)(1 - e^{-t_{ON}/\tau})\right]\right\} \quad \ldots (3.3)$$

By finding the value of t_x, it is possible to find continuous mode or discontinuous mode.

Power Electronics (NMU)   **DC-DC Converter**

If $t_X < T$ then i_o is discontinuous.

If $t_X > T$ then i_o is continuous.

If I_{min} is positive then i_o is continuous, else i_o is discontinuous.

For discontinuous i_o, voltage waveform is as shown in Fig. 3.22. Average output voltage,

$$V_o = \frac{t_{ON}}{T} V + \frac{(T - t_X)}{T} E_b \qquad \ldots (3.4)$$

The RMS output voltage is,

$$V_R = \sqrt{\frac{1}{T} \int_0^T v_o^2 \, dt}$$

$$= \sqrt{\frac{1}{T} \int_0^{t_{ON}} V^2 \, dt + \frac{1}{T} \int_{t_X}^T E_b^2 \, dt} \qquad \ldots (3.5)$$

The output voltage v_o can be expressed by Fourier series and Fourier coefficients are given by,

$$a_n = \frac{2}{T} \int_0^T v_o \cos n\omega t \, dt$$

$$= \frac{V}{n\pi} [1 - \sin n\omega \, t_{ON}] - \frac{E_b}{n\pi} [1 - \sin n\omega \, t_X] \qquad \ldots (3.6)$$

$$b_n = \frac{2}{T} \int_0^T v_o \sin n\omega t \, dt$$

$$= \frac{V}{n\pi} [1 - \cos n\omega \, t_{ON}] - \frac{E_b}{n\pi} [1 - \cos n\omega \, t_X] \qquad \ldots (3.7)$$

$$c_n = \sqrt{a_n^2 + b_n^2} \qquad \ldots (3.8)$$

$$\theta_n = \tan^{-1}\left(\frac{a_n}{b_n}\right) \qquad \ldots (3.9)$$

3.3 FULL BRIDGE DC-DC CONVERTER

- Single switching device choppers are designed for low rating output power. For higher current rating, size of converter component increases and efficiency decreases. The high power chopper operates the magnetic transformer component in the bipolar and push pull mode. It requires two or four switching devices. As transformers are fully utilized magnetically, they tend to be almost half the size of the equivalent single switch isolated converter at power levels above 100 W.

- Fig. 3.23 shows PWM converter with square wave drive on four switching bipolar devices.

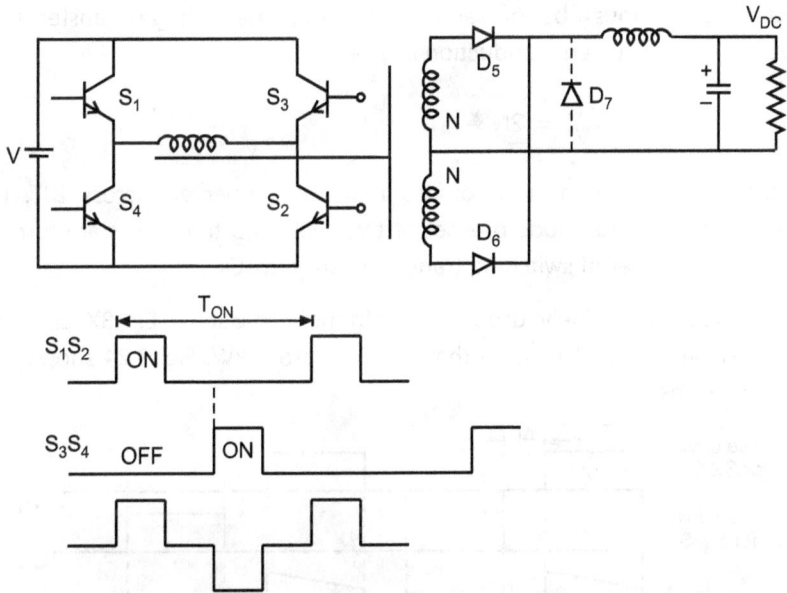

Fig. 3.23 : Full bridge PWM bipolar converter

Pulse width can be changed upto 50% duty cycle, $\delta_{max} = 0.5$.

- This requires some additional energy storage inductor on the output side for smoothing the energy transfer. Freewheeling diode D_7 is added to provide for secondary inductor current to freewheel through the load and thereby reducing the stress on the rectifier. The voltage transfer function of the full bridge PWM converter with continuous conduction is given by,

$$\frac{V_{dc}}{V} = 2N\frac{t_{ON}}{T_{CH}} = 2N\delta$$

- PWM full bridge converter operates as a buck converter. Buck converter is a simplest dc to dc step down converter topology. In case of single switching device, converter voltage rating of the device is 2 V but in bridge converter this rating is V. Total power dissipation is now spread over four controlling devices.

- In case of half bridge converter, two capacitors are used instead of S_2 and S_3. Capacitor branch acts as a voltage divider.

- Voltage transfer function for half bridge converter is,

$$\frac{V_{dc}}{V} = N\frac{t_{ON}}{T_{CH}} = N\delta \qquad \ldots (3.10)$$

- In push pull converter circuit two switching devices and centre tapped transformer are used. Each switch must be of same duty ratio. The voltage transfer function for continuous inductor current conduction is given by,

$$\frac{V_{dc}}{V} = 2N\delta \qquad \ldots (3.11)$$

- In full bridge DC-DC converter, diodes may be connected across BJT. It has two operating modes. In one mode one set of two switching transistors are turn-ON and in other mode second set of switching transistors are turn-ON.

- These converters are widely used in mainframe computers, EPABX and applications where power requirement is more than 500 W upto 2 kW. Fig. 3.24 shows voltage and current waveforms.

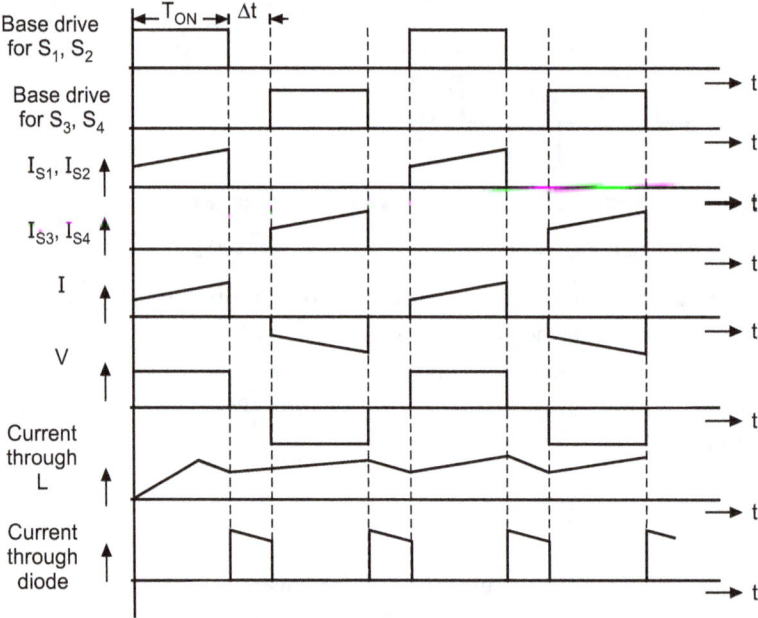

Fig. 3.24 : Voltage and current waveforms of full bridge DC-DC converter

Advantages :

(1) Low ripple and noise in the output.

(2) Better TUF.

(3) Double power than half bridge.

(4) Coupling capacitor can remove flux symmetry problem.

Drawbacks :

- Need four high frequency switching devices and four back up diodes.
- Four switching devices need isolated drive.
- Complex drive circuit.

3.4 SWITCH MODE POWER SUPPLY

- Electronic equipments, computers and instrumentation typically require low dc voltages such as +5 V, ± 12 V etc., in the power range of few watts to few kilowatts. SMPS is a efficient way to convert input ac into several output dc voltages.

- An SMPS is based on a dc chopper with a rectified and possibly transformed output. The output voltage amplitude is controlled by varying the mark-space ratio of the chopper. This may be achieved by means of pulse-width controller or frequency variation with constant pulse width. The circuit technique used for SMPS can be categorised in four ways :

  (1) Flyback SMPS.

  (2) Feed forward SMPS.

  (3) Push-pull SMPS.

  (4) Bridge SMPS.

- Fig. 3.25 shows the block diagram of typically high frequency off line SMPS.

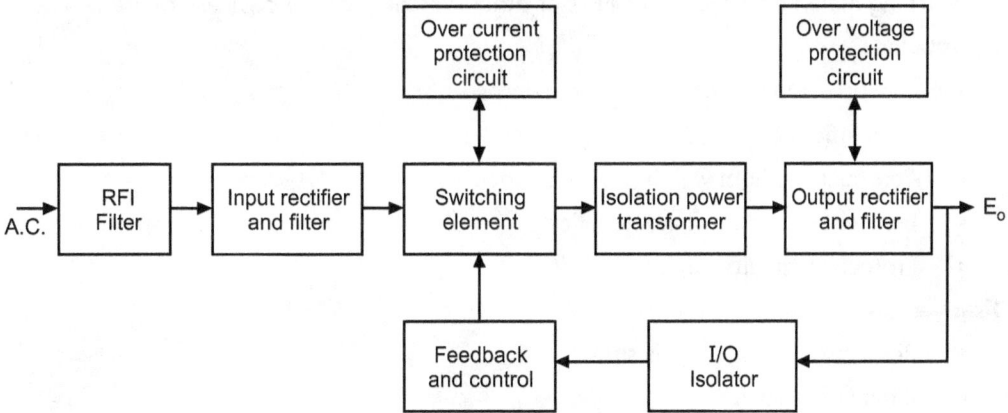

Fig. 3.25 : Functional block diagram of SMPS

- In SMPS the input rectification is done directly off the line without the use of the low frequency isolation power transformer. The AC line is directly rectified and filtered to produce a raw high voltage DC. This DC is fed to the switching element. The switch is operating at high frequency (20 kHz to 1 MHz), chopping the dc voltage into a high frequency square wave. This square wave is fed into the power isolation transformer, stepped down to a predetermined value and then rectified and filtered to produce the required dc output.

- A part of the output is monitored and compared against the fixed reference voltage and error signal is used to control the ON-OFF time of the switch. Thus output gets regulated. Since the switch is either ON or OFF it is dissipating very little energy, resulting in a very high overall power supply efficiency of about 70% to 80%. Other advantage is that size of power transformer is quite small due to high operating frequency. The combination of high frequency and lower magnetics results in light weight power supplies with very high power density as compared to linear power supply.

- In this regulator circuit, switch is connected in series with the load and regulation of output voltage is achieved by ON-OFF switching of the device through feedback circuit. The feedback circuit samples the output voltage and compares it with reference voltage so that the error signal is used to control the duty cycle.

$$V_0 = \delta V_{in} = \left(\frac{t_1}{t_1 + t_2}\right) V_{in} \qquad \ldots (3.12)$$

- If the output voltage tends to decrease below reference voltage V_R then ON time of the pulse is increased. The switching device conducts for long time, so that load voltage increases to desired level. Reverse action occurs, if load voltage tends to increase. For switching action either BJT, MOSFETs or other switching power devices are used.

Advantages :
- Low power dissipation switching devices.
- High efficiency.
- Compact and light weight power supply.
- Excellent operating characteristics.
- Protection circuits can be used.

Disadvantages :
- Response of regulation is slow.
- It may produce noise.
- Many times life is lower than linear power supply.
- Expensive.

- In isolated fly back converter, the ferrite core high frequency transformer is used for electrical isolation between the load and the source. Due to use of transformer it is possible to obtain multiple outputs.

- In discontinuous mode fly back converter, slower diodes can be used on the secondary side for rectification. It requires smaller size transformer as compared to continuous node converter. It does not require filter inductance on the secondary side. It gives fast transient response. This type of discontinuous converter based SMPS requires high peak current rating devices on both sides with large size filter capacitor. Its maximum duty cycle is limited to 50%.

3.5 STEP-UP CHOPPER

- The chopper which is used to produce higher voltage at the load than the input voltage is called as step-up chopper. Chopper element is in parallel with source and load. Fig. 3.26 shows the circuit diagram of step-up chopper. L is a series inductor. It is connected to store energy when SCR (chopping element) is 'ON'. Diode D is used to block reverse flow of current. When the SCR is triggered, the inductor L is connected to the supply E_{dc} and inductor stores energy during the period T_{ON}.

- When SCR is OFF, the inductor current is forced to flow through the diode for a T_{OFF} period. As the current tends to decrease, polarity of the e.m.f. induced in inductor L is reversed. So voltage across the load is

$$V_o = V_{dc} + L\frac{di}{dt} \qquad \ldots (3.13)$$

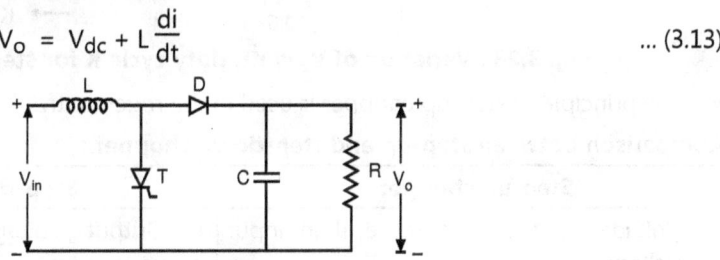

Fig. 3.26 : Step-up chopper

- Inductor voltage adds to source voltage to force the inductor current into the load. High value inductors are used to get less ripples in the output. Fig. 3.27 shows voltage and current waveforms of step-up chopper.

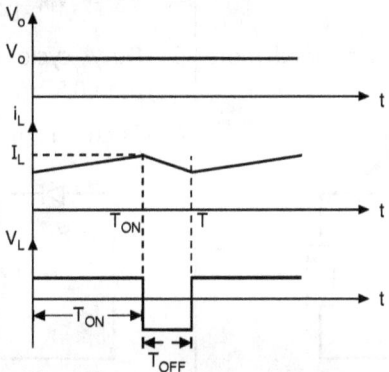

Fig. 3.27 : Voltage and current waveforms of step-up chopper

- During 'ON' time, inductor current increases linearly and during OFF time inductor current decreases linearly. Duty cycle is defined as ratio of T_{ON} to total time T.

$$\text{Duty cycle, } K = \frac{T_{ON}}{T_{ON} + T_{OFF}} = \frac{T_{ON}}{T} \quad \ldots (3.14)$$

- Voltage at the output varies with variation in K. K has a range between 0 to 1. Fig. 3.28 shows the relation between voltage at the output and duty cycle K.

$$V_o = \frac{V_{in}}{1 - K} \quad \ldots (3.15)$$

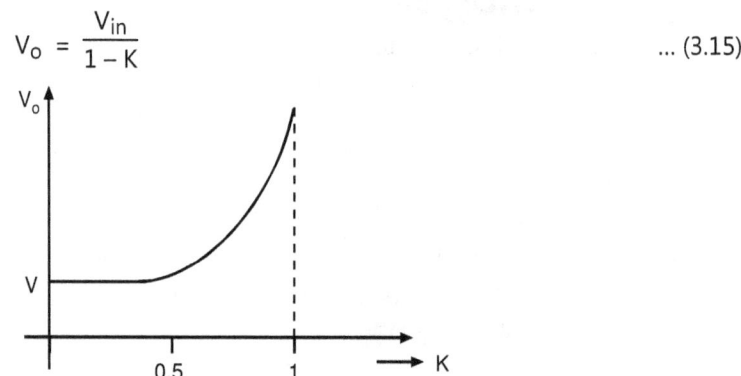

Fig. 3.28 : Variation of V_o w.r.t. duty cycle K for step-up chopper

- The principle of step-up chopper is used in the regenerative breaking of a D.C. motor.

Comparison between step-up and step-down chopper :

Step-up chopper	Step-down chopper
1. Voltage at output is more than input voltage.	1. Output voltage is less than input voltage.
2. Chopping element is in parallel.	2. Chopping element is in series.
3. Inductor is connected in series.	3. Inductor is connected in parallel.
4. $V_o = V_{in} \dfrac{1}{1-K}$	4. $V_o = V_{in} \dfrac{K}{1-K}$
5. Duty cycle is normally maintained more than 0.5 and less than 1.	5. Duty cycle is always maintained less than 0.5.
6. Circuit diagram :	6. Circuit diagram :
Fig. 3.29 (a)	Fig. 3.29 (b)

(Chap. 3.34)

SOLVED EXAMPLES

Example 3.1 : *A single quadrant dc chopper has a resistive load of 10 Ω and an input voltage of 230 V. The chopping frequency is 1 kHz and ON time is 0.4 msec. Determine average load current and power delivered to load.*

Solution : Given : $V_{dc} = 230$ V, $f = 1$ kHz, $T_{ON} = 0.4$ msec

$$\text{The duty cycle} = \frac{0.4 \text{ msec}}{1 \text{ msec}} = 0.4$$

As $f = 1$ kHz, $T = \frac{1}{f}$

∴ $T = 1$ msec

∴ Average load voltage,

$$V_{av} = V_{dc} \times \text{Duty cycle}$$
$$= 230 \text{ V} \times 0.4 = 92 \text{ V}$$

Load power delivered,

$$P_{out} = V_{ar}^2 / R$$
$$V_{ar} = V_{dc} \times \sqrt{K}$$
$$= 230 \times \sqrt{0.4} = 145.46 \text{ V}$$

∴ $$P_{load} = \frac{(145.46)^2}{10 \text{ Ω}}$$

$$= \mathbf{2115.86 \text{ watt}}$$

$$\text{Average load current} = \frac{V_{av}}{R} = \frac{92}{10} = \mathbf{9.2 \text{ A}}$$

Example 3.2 : *A 400 V dc source supplies RL load through a chopper. For the duty cycle of chopper α = 0.25. Find the chopping frequency to limit the amplitude of load current to 10 A. Take L = 0.5 H and R = 0 Ω.*

Solution : Given : $V_{dc} = 400$ V, $\alpha = 0.25$

∴ $V_{out} = \alpha \times V_{dc} = 0.25 \times 400 = 100$ V

$$L\frac{di}{dt} + 100 = 400 \qquad \text{(As per KVL)}$$

∴ $$L\frac{di}{dt} = 300$$

∴ $$L \times \frac{10}{T_{ON}} = 300$$

(Chap. 3.35)

$$T_{ON} = \frac{0.5 \times 10}{300} = 16.67 \text{ msec}$$

But
$$\frac{T_{ON}}{T} = \alpha$$

∴
$$T = \frac{16.67}{0.25} = 66.68 \text{ msec}$$

$$\text{Chopping frequency, } f = \frac{1}{T} = \frac{1}{66.68 \times 10^{-3}} = \mathbf{15 \text{ Hz}}$$

Example 3.3 : *A step-up chopper has input voltage of 230 V and output voltage 660 V. If the OFF time of the chopper is 100 μsec. Calculate pulse width of the output voltage. In case the pulse width is reduced by 50% find new output voltage.*

Solution : (a) Output voltage 660 V = $V_{in}\left(\frac{1}{1-\alpha}\right)$

$$660 \text{ V} = 230 \frac{1}{1-\alpha}$$

∴
$$1 - \alpha = \frac{230}{660}$$

∴
$$\alpha = 1 - \frac{230}{660} = 0.65152$$

$$\alpha = \frac{T_{ON}}{T_{ON} + T_{OFF}}$$

$$0.65152 = \frac{T_{ON}}{T_{ON} + 100 \text{ μsec}}$$

$$0.65152 \, T_{ON} + (100 \times 0.65152) \times 10^{-6} = T_{ON}$$

∴
$$(65.152) \times 10^{-6} = T_{ON} - 0.65152 \, T_{ON}$$

$$= 3484 \, T_{ON}$$

∴
$$T_{ON} = 200 \text{ μsec}$$

∴
$$T = \mathbf{300 \text{ μsec}}$$

(b) If T_{ON} is reduced by 50%.

New T_{ON} = 100 μsec   at T = 300 μsec

∴ New output voltage = $230 \left(\dfrac{1}{1 - \dfrac{1}{3}}\right) = 230 \left(\dfrac{1}{1 - 0.33}\right)$

$$= \mathbf{243.28 \text{ V}}$$

Example 3.4 : *A dc chopper is connected to an inductive load with a resistance of 5 Ω and an input voltage of 300 V. The ON time and OFF time are 20 msec and 10 msec respectively. Determine duty cycle, chopping frequency, average load voltage and average load current.*

Solution : Duty cycle, $K = \dfrac{T_{ON}}{T_{ON} + T_{OFF}} = \dfrac{20}{20 + 10}$

$$= \dfrac{20}{30} = \mathbf{0.667}$$

Chopping frequency $= \dfrac{1}{T_{ON} + T_{OFF}} = \dfrac{1}{30 \text{ msec}}$

$$= \mathbf{33.33 \text{ Hz}}$$

Load voltage $= K \times V_{dc}$

$$= 0.667 \times 300$$

$$= \mathbf{200.1 \text{ V}}$$

Load current $= \dfrac{200.1}{5} = \mathbf{40.02 \text{ A}}$

Example 3.5 : *A step down chopper operating frequency is 2 kHz with a dc source supply of 250 V and load resistance 12 Ω. The time constant of the load circuit is 10 msec. If the average load voltage is 150 V, calculate (a) the on-time, (b) the average and RMS values of load current, (c) peak-to-peak ripple current.*

Solution : The period of chopper, $T = \dfrac{1}{f} = \dfrac{1}{2 \times 1000} = \dfrac{1}{2000} = 0.5$ msec

Since the time constant of the load circuit (L/R) is 10 msec, which is very large as compared to T, the load current may be taken to be continuous.

(a) T_{ON} and duty cycle K :

For duty cycle,

Output average voltage $= K \times V_{dc}$

$\therefore \qquad K = \dfrac{\text{Output voltage}}{V_{dc}} = \dfrac{150 \text{ V}}{250 \text{ V}} = 0.6$

Duty cycle $= 0.6$

As duty cycle $= \dfrac{T_{ON}}{T}$

$\therefore \qquad 0.6 = \dfrac{T_{ON}}{0.5}$

$\therefore \qquad T_{ON} = 0.6 \times 0.5 = \mathbf{0.3 \text{ msec}}$

(b) RMS value of load current and average load current :

$$\text{Average load current} = I_o = \frac{V_o}{R} = \frac{150}{10} = 15 \text{ A}$$

RMS value of the load current,

$$I_R = \frac{V_{rms}}{R} = \frac{\sqrt{0.6} \times 250}{10} = \textbf{19.37 A}$$

(c) For peak-to-peak current :

$$\text{Time constant, } T = \frac{L}{R} = 10 \text{ msec}$$

Peak-to-peak current,

$$\Delta I = \frac{V(1-\delta)\delta T}{L} = \frac{250(1-0.6) \, 0.6 \times 0.5 \times 10^{-3}}{0.1}$$

$$= \textbf{0.3 A}$$

Example 3.6 : *In the step-up chopper, input voltage is 120 V, load voltage 250 V. If the average power is 25 kW, calculate (a) duty cycle, (b) effective load resistance, (c) average source current.*

Solution : Value of input current,

$$I_{in} = \frac{P_{out}}{V_{in}} = \frac{25 \times 10^3}{120} = 208.33 \text{ A}$$

Average current through load,

$$I_{out} = \frac{P_o}{V_{out}} = \frac{25 \times 10^3}{250} = \textbf{100 A}$$

Output voltage, $\qquad V_{out} = \dfrac{V_{in}}{1-\delta}$

where $\qquad \delta$ = Duty cycle

$$250 = \frac{120}{1-\delta}$$

$$\therefore \qquad 250 - 250\,\delta = 120$$

$$\therefore \qquad \frac{250-120}{250} = \delta$$

$$\therefore \qquad \delta = \textbf{0.52}$$

The effective load resistance,

$$R_{eff} = \frac{V_{in}}{I_{in}} = \frac{120}{208.33} = \textbf{0.57 } \Omega$$

Example 3.7 : *A step up dc chopper has an input voltage of 200 V and an output voltage of 250 V. The blocking period in each cycle of operation is 0.6 msec. Find the period of conduction in each cycle.*

Solution : Output voltage $= \dfrac{V_{in}}{1-\delta}$

$$250 \text{ V} = \dfrac{200}{1-\delta}$$

$\therefore \quad \delta = \dfrac{250-200}{250} = \dfrac{50}{250} = 0.2$

As $\quad \delta = \dfrac{T_{ON}}{T_{ON}+T_{OFF}}$

$\therefore \quad T_{ON} = \dfrac{\delta \times T_{OFF}}{1-\delta} = \dfrac{0.2 \times 0.6}{1-0.2} =$ **0.15 msec**

$\therefore$ Period of conduction in each cycle is 0.15 msec.

Example 3.8 : *A step up chopper has an input voltage of 220 V and an output voltage of 660 V. If the non-conducting time of SCR chopper is 100 μsec, calculate the pulse width of the output voltage. In case the pulse width is reduced by 50% for constant frequency operation, find the new output voltage.*

Solution : Duty cycle, $\delta = 1 - \dfrac{V_{in}}{V_{out}} = 1 - \dfrac{220}{660} = 0.67$

$$\delta = \dfrac{T_{ON}}{T_{ON}+T_{OFF}}$$

$\therefore \quad T_{ON} = \dfrac{\delta T_{OFF}}{1-\delta} = \dfrac{0.67 \times 100}{1-0.67}$

$\qquad =$ **203 μsec**

$\therefore$ Chopper frequency, $f = \dfrac{1}{T} = \dfrac{1}{200+103 \text{ μsec}} = \dfrac{1}{303 \text{ μsec}} =$ **3.33 kHz**

When the pulse width is reduced by 50% and chopper frequency constant then $t_{ON} = \dfrac{203}{2} = 101.5$ μsec.

$\therefore \quad t_{OFF} = 303 - 101.5 = 201.5$ μsec

$\therefore \quad \delta_{new} = \dfrac{101.5}{303} = 0.335$

$\therefore \quad$ Output voltage $= \dfrac{220}{1-\delta} = \dfrac{220}{1-0.335} =$ **330.8 V**

REVIEW QUESTIONS

1. Draw basic diagram of chopper and sketch input and output waveforms.
2. Describe the working of Jones chopper with circuit diagram.
3. Classify choppers according to direction of output voltage and current. Draw their configuration.
4. Explain with waveforms the constant frequency system and variable frequency system for chopper control.
5. Draw the voltage and current waveforms and explain with circuit diagram load commutation method in chopper.
6. Compare step-up chopper and step-down chopper on the basis of output voltage, effect of duty cycle, chopping element position and circuit configuration.
7. State the working principle of chopper.
8. List out any four features of chopper and state any four applications of chopper.
9. Explain the role of inductor in step-down and step-up chopper.
10. What is PWM chopper ? State its advantages.
11. What is frequency modulation chopper control ? State two methods for this control. List drawbacks of this control method.
12. How choppers are classified according to output voltage level, output voltage control, commutation method, quadrant operation and number of chopping elements ?
13. Explain with circuit diagram class-B chopper.
14. Compare class-C and class-D chopper.
15. How many SCRs are required in type-E chopper ? Explain its operation with circuit diagram.
16. What is commutation ? How commutation is done in chopper circuits ?
17. State advantages and drawbacks of voltage commutated chopper.
18. Sketch circuit diagram of current commutated chopper. Explain its operation using related waveforms.
19. Compare inverter circuit with chopper circuit.
20. What is TRC ? Explain its operation.
21. What is SMPS ? Explain with block diagram operation of SMPS.
22. State advantages and drawbacks of SMPS.

Chapter 4
INVERTER

| Weightage of Marks = 16, Teaching Hours = 08 |

Contents

- Introduction
  - Need of inverter
  - Classification
- Series inverter
  - Basic series inverter
  - Modified series inverter
- Parallel inverter
  - Basic parallel inverter
- Single phase bridge inverter
  - Single phase half bridge inverter
  - Single phase full bridge inverter
  - PWM inverter
- Harmonic reduction techniques
- Three phase bridge inverter
- Advantages of MOSFET inverter
- Inverter selection factors

Objectives

After learning this chapter, reader will be able to :

- Describe features of inverter.
- State classification of inverters.
- State and explain need of modification of basic series inverter.
- Explain parallel inverter.
- Describe half and full bridge inverter.
- State need and method of output voltage control of inverter.
- List PWM technique for voltage and waveform control of inverter.
- Explain harmonic reduction techniques.
- Explain three phase bridge inverter.
- List advantages of MOSFET inverter.
- List specifications of inverter.

4.1 INTRODUCTION

4.1.1 Need to Inverter

- A static power converter that converts D.C. input power into A.C. output power at any specified voltage and frequency is called an inverter. These are also called as D.C. to A.C. static converters. For inverter switching BJT, MOSFETs, IGBTs, MTC (MOS controlled thyristors), SITH (Static Induction thyristors), GTO and SCR can be used.

- For low and medium power output, power transistors and other power devices are used.

- For high power applications, thyristors should be used. Table 4.1 indicates comparison between transistorised and SCR inverters.

Table 4.1

Sr. No.	Transistorised Inverter	SCR Inverter
1.	It is suitable for low and medium power output.	It is suitable for high power output.
2.	Higher switching speed.	Lower switching speed.
3.	It requires simple control circuit. No need of trigger circuit.	It requires complex control circuit. It requires separate trigger circuit.
4.	It has high efficiency.	It has low efficiency.
5.	It has greater reliability.	It is less reliable.
6.	No additional circuit is required for commutation.	It requires additional circuit for commutation.
7.	Lower output current.	Higher output current.
8.	Small size, less weight and less expensive.	Larger size, higher weight and expensive.

- The output voltage waveform of an ideal inverter should be sinusoidal. The voltage waveforms of practical inverter are non-sinusoidal and contain harmonic distortion. The output frequency of an inverter depends on switching rate of semiconductor device.

- The D.C. power input to the inverter may be battery, fuel cell, solar cell or other D.C. source. The quality of an inverter is normally evaluated in terms of following performance factors :
  1. The harmonic factor
  2. The distortion factor
  3. The total harmonic distortion factor
  4. The lowest order harmonic.

Some important applications of inverters are
- Adjustable speed A.C. drive
- Induction heating
- Stand-by aircraft power supplies
- UPS (Uninterrupted power supply)
- HVDC
- Satellite power supply
- Astranout suits cooling system
- Illumination system
- Domestic electric supply
- Ultrasonic generator
- SONAR transmitter

4.1.2 Inverter Classification

- The inverter circuits can be classified into many groups on the basis of different criteria.

    1. **Based on the number of output phases :**

        (a) Single phase

        (b) Three phase

    2. **Based on the method of commutation :**

        (a) Line commutation : Inverters based on natural commutation are called as line commutated inverters.

        (b) Forced commutation : In case of D.C. circuits since the supply voltage does not go through the zero point, some external circuit is required to commutate the SCRs. Inverters based on this principle are called forced commutated inverters. These type of inverters require complex commutation circuits. It is a stand-alone inverter. It can provide variable voltage and variable frequency A.C. supply. These are having wide range of applications.

    3. **Based on the connections of thyristor and commutating elements :**

        (a) Series inverter

        (b) Parallel inverter

        (c) Bridge inverter

    4. **Based on the nature of D.C. source at input :**

        (a) Voltage fed inverter

        (b) Current fed inverter

Table 4.2 shows the comparison between voltage fed inverter and current fed inverter.

Table 4.2 : Comparison of voltage fed inverter and current fed inverter

Sr. No.	Voltage Fed Inverter	Current Fed Inverter
1.	It is also called as Voltage Source Inverter (VSI).	It is also called as Current Source Inverter (CSI).
2.	Source voltage is constant and independent of load.	Source current is constant and independent of load.
3.	D.C. source has small or negligible impedance.	D.C. source has high impedance.
4.	Suitable for single motor or multimotor drive.	Not suitable for multimotor drive.
5.	Load voltage is determined by inverter. Load current waveform depends on load.	Load current depends on inverter load and voltage depends on load parameter.

4.1.3 Series Inverter

- In a series inverter, commutating components L and C are connected in series with the load. Load resistor R, commutating components L and C form an underdamped circuit.
- This type of SCR based inverter produces an approximately sinusoidal waveform at a high output frequency, output signal frequency may range from 200 Hz to 100 kHz for efficient operation at higher frequencies.
- The series inverter has many advantages over parallel inverter. As switching frequency increases, size of commutating component decreases.

Applications of series inverter are

- Ultrasonic generators
- Induction heating
- Sonar transmitter
- Fluorescent lighting.

Basic Series Inverter :

- Basic series inverter consists of two thyristors T_1 and T_2. There are two produced positive half cycle and negative half cycle at the output.
- L and C are commutating elements and these are connected in series with the load.

Fig. 4.1 (a) shows the circuit diagram and Fig. 4.1 (b) shows the associated waveforms.

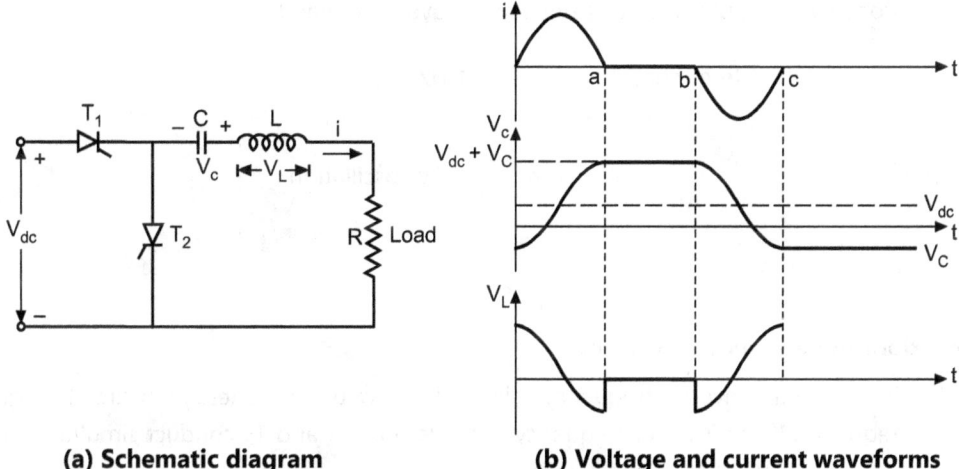

(a) Schematic diagram   (b) Voltage and current waveforms

Fig. 4.1 : Basic series inverter

This is the basic circuit operation mode. Value of L and C are selected such that $R^2 < \frac{4L}{C}$.

... (4.1)

Mode 1 :

- When V_{dc} is applied and T_1 is turned ON, then current flows through R-L-C circuit. Capacitor C charges to V_C level.
- Current increases gradually to peak value. The voltage across C is approximately the supply voltage V_{dc}.
- After this current starts decreasing. Finally current becomes zero.
- Now voltage across the capacitor is maximum and it is $V_{dc} + V_C$. As soon as current becomes zero, thyristor T_1 turns OFF.

Mode 2 :

- In this mode both T_1 and T_2 SCRs are in OFF state. Voltage across the capacitor will be held constant. This OFF period ensures proper turn OFF for T_1.

Mode 3 :

- Voltage on capacitor makes anode of T_2 as positive.
- Now gate pulse is applied to T_2. Capacitor C discharges through T_2.
- So current flows through the load in opposite direction.
- It forms a negative half cycle.
- This current increases to negative peak and decreases to zero.

- SCR T_2 will then be turned OFF. Again after time delay T_{OFF}, T_1 is fired. So by repeating the process at the output, almost sinusoidal wave is obtained.

$$\text{Output frequency, } f = \frac{1}{\left[\frac{T}{2} + T_{OFF}\right]} \text{ Hz} \quad \ldots (4.2)$$

where $\quad T = $ Time period of oscillation

$$\frac{T}{2} = \frac{\pi}{\sqrt{\frac{1}{LC} - \frac{R^2}{4L^2}}}$$

Limitations of basic series inverter :

1. The maximum inverter frequency is limited to a value that is less than circuit ranging frequency. If the inverter frequency exceeds both T_1 and T_2 conduct simultaneously and D.C. source gets short circuited.
2. The load voltage waveform has more distortion due to T_{OFF} time delay.
3. High rating of commutating component is required as they carry load current.
4. Load current is drawn from D.C. source only during positive cycle, so its peak current rating increases and more ripples are present in it.
5. Circuit shows poor output regulation.

These limitations are overcome by modifying the basic inverter circuit.

Modified Series Inverter :

- To overcome maximum frequency limitation, inductance of basic series inverter is divided into two inductors L_1 and L_2 having same inductance and closely coupled.
- Now T_2 can be triggered even before load current reduces to zero or T_1 has been turned OFF.
- This increases the frequency range. Fig. 4.2 shows modified series inverter with coupled inductor.

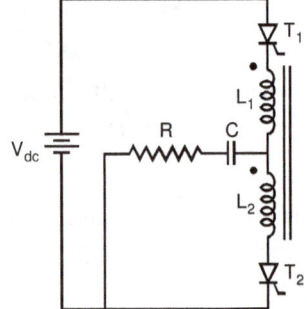

Fig. 4.2 : Series inverter with coupled inductors

- In the basic series inverter and in modified series inverter for maximum frequency, current from d.c. source is intermittent. This drawback is overcome by using half bridge improved series inverter.

Fig. 4.3 shows half bridge modified series inverter.

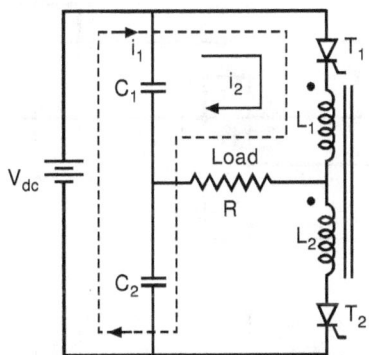

Fig. 4.3 : Half bridge modified series inverter

- In this circuit, power is drawn from the input during both the half cycles of output. In this inverter, $L_1 = L_2$ and $C_1 = C_2$. Total voltage across C_1 and C_2 should be equal to V_{dc}.

- As T_1 is turned ON, two currents flow through T_1 and load R. Current i_1 flows through path $V_{dc+} - T_1 - L_1 - R - C_{2+} - C_2 - V_{dc}$. It charges C_2. Capacitor C_1 provides second current i_2. This i_2 has path $C_{1+} - T_1 - L_1 - R - C_1$. As input voltage for both capacitors are equal, so 50% of load current is drawn from the input source and 50% from the discharge of the capacitor.

- In both cycles, above process repeats. Hence, input D.C. supply no more remains intermittent in nature and ripples are reduced to the minimum.

4.1.4 Parallel Inverter

- In parallel inverter, capacitor is connected in parallel with the load to commutate a conducting thyristor. In class-D complementary commutation method is used. Fig. 4.4 shows a basic parallel inverter.

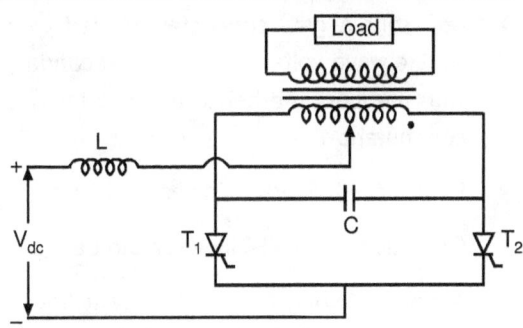

Fig. 4.4 : Basic parallel inverter

Operation of Basic Parallel Inverter Circuit :

- This basic parallel inverter circuit produces A.C. square wave output from D.C. input source. Once the SCRs are turned ON alternately, load is connected across secondary of the transformer.

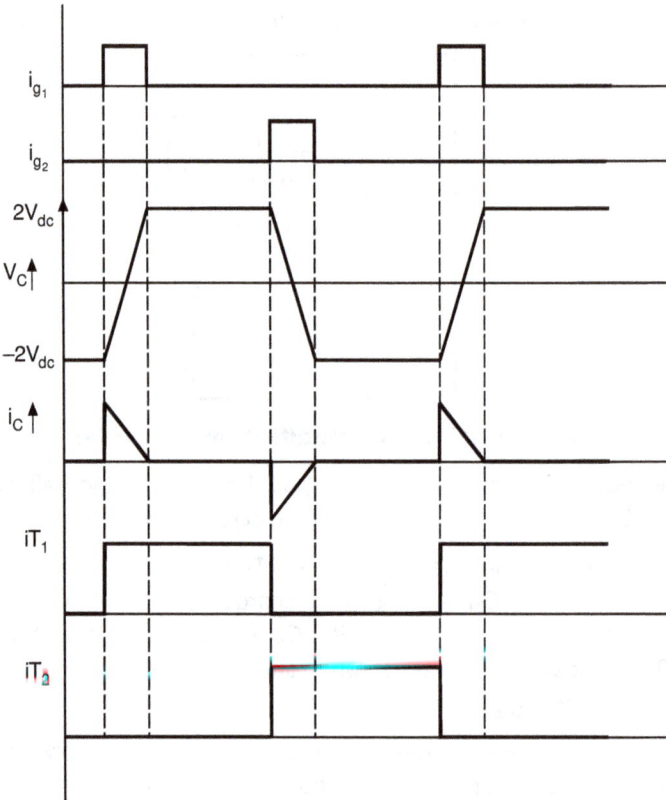

Fig. 4.5 : Waveforms of parallel inverter

- D.C. source gets connected to half of primary of transformer alternately. It induces square wave voltage across the secondary. The commutating capacitor comes in parallel with the load and hence the inverter is called as parallel inverter. Capacitor is used for commutation.

- Inductance L prevents instant discharge of capacitor C. Fig. 4.5 shows related waveforms.

- Operation of parallel inverter can be explained using three modes.

- **Mode 1 :** When T_1 is fired current flows through the inductance L, SCR T_1, half part of the primary of transformer. D.C. source voltage V_{dc} appears across half the primary of transformer. Total primary voltage becomes $2V_{dc}$.

- **Mode 2 :** When T_2 SCR is fired, commutating capacitor applies $-2V_{dc}$ voltage across T_1 SCR. So T_1 will be turned OFF. Now T_2 is conducting current flow V_{dc}^+, L, primary half of transformer and T_2. Again $2V_{dc}$ voltage appears across the capacitor.

- **Mode 3 :** Again T_1 SCR is turned ON. Commutating capacitor applies $-2V$ dc voltage across SCR T_2. Now T_2 will be turned OFF.

- Approximately square wave will be obtained at the transformer output terminals. Shape of the output waveform depends on the magnitude of load. Output signal frequency depends on the frequency of trigger pulse. Drawbacks of basic parallel inverter are :

    1. The circuit turn-OFF time increases as load decreases.
    2. For lower load SCR, reverse blocking peak voltage rating increases.
    3. High value commutating capacitors are required.
    4. The output voltage signal shape is load dependent.

- To overcome these limitations, modified parallel inverter circuit is used. In this inverter, feedback diodes D_1 and D_2 are connected. Inductor is shifted to cathode series position.

- In this circuit, L and C are not load dependent. Fig. 4.6 shows the modified parallel inverter.

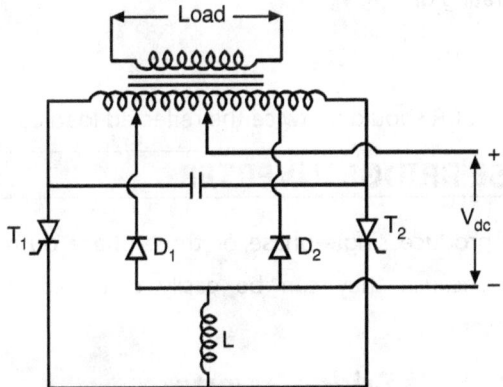

Fig. 4.6 : Modified parallel inverter

- The load voltage waveform is not affected by load current. This circuit can work with wide range of reactive load.

- Parallel inverter operates in three operating modes. In mode 1, thyristor T_1 is triggered. Mode 2 begins with triggering of T_2. Mode 3 is for commutating T_2 and when load current becomes zero. Fig. 4.7 shows load voltage and current waveform for parallel inverter.

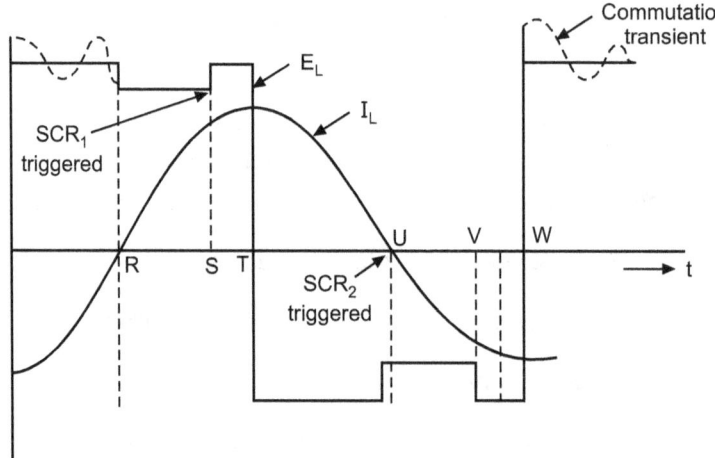

Fig. 4.7 : Load voltage and current waveform for parallel inverter

- For parallel inverter voltage rating of the capacitor is $V_c \gg 2E_{dc}$ and current rating of the inductor is $\gg 2I_L$.

- For blocking voltage rating of SCR, V_{BO},

$$V_{BO} \gg 2E_{dc}$$

- Peak current rating of SCR should be twice the reflected load current.

4.2 SINGLE PHASE BRIDGE INVERTER

- Bridge inverter can produce single-phase or three-phase output. Bridge inverters are more widely used because they can be easily extended to three phase. Output transformer is not essential.

4.2.1 Single-phase Half Bridge Inverter

- Fig. 4.8 shows a half-bridge inverter configuration. The D.C. input to the half bridge is from a split D.C. power supply. It is a three wire D.C. power supply. Two SCRs S_1 and S_2 are used along with two diodes D_1 and D_2. These are feedback diodes.

- The positive cycle of the output voltage appears across the load when SCR_1 is turned ON. Output voltage $V_o = V/2$. During negative cycle, SCRs are turned ON. For resistive load, load voltage is in phase with the load current. Before switching ON one SCR, other SCRs must be turned OFF, else they cause short circuit in D.C. supply.

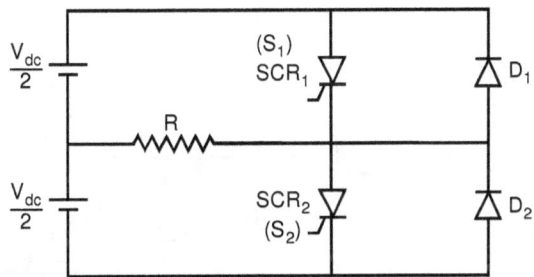

Fig. 4.8 : Half bridge inverter

- For inductive load, current lags voltage. The diode conducts load current when SCR_1 and SCR_2 are OFF. Load reactive energy is fed back to the supply. Therefore these are called as feedback diodes. Fig. 4.9 shows related waveforms.

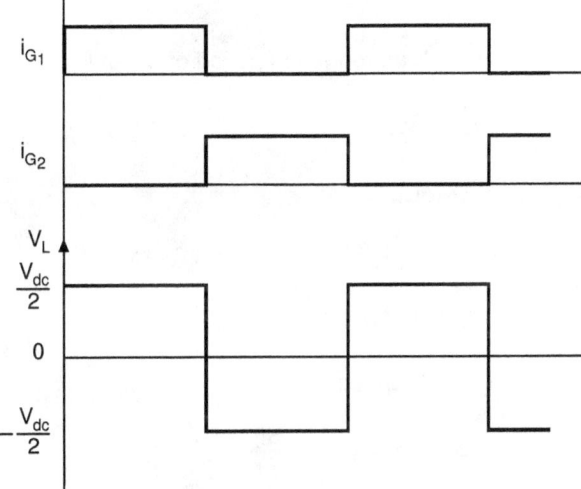

Fig. 4.9 : Half-bridge inverter waveforms

- A positive output voltage appears across the load when either S_1 or D_1 is conducting. The in-phase current flows through the main SCR and out of phase current flows through the diode.
- A negative output voltage appears when either S_2 or D_2 is ON. The in-phase current is carried by S_2 and out of phase current by D_2 that is SCR conducts when voltage and current are of the same polarity and the feedback diode conducts when the load voltage and load current are out of phase. SCR triggering frequency = $f = \frac{1}{T}$, where T = Triggering period of SCRs.
- For commutation, inductors and capacitors are used. Inductors are closely coupled. So complementary commutation occurs. This circuit is known as McMurry Bedford half bridge inverter (complementary commutated inverter). Fig. 4.10 shows half bridge McMurry Bedford inverter.

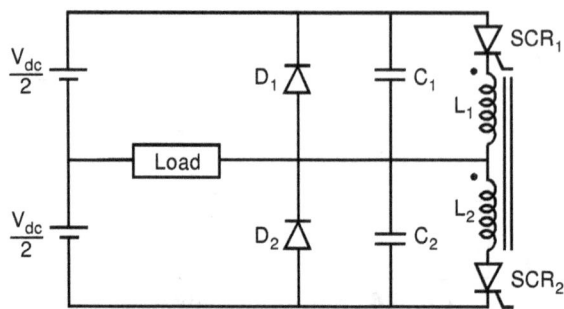

Fig. 4.10 : McMurry Bedford half bridge inverter

- Main drawback of half bridge inverter circuit is the requirement of three wire D.C. supply.
- Output signal frequency depends on triggering period of the thyristor.

$$\omega = \frac{2\pi}{T}$$

Output is a rectangular waveform.

Load current, $\quad i_L = -I_L$ for $t = 0, T, 2T$

$$i_L = I_L \text{ for } t = \frac{T}{2}, \frac{3T}{2}$$

For duration $0 < t < t/2$ the voltage equation,

$$E_L = \frac{E_{dc}}{2} = Ri_L + L\frac{di_2}{dt} + \frac{1}{C}\int_0^t i_L \, dt + V_{CO}$$

where $\quad V_{CO}$ = Voltage across the capacitor at $t = 0$.

- The output signal nature depends on the circuit damping and load characteristics.
- If the load is under damped, the current of thyristor T_1 becomes zero and SCR turns OFF before SCR_2 is triggered. Now diode D_1 conducts freewheeling current i_{D_1}. When T_2 is triggered, diode D_1 reverse biased and current is transformed from D_1 to D_2.
- When the load is over damped, T_1 is forced to switch OFF at $T/2$ while it is carrying current. So the voltage across L component of load reverses causing diode D_2 to forward bias and it conducts the freewheeling current when T_2 is triggered at $T/2$, T_2 conducts and D_2 switches to OFF state.
- Fig. 4.11 shows the equivalent circuit model and current-voltage waveform at load when the load is overdamped, underdamped, RL load and R load.

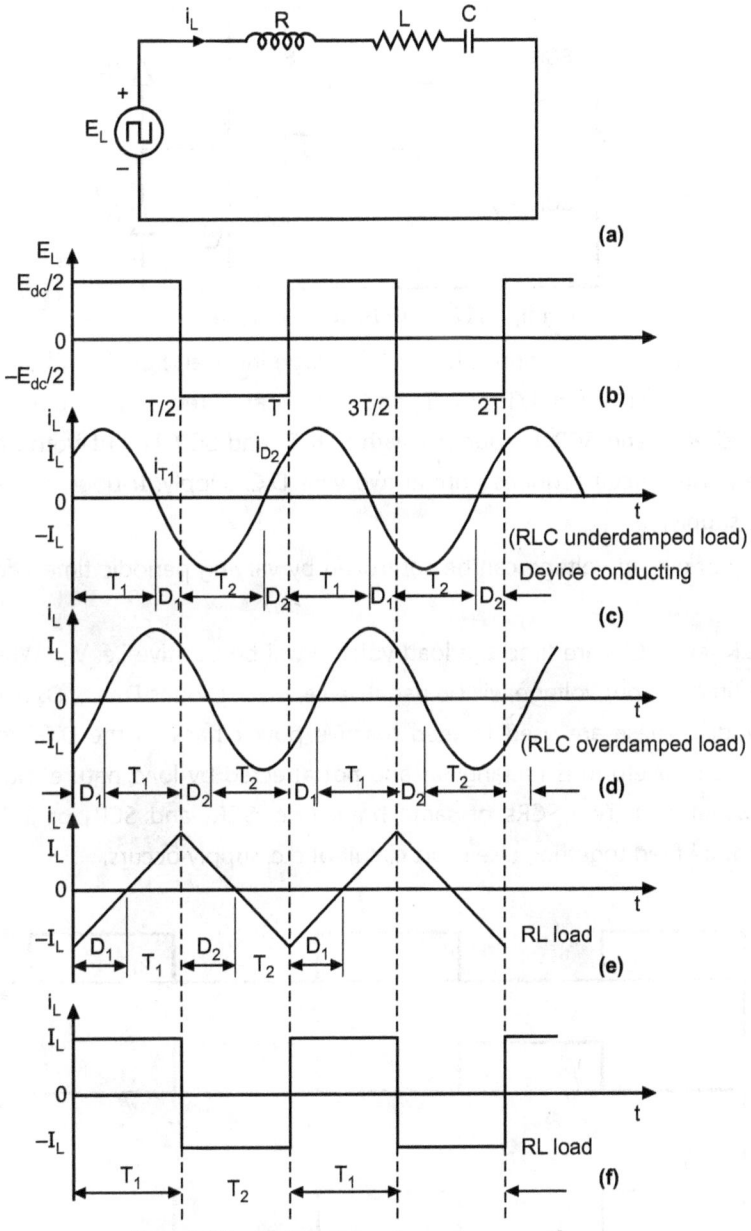

Fig. 4.11 : Half bridge inverter waveforms

4.2.2 Full Bridge Inverter
- It overcomes the drawback of half bridge single-phase inverter.
- The full bridge inverter requires four SCRs and four diodes. Amplitude of output voltage is doubled.

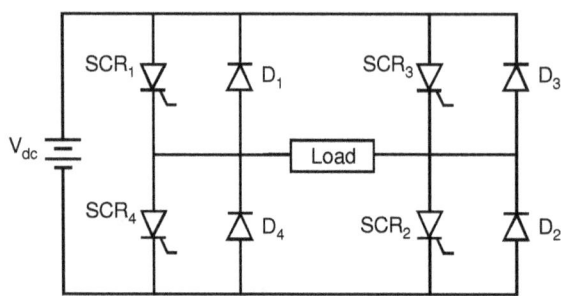

Fig. 4.12 : Full bridge inverter

Fig. 4.12 shows the circuit connection of full bridge inverter. SCR T_1 and SCR T_2 are fired together at frequency f = 1/T. SCR T_3 and SCR T_4 are fired at 180° out of phase with these. i.e. SCR T_1 and SCR T_2 together with SCR T_3 and SCR T_4. But both pairs are fired alternately. This circuit requires normal two wire D.C. supply. It does not require three wire D.C. supply.

- Frequency of output voltage can be controlled by varying periodic time T for triggering of SCRs.
- When SCR_1 and SCR_2 are fired the load voltage will be positive i.e. V_{dc}. When SCR_3 and SCR_4 are fired, output voltage will be negative i.e. $-V_{dc}$. Diodes D_1, D_2, D_3 and D_4 are free wheel diodes. These are used to feed reactive power back to the D.C. power supply. Load voltage waveform is rectangular and not affected by load nature. Fig. 4.13 shows related waveforms. Two SCRs of same branch i.e. SCR_1 and SCR_4 or SCR_3 and SCR_2 should not be fired together, else short circuit of d.c. supply occurs.

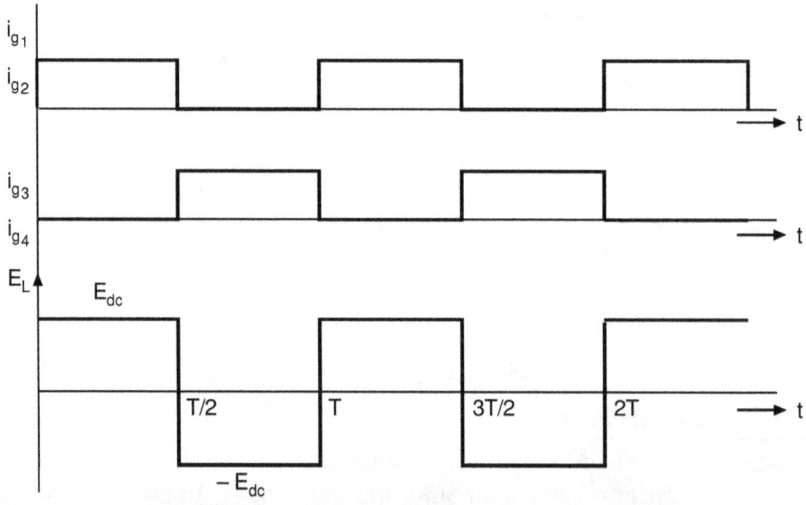

Fig. 4.13 : Waveforms of full bridge inverter

- In the full bridge inverter, diodes are essential only when the load is RL or RLC type. For pure resistive load, diodes are not essential.

- The commutation scheme for full bridge inverter consists of auxiliary thyristor. This inverter is known as McMurry inverter. It is an impulse commutated inverter. L.C. and auxiliary thyristor are used for commutation.

Fig. 4.14 shows the circuit diagram of McMurry full bridge inverter.

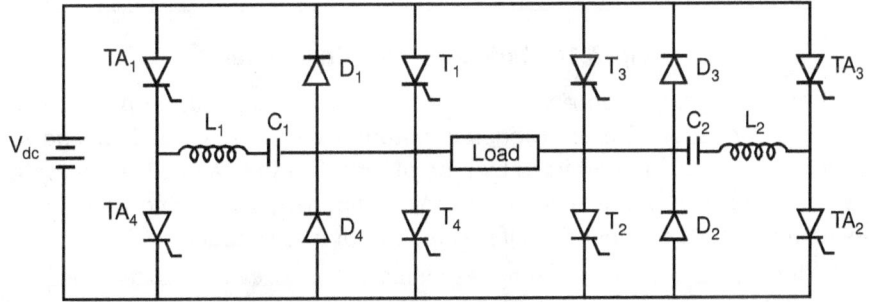

Fig. 4.14 : McMurry full bridge inverter

- In McMurry inverter, at the end of commutation excess charge occurs across the capacitor. In high voltage inverter, this excess charge develop stresses or inverter component. To overcome this drawback, modified McMurry inverter circuit is used. It consists of resistances R_1, R_2 and four auxiliary diodes as additional components. Fig. 4.15 shows the modified McMurry full bridge inverter.

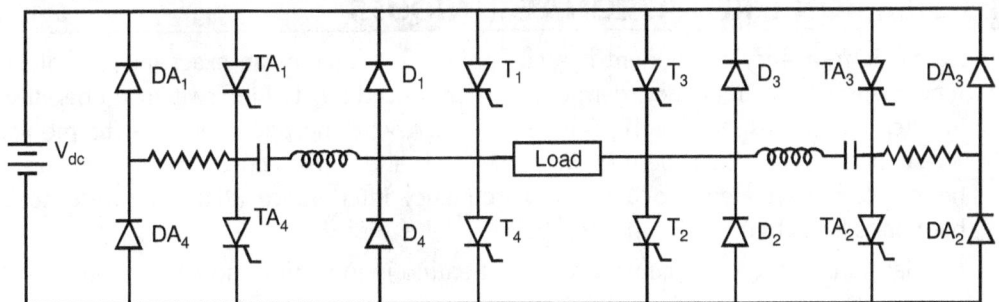

Fig. 4.15 : Modified McMurry full bridge inverter

- Another scheme for commutation of SCRs of full bridge inverter is complementary commutation. This type of circuit is known as McMurry Bedford full bridge inverter. It consists of two closely coupled inductors. Firing of one SCR commutates other SCR. Fig. 4.16 shows the circuit connection of McMurry Bedford inverter.

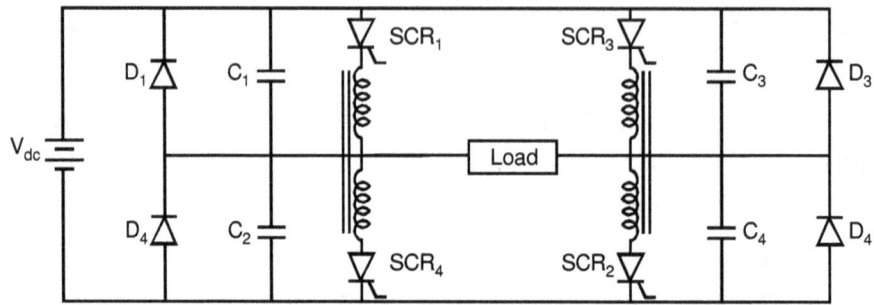

Fig. 4.16 : McMurry Bedford inverter

- In full bridge inverter, when one set of two SCRs are triggered, output is positive and when the other set of SCRs are triggered, output is negative. So load voltage waveform is rectangular and it is not affected by type of load. The load and current waveforms are same as that for half bridge inverter but the component conducting period is different. Every time two SCRs conduct and alternately two diodes conduct.
- For McMurry inverter, commutating elements L and C can be determined using the following formulae :

$$L = \frac{0.397 \, E_{dc \, (min)} \, t_{off}}{I_{L \, max}} \qquad \ldots (4.3)$$

$$C = \frac{0.893 \, t_{off} \, I_{L \, (max)}}{E_{dc \, (min)}} \qquad \ldots (4.4)$$

where $I_{L \, (max)}$ = Maximum load current
t_{off} > SCR turn-OFF time

4.3 HARMONIC REDUCTION TECHNIQUES

- Harmonic frequency component is a component of signal of an exact multiple of the fundamental signal frequency. Harmonics are produced due to high switching operation. Inverter circuit consists of high power SCRs. Their switching operation gives harmonics. These harmonics affect performance of load and other equipment. High order harmonics are radiated and give radio frequency interference (RFI). The presence of harmonics leads to the following drawbacks.

    (a) Harmonic current will cause excessive heating in induction motor connected with thyristor system. It reduces load carrying capacity of the motor.

    (b) Harmonic from power side affect operation and performance of control and regulation circuit. For this purpose, proper shielding is essential, else circuit shows unreliable operation.

    (c) On critical loads, torque pulsation produced by the harmonic current can be harmful.

    (d) Harmonic current causes losses in the A.C. system and sometimes produce resonance in the system.

- There are many industrial applications which allow maximum 5% harmonic content at inverter output. Inverter output may have more than 5% harmonic. So harmonic reduction is essential.

Various methods for harmonic reduction are as follows :
- Single pulse width modulation
- Transformer connection
- Uses of filter
    - LC filter
    - Resonant filter
    - OTT filter
- Multiple commutation in each half cycle.
- Stepped wave inverter
- Resonating the load.

4.3.1 Harmonic Reduction by Single Pulse Width Modulation

- In this method, width of pulse is adjusted to reduce the harmonic. By this method, only one harmonic can be eliminated at a time. To reduce higher order harmonic, pulse width should be reduced. For lower harmonic elimination, required pulse width must be larger.

$$E_{Ln} = \frac{2\sqrt{2}\, E_{dc}}{n\pi} \sin \frac{np}{2} \qquad \ldots (4.5)$$

where
E_{Ln} = Amplitude of nth harmonic, for its elimination, it is considered as zero

E_{dc} = Input D.C. voltage

n = n^{th} harmonic

p = Width of the pulse

For 3rd harmonic, p = 120°
For 5th harmonic, p = 72°

4.3.2 Harmonic Reduction by Transformer Connection

- Output voltage from two or more inverters can be combined using the transformer to get a net output voltage with reduced harmonic content.
- Output voltage waveform from the inverter must be similar but phase shifted from each other.
- Transformer have a turns ratio of 1 : 1. The phase shifting of π/3 and combining voltage by transformer connection, it is possible to eliminate third harmonics. Along with third harmonics, multiples of third harmonics such as 9th, 12th are also eliminated.
- The main drawback of this method is that, it requires more number of inverters and transformer of similar rating.

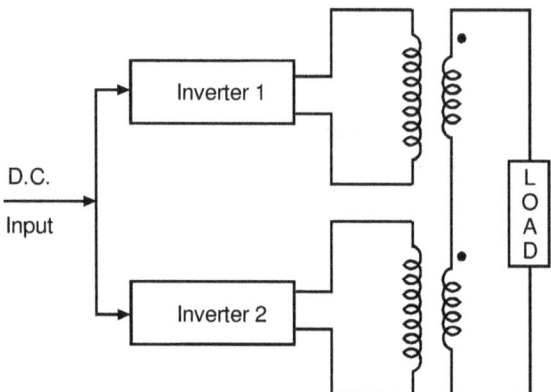

Fig. 4.17 : Harmonic reduction by transformer connection

4.3.3 Harmonic Reduction by using Filter

- Output of inverter is either square or quasi-square waveform. To attenuate harmonic component of these waveforms, filters are used. Following types of filters are normally used with inverter :
  1. LC filter
  2. Resonant filter
  3. OTI filter

(a) LC Filter :
- L and C components are normally used for filter as

$$X_L = 2\pi f L \quad \ldots (4.6)$$

and

$$X_C = \frac{1}{2\pi f C} \quad \ldots (4.7)$$

- The inductance offers a high impedance to harmonic voltage. As order of harmonic component increases, impedance of inductance also increases. The capacitance offers a shunt path for the harmonic content.
- As higher order harmonic frequency is more, X_C will be lower and content will be passed.
- This type of filter can attenuate higher frequencies more easily. This LC filter may be single stage or cascaded type. Fig. 4.18 shows the LC filter.

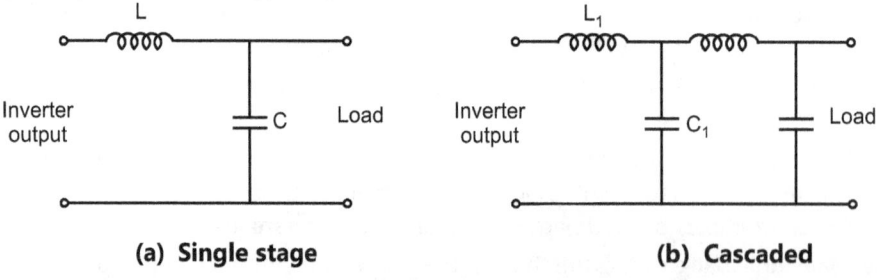

(a) Single stage   (b) Cascaded

Fig. 4.18 : LC filter

- Cascaded filters are used for higher attenuation. For same kVA rating of L and C, cascaded filter gives a better attenuation but it becomes expensive.

(b) Resonant Filter :

- Sometimes for specific applications, sine wave output inverter is essential. A sinusoidal output voltage can be realized by means of a combined series-parallel resonant filter. This resonant filter must be tuned to the fundamental frequency of the output voltage.
- These are used for elimination of low order harmonic component. Both series L, C and parallel L, C are tuned to the fundamental frequency. The series arm presents zero impedance to fundamental frequency component. It gives finite and increasing impedance to the higher frequencies. The shunt arm offers infinite impedance to fundamental frequency component but low impedance for higher frequencies. Fig. 4.19 shows the circuit for resonant filter.

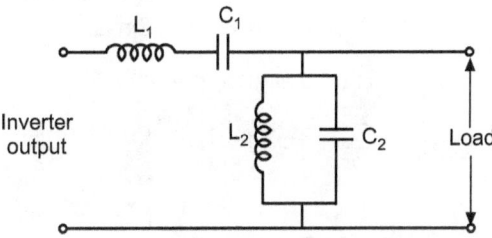

Fig. 4.19 : Resonant filter

(c) OTT Filter :

- It is used with parallel inverter. It eliminates harmonics and provides sine wave output. It gives good load regulation. It maintains capacitive load to the inverter. It helps in SCR commutation.

Advantages of OTT Filter :

(a) The input impedance remains capacitive.
(b) As long as the normalized load impedance magnitude exceeds Z, the input impedance is capacitive.
(c) Infinite load impedance.
(d) It helps to operate protective devices when fault occurs in load. It is a LC filter.

Fig. 4.20 shows the circuit diagram of OTT filter.

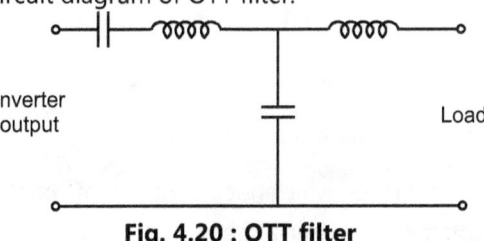

Fig. 4.20 : OTT filter

For OTT filter, $R_L = \dfrac{E_L^2 \times P_f^2}{P_o^2} \, \Omega$

where E_L = Output RMS voltage

P_f = Output power factor

P_o = Output power

Load impedance, $Z_L = \sqrt{R_L^2 \times X_L^2} \, (\Omega)$

$\angle Z_L = \cos^{-1} P_f$

Filter elements, $C_1 = \dfrac{1}{6 Z_D \, \omega_D}$

where ω_D = Radian frequency = $2\pi f$

Z_D = Filter design impedance

$Z_D = \dfrac{|Z_L|}{2}$

$C_2 = \dfrac{1}{3 Z_D \, \omega_D}$

$L_1 = \dfrac{9 Z_D}{2 \omega_D}$

$L_2 = \dfrac{Z_D}{\omega_D}$

4.4 OUTPUT VOLTAGE AND FREQUENCY CONTROL

4.4.1 Necessity of Control of Output Voltage

- Inverter output voltage control is done by inverter gain control. The inverter gain is defined *as the ratio of output A.C. voltage to input D.C. voltage.* This output voltage control is necessary due to following reasons :

    - To compensate for the variation in the input voltage.

    - To compensate for the regulation of inverter.

    - To supply some special loads which need variation of voltage with frequency such as an induction motor. It is a volt/hertz speed control method of induction motor.

- Various techniques are available for the control of output voltage of single-phase inverter. These methods are as follows :
  1. External control of the A.C. output voltage.
  2. External control of the D.C. input voltage.
  3. Internal control of the inverter output voltage

First two methods require the use of peripheral components whereas the third method requires no peripheral components.

4.4.2 Methods for Output Voltage Control

4.4.2.1 External Control of A.C. Output Voltage

- For this method, A.C. voltage controller is inserted between output terminal of inverter and load. By changing the firing angle of thyristor used in A.C. voltage controller, the voltage input to the A.C. load is regulated.
- This method is not suitable at low level A.C. output voltage as the circuit increases harmonic content at the A.C. output voltage at low level.
- This method is therefore rarely used for high power application.
- It is suitable for low power application.

Fig. 4.21 shows scheme for external A.C. voltage control method.

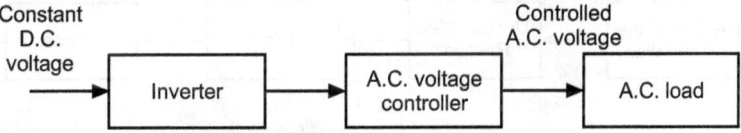

Fig. 4.21 : External A.C. voltage control

- Output voltage of two inverters can be added by using transformer to obtain adjustable A.C. output voltage. Inverter outputs are fed to primary of two transformers. Their secondaries are connected in series. For this method both inverter outputs must have same frequencies. This method does not add harmonic content even at low output voltage level. Fig. 4.22 shows the external A.C. voltage control using series connection of inverter.

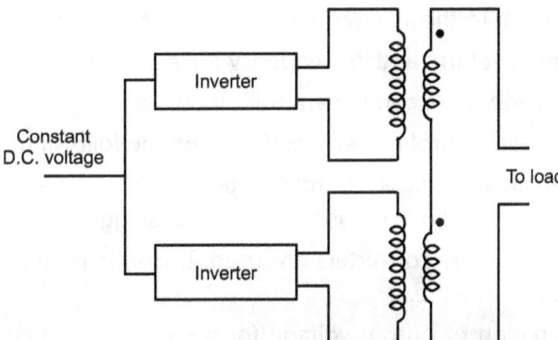

Fig. 4.22 : Output AC voltage control using series connection of inverter

4.4.2.2 External Control of D.C. Input Voltage

- In this method, input D.C. voltage may be altered to vary the A.C. output voltage. This can be done using a phase controlled rectifier or by using chopper. Input D.C. voltage can be controlled by A.C. voltage controller and uncontrolled rectifier by the use of chopper at input, it is possible to control input D.C. voltage. Fig. 4.23 shows block diagram for all four methods of external D.C. input voltage control to control inverter gain.

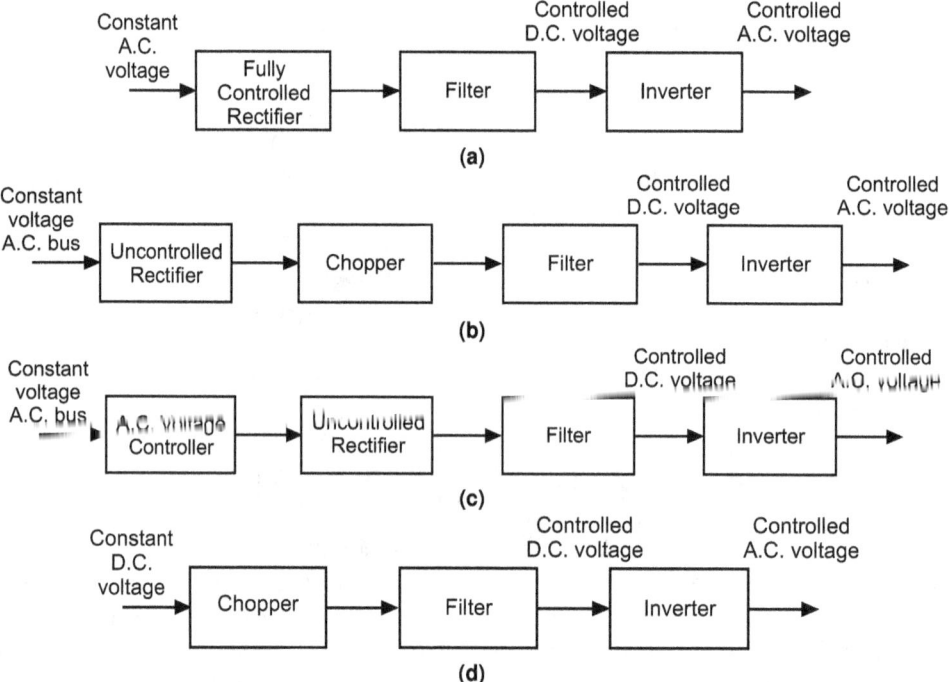

Fig. 4.23 : Various methods for external input D.C. voltage control

- Input voltage control technique in which D.C. voltage input to the inverter is controlled by external component to the inverter has following advantages :
  1. Output voltage waveform and its frequency are not affected.
  2. Less power loss and more component utilization.

- This method of voltage control however suffers from the following disadvantages.
  (1) In all methods, filter circuit is essential. Filter circuit increases cost, weight and size. It reduces efficiency and make transient response sluggish.
  (2) More number of power converters are used. It results in more losses and reduced efficiency of entire scheme.
  (3) For a large variation of output voltage for a constant load current, control of D.C. input voltage is not desirable.

4.4.2.3 Internal Control

- The output voltage from an inverter can also be adjusted by adding a control mechanism within the inverter itself. The most efficient method for doing this is by pulse width modulation (PWM) control. In PWM method, fixed D.C. input voltage is given to the inverter and a controlled A.C. output voltage is obtained by adjusting the ON and OFF period of inverter components.
- Advantages of PWM control method are as follows :
  1. Additional components are not required.
  2. Lower order harmonics can be eliminated.
- Main drawback of this scheme is that, it requires expensive inverter grade SCRs. Inverter grade SCRs are fast switching SCRs. They are having very less turn-ON time and turn-OFF time.

4.4.3 Pulse Width Modulation (PWM)

- PWM inverter shows better performance. Constant amplitude variable width pulses are used to control output voltage of inverter. Different PWM control techniques are as follows.
  - Single Pulse Width Modulation [SPWM]
  - Multiple Pulse Width Modulation [MPWM]
  - Sinusoidal Pulse Width Modulation [Sin PWM]
- Forced commutation is used in all PWM inverters. All these three techniques differ from each other by amount of harmonic content at output voltage.

4.4.3.1 Single Pulse Width Modulation Control (SPWM)

- In SPWM control there is only one pulse per half cycle and width of the pulse is changed to control inverter output voltage. Pulse width can be varied from 0° to 180°.

  Fig. 4.24 shows gating signal and output voltage of SPWM full bridge inverter.

- The gating signal is generated by comparing rectangular reference signal of amplitude E_R with triangular carrier signal of amplitude E_C. Output signal frequency depends on frequency of the reference signal.
- This type of voltage control method gives less harmonic content at low output voltage level. Positive and negative half cycles are identical, pulse width can be varied by changing E_R. The ratio of E_R and E_C is the control variable. It is also called as amplitude modulation index.

$$m = \frac{E_R}{E_C} \quad \ldots (4.8)$$

- When pulse width is maximum i.e. π then output voltage

$$E_L = \frac{4E_{dc}}{\pi} \quad \ldots (4.9)$$

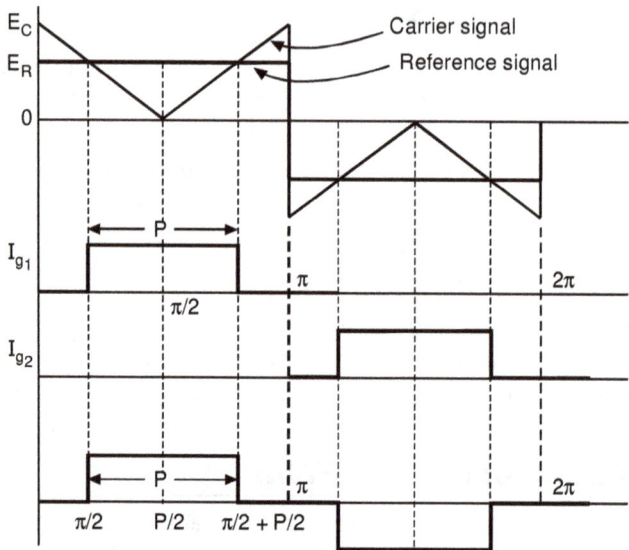

Fig. 4.24 : Single pulse width modulation

4.4.3.2 Multiple Pulse Width Modulation (MPWM)

- In this method of pulse width modulation, the harmonic content can be reduced using multiple pulses in each half cycle of output voltage.

- To generate gating signal, rectangular reference signal is compared with carrier triangular wave. The carrier frequency f_c determines the number of pulses per half cycle. Frequency of output signal depends on frequency of reference signal.

- The modulation index controls the output voltage. This technique is also known as symmetrical pulse width modulation or uniform pulse width modulation.

- Number of pulses per half cycle

$$N_P = \frac{f_c}{2f_0} = \frac{m_f}{2} \quad \ldots (4.10)$$

m_f is a ratio of f_c and f_0. It is called as frequency modulation index. As more time switching occurs, so switching loss is more. Larger pulse per half cycle reduces the amplitude of lower order harmonics but increases the amplitude of some higher order harmonics, such higher order harmonics produce negligible ripple and can easily be filtered out. Fig. 4.25 shows the related waveforms for multiple pulse width modulation.

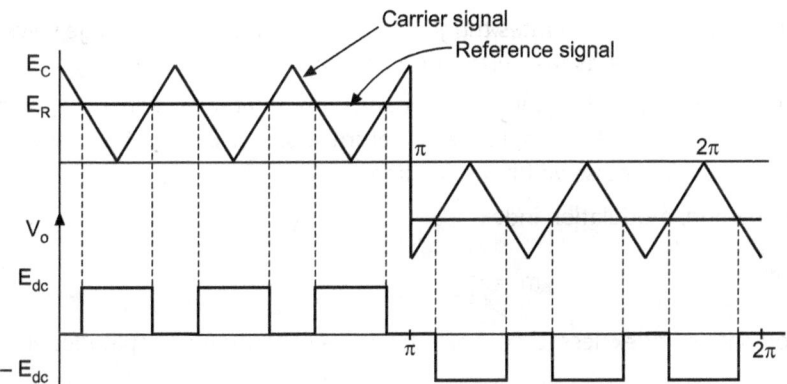

Fig. 4.25 : Multiple pulse width modulation

- This method has more advantages as compared to single pulse width modulation. This method requires more expensive inverter grade SCRs.

4.4.3.3 Sinusoidal Pulse Width Modulation

- In this PWM control same as multiple pulse width modulation, many pulses per half cycle are used. In multiple pulse width modulation, all the pulses are of equal width.
- But in sinusoidal pulse width modulation, pulse width variation occurs as a sinusoidal function.
- In sinusoidal pulse width modulation, high frequency triangular carrier wave is compared with a sinusoidal reference wave. The intersection of these two waves determine the switching instant and commutation.

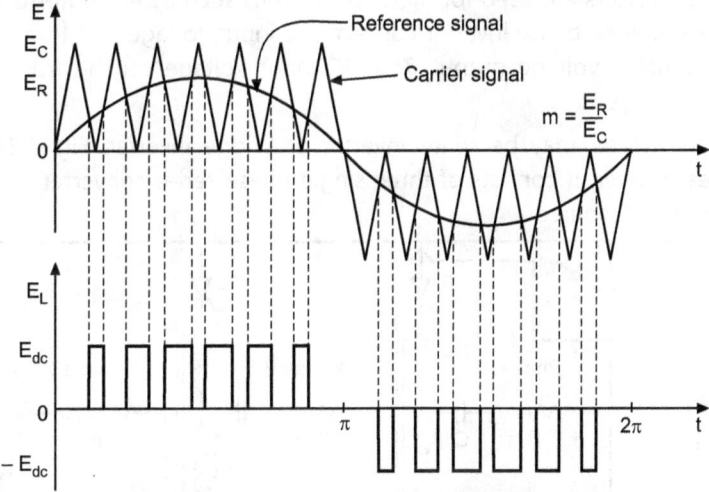

Fig. 4.26 : Sinusoidal pulse width modulation

- The corner and reference wave are mixed in a comparator when sinusoidal wave has a magnitude higher than that of the triangular wave, the comparator output is high, otherwise output is low.

- The comparator output operates trigger circuit such that output voltage wave of inverter has a pulse width same as the pulse width of comparator output.
- Inverter output signal frequency f_0 depends on reference signal f_r. Inverter output voltage depends on peak amplitude of return a signal E_r. Fig. 4.26 shows waveforms related to sinusoidal pulse width modulation.
- For this method, modulation index

$$m = \frac{E_R}{E_C} \quad \ldots (4.11)$$

- For modulation index less than one, the largest harmonic amplitudes in the output voltages are associated with harmonic or order $\frac{f_c}{f_r} + 1$ or $\frac{f_c}{f_r} - 1$. It depends on number of pulses per half cycle. Therefore by increasing number of pulses per half cycle, the order of the dominant harmonic frequencies can be increased. High order harmonics can be filtered out easily.
- To obtain large number of pulses per half cycle, more fast switching is essential.
- Higher switching frequency thyristors are more expensive and also more switching losses occur. This method is used to minimize the lower order harmonics.

4.5 THREE PHASE BRIDGE INVERTER

- Power rating limitations of single phase inverter are overcome by three phase inverter. Three phase inverters are used for high applications such as AC motor drives, induction heating, UPS. A three phase inverter converts DC input voltage to a three phase variable frequency, variable voltage output. The DC input voltage can be from DC source or rectified AC voltage.
- Three phase inverter may be series inverter or bridge inverter. Fig. 4.27 shows three phase series inverter. It consists of three single phase series converter with three phase load and single DC source.

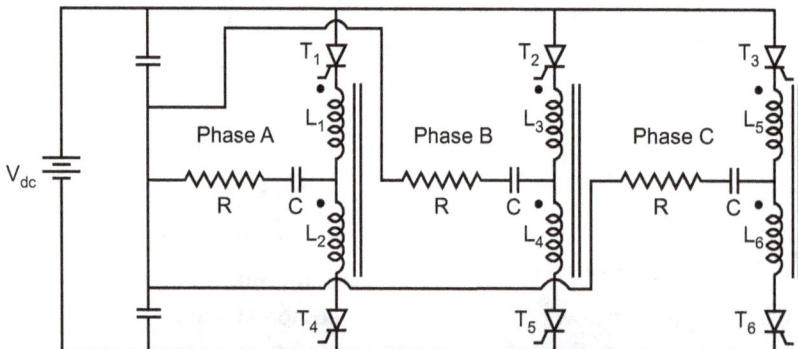

Fig. 4.27 : Three phase series inverter

- Each phase acts as a separate series inverter. Values of L and C must be selected as those for series inverter. In this circuit $L_1 = L_2 = L_3 = L_4 = L_5 = L_6$. Thyristor triggering sequence is T_1, T_6, T_2, T_4, T_3 and T_5. The firing frequency is six times the output frequency. Interval between successive firing will be T/6. T is the period of output signal.

- Fig. 4.28 shows the three phase bridge inverter. A three phase bridge inverter can be constructed by combining three single phase half bridge inverter.

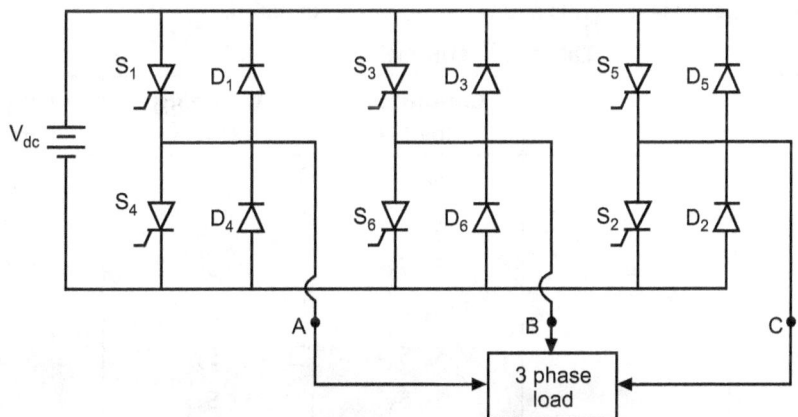

Fig. 4.28 : Three phase bridge inverter

- Three phase load may be star connected or delta connected. The circuit consists of six power thyristor SCRs with six freewheeling diodes. These SCRs are turned ON and OFF periodically in the proper sequence to produce the desired output waveform. Output frequency of the inverter depends on the rate of switching. Fig. 4.29 shows star and delta type load.

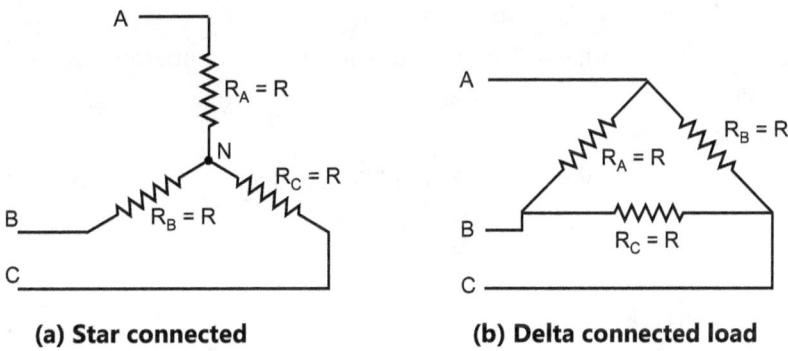

(a) Star connected   (b) Delta connected load

Fig. 4.29 : Three phase load

- Two modes of operating three phase bridge inverter are (i) 180° conduction mode and (ii) 120° conduction mode.

4.5.1 Three Phase Bridge Inverter with 120° Conduction Mode

- In this mode each SCR conducts for 120°. At any time only SCRs remains in conduction. In each cycle, six commutation pulses are required. One period of inverter operation has been divided into six intervals. This mode requires six steps each of 60° duration for completing one cycle of the output AC voltage. Table 4.3 shows conducting SCRs, outgoing SCRs and incoming SCR for each interval. All these six intervals form one cycle. For each cycle these intervals and operations are repeated.

Table 4.3 : Operating mode table

Sr. No.	Interval	Conducting devices	Incoming device	Outgoing device
1.	I	S_6, S_1	S_1	S_5
2.	II	S_1, S_2	S_2	S_6
3.	III	S_2, S_3	S_3	S_1
4.	IV	S_3, S_4	S_4	S_2
5.	V	S_4, S_5	S_5	S_3
6.	VI	S_5, S_6	S_6	S_4

- In this table S_1, S_2, S_3, S_4, S_5 and S_6 are $SCR_1, SCR_2, SCR_3, SCR_4, SCR_5$ and SCR_6.
- Fig. 4.30 shows waveforms for three phase bridge inverter for 120° conduction mode. Waveform shows gate pulses for SCR_1 SCR_2, SCR_3, SCR_4, SCR_5 and SCR_6. V_{AN}, V_{BN} and V_{CN} are each phase voltage waveforms. V_{AB}, V_{BC} and V_{CA} indicate waveforms for voltages w.r.t. other phase. Conduction period for each switch is 120°. The phase shift between the triggering of every two adjacent switches is 60°. Line voltages V_{AB}, V_{BC} and V_{CA} are six-step waves with step amplitudes V_{DC} and $V_{DC}/2$. These line voltages are phase shifted by 120°. The line voltage V_{AB} leads V_{AN} by 30°.
- Two SCRs conduct at a time. Out of these two one from upper group and other from lower group.

In 120° conduction mode :

- During interval I i.e. $0 \leq \omega t \leq \pi/3$, SCR_1 and SCR_6 conduct.

$$E_{AN} = \frac{E_{dc}}{2}, \quad E_{BN} = 0, \quad E_{CN} = 0$$

- During interval II i.e. $\pi/3 \leq \omega t \leq \frac{2\pi}{3}$

$$E_{AN} = \frac{E_{DC}}{2}, \quad E_{BN} = 0, \quad E_{CN} = -\frac{E_{dc}}{2}$$

In this interval SCR_1 and SCR_2 conduct.

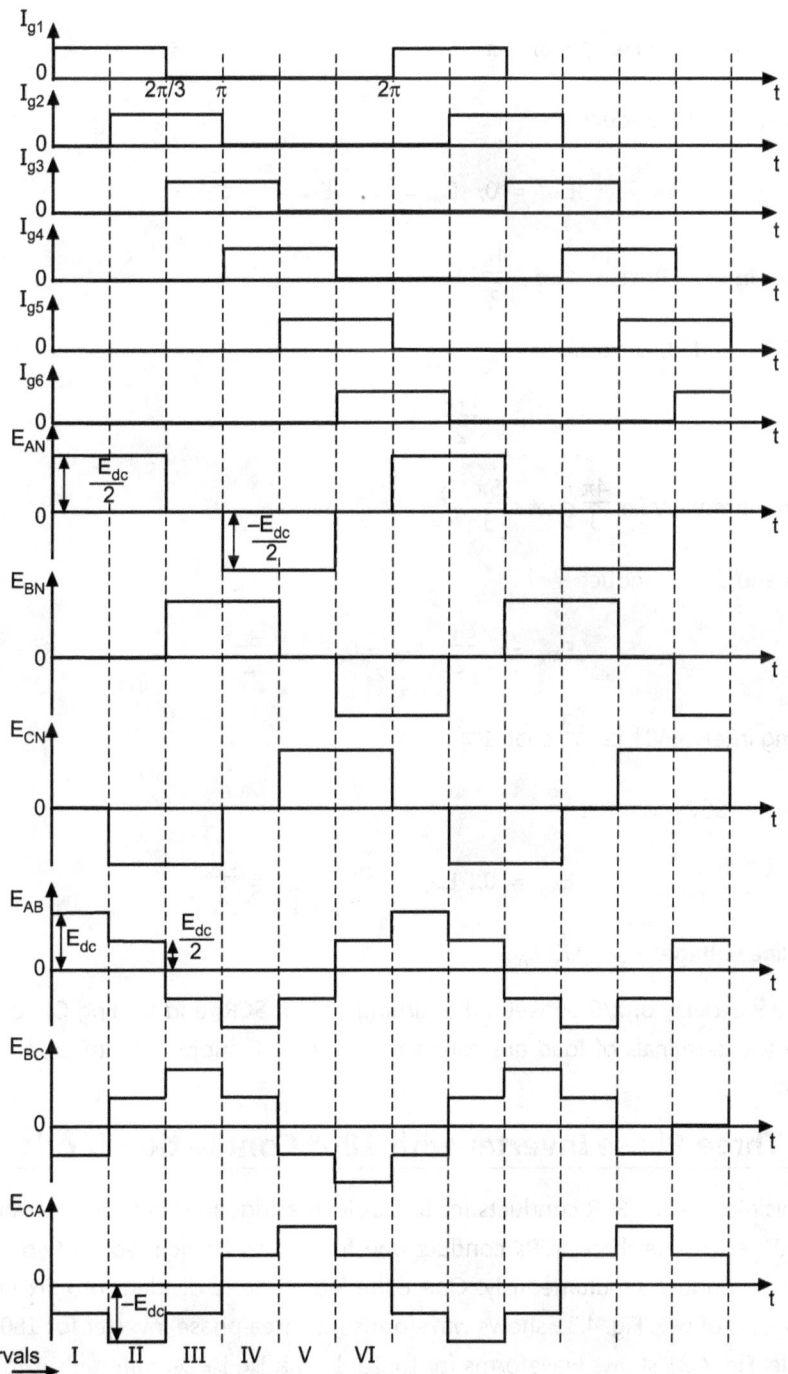

Fig. 4.30 : Three phase inverter for 120° conduction mode
(Chap. 4.29)

- During interval III i.e. $\frac{2\pi}{3} \leq \omega t \leq \pi$.

    SCR$_2$ and SCR$_3$ conduct.

    $$E_{AN} = 0, \quad E_{BN} = \frac{E_{DC}}{2}, \quad E_{CN} = -\frac{E_{DC}}{2}$$

- During interval IV i.e. $\pi \leq \omega t \leq \frac{4\pi}{3}$

    SCR$_3$ and SCR$_4$ conduct.

    $$E_{AN} = -\frac{E_{DC}}{2}, \quad E_{BN} = \frac{E_{DC}}{2}, \quad E_{CW} = 0$$

- During interval V i.e. $\frac{4\pi}{3} \leq \omega t \leq \frac{5\pi}{3}$

    SCR$_4$ and SCR$_5$ conduct.

    $$E_{AN} = -\frac{E_{DC}}{2}, \quad E_{BN} = 0, \quad E_{CN} = \frac{E_{DC}}{2}$$

- During interval VIth i.e. $\frac{5\pi}{3} \leq \omega t \leq \frac{6\pi}{3}$

    SCR$_5$ and SCR$_6$ conduct.

    $$E_{AN} = 0, \quad E_{BN} = -\frac{E_{DC}}{2}, \quad E_{CN} = \frac{E_{DC}}{2}$$

The line voltages $E_{AB} = \sqrt{3}\, E_{AN}$.

There is a delay of $\pi/6$ between the turning OFF of SCR$_1$ and turning ON of SCR$_2$. At any time two terminals of load are connected to the DC supply and third terminal remains open.

4.5.2 Three Phase Inverter with 180° Conduction Mode

- In this mode each SCR conducts for 80°. SCRs are triggered in sequence with an interval of 60°. At a time three SCRs conduct one from each branch. So no two SCRs of same branch conduct simultaneously. One complete cycle is divided into six intervals. Each interval is of 60°. Fig. 4.31 shows waveforms for three phase inverter for 180° conduction mode. Fig. 4.31 shows waveforms for $I_{g1}, I_{g2}, I_{g3}, I_{g4}, I_{g5}, I_{g6}$ i.e. gate pulses for all six SCRs. Phase voltages are E_{AN}, E_{BN} and E_{CN} and line voltages are E_{AB}, E_{BC} and E_{CA}.

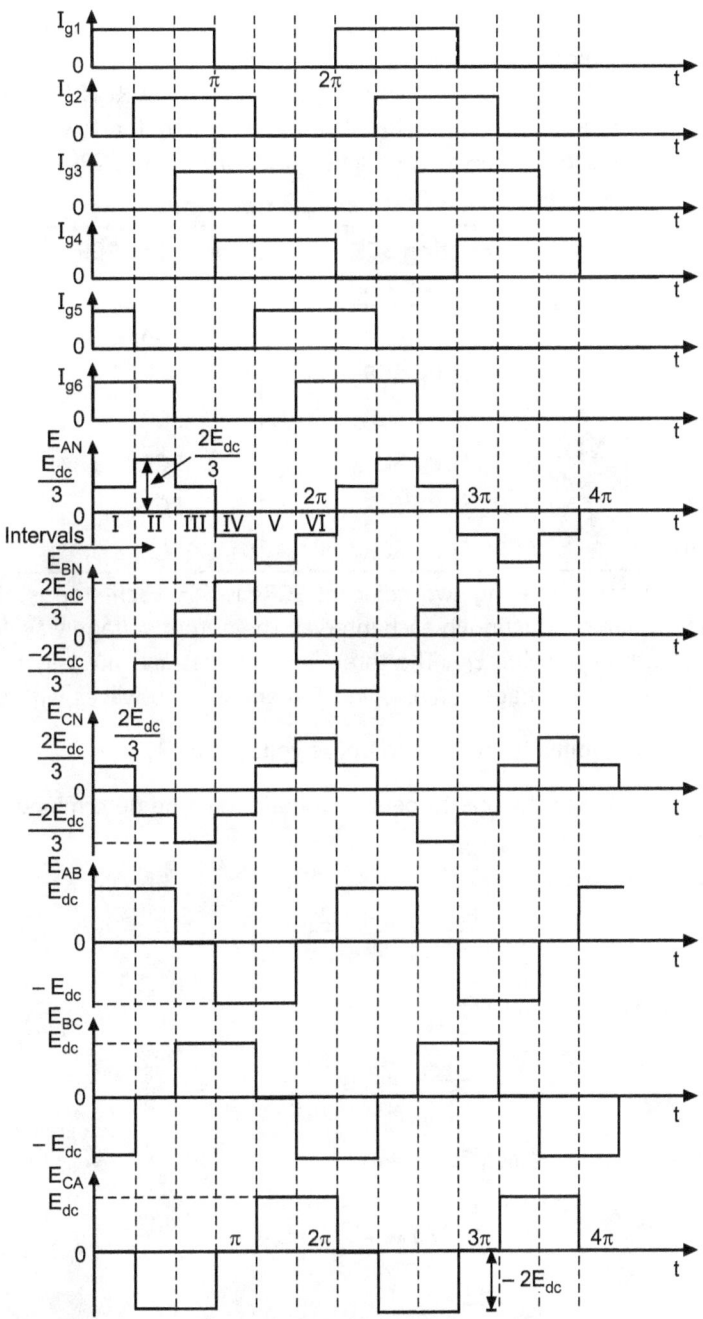

Fig. 4.31 : Bridge inverter three phase type with 180° conduction mode

- SCR pair of each branch S_1, S_4, S_3, S_6 and S_5, S_2 are turned ON with a time interval of 180°. SCR_1 conducts for 180° and SCR_4 conducts for next 180°. SCRs in the upper group i.e. SCR_1, SCR_3 and SCR_5 conduct at an interval of 120°. If SCR_1 is fired at 0° then SCR_3 must be triggered at 120° and SCR_5 at 240°. Similarly, for lower group SCRs are triggered. Table 4.4 shows interval, conducting SCRs, incoming SCRs and outgoing SCRs.

Table 4.4 : 180° conduction mode

Sr. No.	Interval	Conducting SCR	Incoming SCR	Outgoing SCR
1.	I	SCR_5, SCR_6, SCR_1	SCR_1	SCR_4
2.	II	SCR_6, SCR_1, SCR_2	SCR_2	SCR_5
3.	III	SCR_1, SCR_2, SCR_3	SCR_3	SCR_6
4.	IV	SCR_2, SCR_3, SCR_4	SCR_4	SCR_1
5.	V	SCR_3, SCR_4, SCR_5	SCR_5	SCR_2
6.	VI	SCR_4, SCR_5, SCR_6	SCR_6	SCR_3

- Phase shift between triggering two adjacent SCRs is 60°. Each step is of 60° duration. Only three SCRs are conducting in each interval. The output voltage waveforms are quasi square wave with peak value E_{DC}. The three line voltages are mutually phase shifted by 120°. The three phase voltage E_{AN}, E_{BN} and E_{CN} are six-step waves with step amplitude $\frac{E_{DC}}{3}$ and $\frac{2}{3} E_{DC}$. Line voltages are leading phase voltages by 30°.
- For star connected load the line to neutral voltage must be determined to find the line or phase current.
- During interval I i.e. $0 \leq \omega t \leq \pi/3$,

$$E_{AN} = \frac{E_{DC}}{3}, \quad E_{BN} = -\frac{2E_{DC}}{3}, \quad E_{CN} = \frac{E_{DC}}{3}$$

- During interval II i.e. $\pi/3 \leq \omega t \leq \frac{2\pi}{3}$,

$$E_{AN} = \frac{2E_{DC}}{3}, \quad E_{BN} = -\frac{E_{DC}}{3}, \quad E_{CN} = -\frac{E_{DC}}{3}$$

- During interval III i.e. $\frac{2\pi}{3} \leq \omega t < \pi$,

$$E_{AN} = \frac{E_{DC}}{3}, \quad E_{BN} = \frac{E_{DC}}{3}, \quad E_{CN} = -\frac{2E_{DC}}{3}$$

- During interval IV i.e. $\pi \leq \omega t \leq \frac{4\pi}{3}$,

$$E_{AN} = -\frac{E_{DC}}{3}, \quad E_{BN} = \frac{2E_{DC}}{3}, \quad E_{CN} = -\frac{E_{DC}}{3}$$

- During interval V i.e. $\frac{4\pi}{3} \leq \omega t \leq \frac{5\pi}{3}$,

$$E_{AN} = -\frac{2E_{DC}}{3}, \quad E_{BN} = \frac{E_{DC}}{3}, \quad E_{CN} = -\frac{E_{DC}}{3}$$

- During interval VI i.e. $\frac{5\pi}{3} \leq \omega t \leq 2\pi$,

$$E_{AN} = -\frac{E_{DC}}{3}, \quad E_{BN} = -\frac{E_{DC}}{3}, \quad E_{CN} = \frac{2E_{DC}}{3}$$

- The line voltage $E_{AB} = E_{AN} - E_{BN}$ is obtaining by reversing E_{BN} and adding it to E_{AN}.

  Line voltage $E_{BC} = E_{BN} - E_{CN}$

  Line voltage $E_{CA} = E_{CN} - E_{AN}$

- Phase voltages have six steps per cycle and line voltages have one positive pulse and one negative pulse per cycle. The phase and line voltages are out of phase by 120°.
- Table 4.5 shows comparison between 180° and 120° operating modes of three phase inverter.

Table 4.5

180° conduction mode	120° conduction mode
1. No time is provided between commutation and turning ON of SCR pair.	1. 60° time interval is provided between commutation and turn ON process.
2. Less reliable commutation.	2. More reliable commutation.
3. More utility factor.	3. Less utility factor.
4. Inverter output is 33.33%.	4. Inverter output is 28.9%.

- A three phase inverter may be considered as a three, single phase inverter with phase shift of 120° in output of each phase. The voltage control techniques for single phase inverter are applicable for three phase inverter. In case of sine wave PWM control, there are three sine waves as reference waves and shifted by 120°. A carrier wave is compared with the reference signal corresponding to a phase to generate the trigger signal for that phase.

4.6 ADVANTAGES OF MOSFET INVERTER

Thyristor-based inverter require commutation circuit to turn-OFF thyristor. MOSFET-based inverter has following advantages :
- Very high switching speed.
- Requires very low driving power.
- Minimum thermal runaway problem.
- They can be used in parallel for greater power capability.
- No need of commutation circuit.

4.7 INVERTER SPECIFICATIONS

For many domestic and industrial applications, following are the important specifications for inverter. These factors are considered for selecting inverter for particular application.

- Rated power output
- Number of phases
- Maximum output current
- Power factor at rated output
- Minimum operating voltage at input.
- Normal operating input D.C. voltage
- Maximum open-circuit voltage
- Maximum operating current
- Peak efficiency
- Tare losses
- Ambient temperature
- Audible noise
- Enclosure standard
- Dimensions and weight
- Operating voltage
- Frequency of output signal
- Harmonic current distortion at rated output

SOLVED EXAMPLES

Example 4.1 : *For single phase full bridge inverter, input voltage V = 60 V, R = 5 Ω, calculate : (a) the RMS output voltage at fundamental frequency, (b) The output power, (c) the average and peak current of each SCR, (d) the peak reverse blocking voltage of SCR, (e) the total harmonic distortion, (f) the harmonic factor and distortion factor of the lowest order harmonic.*

Solution : (a) The RMS output voltage at fundamental frequency is,

$$V_{iR} = 0.9\ V = 0.9 \times 60 = \textbf{54 V}$$

(b) The output power is,

$$P_o = \frac{V_R^2}{R} = \frac{60^2}{R} = \textbf{720 W}$$

(c) The peak current of each SCR,

$$I_{SCR\ (peak)} = \frac{60}{5} = 12\ A$$

As $\quad R = 5\ \Omega$

The average current of each SCR,

$$I_{SCR\ (av)} = \frac{12}{2} = \textbf{6 A}$$

(d) Reverse blocking voltage,
$$V_{RB} = V = \mathbf{60\ V}$$

(e) $$THD = \frac{\sqrt{V^2 - V_{iR}^2}}{V_{iR}} = \frac{\sqrt{60^2 - 54^2}}{54}$$
$$= 0.4841 = \mathbf{48.41\%}$$

RMS value of nth harmonic,
$$V_{nR} = \frac{V_{iR}}{n} = \frac{54}{n}$$

Distortion factor, $DF = \frac{1}{V_{iR}} \sqrt{\left(\frac{V_{iR}}{3^2}\right)^2 + \left(\frac{V_{in}}{5^2}\right)^2 + \left(\frac{V_{in}}{7^2}\right)^2}$

∴ $DF = \frac{V_{in\,R}}{V_{iR}} \sqrt{\left(\frac{1}{3^2}\right)^2 + \left(\frac{1}{5^2}\right)^2 + \left(\frac{1}{7^2}\right)^2}$

$$= \sqrt{\frac{1}{3^2} + \frac{1}{5^2} + \frac{1}{7^2}}$$

$$= \frac{1}{9} + \frac{1}{25} + \frac{1}{49} = 0.17152 = \mathbf{17.15\%}$$

(f) Harmonic factor for 3rd harmonic,
$$HF_3 = \frac{1}{3} = \mathbf{33.33\%}$$

Distortion factor for 3rd harmonic,
$$DF_3 = \frac{HF_3}{3^2} = \frac{0.33}{9} = \mathbf{3.67\%}$$

Example 4.2 : *The three phase bridge inverter is supplying a balanced star connected resistive load with a resistance of 10 Ω per phase. If the DC supply voltage is 440 V, calculate : (a) the RMS load current, (b) the power output, (c) peak, average and RMS values of current through the SCR. Assume 180° conduction.*

Solution : The effective load resistance,
$$R_{eq} = R + \frac{R}{2} = \frac{3R}{2} = \frac{3 \times 10}{2} = 15\ \Omega$$

∴ The current supplied by the source which is constant at all intervals is,
$$I = \frac{V}{R_{eq}} = \frac{440\ V}{15} = 29.3\ A$$

The phase current = Line current
$$i_o = \frac{V_{am}}{R}$$

The RMS value of the current,

$$I_{RMS} = \sqrt{\frac{1}{T}\int_0^T i_{av}^2 \, dt}$$

$$= \sqrt{\frac{2}{T}\left(\frac{I^2 T}{6} + \frac{0.2\, TI^2 \times 2T}{6}\right)}$$

By putting I = 29.3 A,

$$I_R = \sqrt{2\left(\frac{29.3^2}{6} + \frac{0.25 \times 29.3^2 \times 2}{6}\right)}$$

$$= 20.72 \text{ A}$$

The power output, $P_o = 3I_R^2 R = 3 \times 20.72^2 \times 10 =$ **12879.6 watt**

(c) RMS value of current through each SCR,

$$I_{SCR\,(RMS)} = \sqrt{\frac{1}{T}\left(\frac{I^2 T}{6} + \frac{0.25 I^2 \times 2T}{6}\right)}$$

$$= \sqrt{\frac{29.3^2}{6} \times \frac{0.25 \times 29.3^2 \times 2}{6}}$$

$$= 14.65 \text{ A}$$

$$I_{SCR\,(av)} = \frac{1}{T}\left(\frac{2 \times 0.5 \times I \times T}{6} + \frac{I \times T}{6}\right)$$

$$= \left(\frac{2 \times 0.5 \times 29.3}{6} + \frac{29.3}{6}\right)$$

$$= 9.77 \text{ A}$$

Example 4.3 : *The three phase bridge inverter is supplying a balanced star connected resistive load with a resistance of 10 Ω per phase. If the DC supply voltage is 440 V, calculate current supplied by the source, the RMS value of current, the output power, RMS value of current through, SCR and average value of current through each SCR. Assume conduction angle as 120°.*

Solution : (a) At any instant load resistance of any two phases are in series, so the current supplied by the source,

$$I = \frac{V}{2R} = \frac{440}{2 \times 10} = 22 \text{ A}$$

Phase current = Line current

$$i_a = i_{av} = \frac{V_{av}}{2}$$

The RMS value of current,

$$I_R = \sqrt{\frac{1}{T}\int_0^T i_{av}^2 \, dt}$$

$$= \sqrt{\frac{2}{T}\left(\frac{I^2 \, 2T}{6}\right)} = \sqrt{\frac{22^2 \times 2}{3}}$$

$$= 17.96 \text{ A}$$

(b) The output power, $P_o = 3I_R^2 R = 3 \times 17.96^2 \times 10$

$$= 9680 \text{ watt}$$

(c) RMS current through SCR,

$$I_{R(SCR)} = \sqrt{\frac{1}{T}\left(\frac{I^2 \, 2T}{6}\right)}$$

$$= \sqrt{\frac{22^2}{3}} = 12.7 \text{ A}$$

$$I_{av(SCR)} = \frac{1}{T}\left(\frac{I \times 2T}{6}\right) = \frac{22}{3} = 7.33 \text{ A}$$

Example 4.4 : *A single phase full wave bridge inverter consists of single pulse width modulator technique to control output voltage. What will be the pulse width for the RMS value of the fundamental component of the output voltage to the 80% of the DC input voltage.*

Solution : $V_{iR} = 0.8 \, V_{in}$

$\therefore \quad \dfrac{4V}{\sqrt{2}\,\pi} \sin\dfrac{\delta}{2} = 0.8 \text{ V}$

$\therefore \quad \delta = 2\sin^{-1}\left(\dfrac{0.8 \times \pi \times \sqrt{2}}{4}\right)$

$$= 125.39°$$

Example 4.5 : *A single phase full wave bridge inverter uses multiple pulse width modulation with 6 pulses per half cycle. The width of each pulse is 20°. If the DC input voltage to the inverter is 230 V, calculate the RMS output voltage.*

Solution : Number of pulses = 6 = P, Pulse width $\delta = 20°$.

RMS output voltage, $V_R = V_{in} \times \sqrt{\dfrac{P \times \delta}{\pi}}$

$$= 230 \times \sqrt{\dfrac{6 \times 20}{180}}$$

$$= 187.8 \text{ V}$$

Example 4.6 : *If the input voltage is increased from 230 V by 10%, what would be the pulse width required to maintain the output voltage as 187.8 V ?*

Solution : Input DC voltage increased by 10% from 230 V.

$$\therefore \quad V = 1.1 \times 230 = 253 \text{ V}$$

If the output power is to be maintained at 187.8 V then to calculate δ,

$$187.8 = V_{in} \sqrt{\frac{6 \times \delta}{180}}$$

$$\therefore \quad \delta = \frac{(187.8/253)^2}{6} \times 180$$

$$= 16.53°$$

Example 4.7 : *A single phase full bridge inverter is operated from a 48 V battery and supplying power to a pure resistive load of 15 Ω. Calculate*

(a) The fundamental output voltage and the first 3 harmonics.

(b) RMS values by direct integration and harmonic summation method.

(c) Output RMS power and output fundamental power.

Solution : $\quad V_{dc} = 40 \text{ V} \quad$ and $\quad R = 15 \text{ Ω}$

(a) $\quad V_{o\,(f_{ON})} = \frac{2\sqrt{2}}{\pi} V_{dc}$

$$= \frac{2\sqrt{2}}{\pi} \times 48 = 43.22 \text{ V}$$

n^{th} harmonic voltage

$$V_{o\,(n^{th})} = \frac{V_{o\,(f_{ON})}}{n}$$

$$\therefore \quad V_{o\,(3^{rd})} = \frac{43.22}{3} = \textbf{14.40 V}$$

$$\therefore \quad V_{o\,(5^{th})} = \frac{43.22}{5} = \textbf{8.64 V}$$

$$V_{o\,(7^{th})} = \frac{43.22}{7} = \textbf{6.17 V}$$

(b) $\quad V_{o\,(RMS)} = V_{dc} = 48 \text{ V}$

$$V_{o\,(RMS)} = \sqrt{V_o^2 + V_{o\,(3)}^2 + V_{o\,(5)}^2 + V_{o\,(7)}^2}$$

$$= \sqrt{(43.22)^2 + (14.40)^2 + (8.64)^2 + (6.17)^2}$$

$$= \textbf{46.72 V}$$

If we consider higher harmonic then this difference decreases.

(c) Output RMS power $= P_{RMS} = \dfrac{V_{o\,RMS}^2}{R} = \dfrac{48^2}{15} = 153.6$ watt

Output fundamental power,

$$P_{o\,(f_{ON})} = \dfrac{V_{o\,(f_{ON})}^2}{R}$$

$$= \dfrac{(43.22)^2}{15}$$

$$= \mathbf{124.53\ watt}$$

Example 4.8 : *A full bridge bipolar PWM inverter is fed from a 120 V battery and driving RL load. If modulation index is 0.8, calculate :*

(a) Total RMS output voltage.

(b) Fundamental output voltage.

(c) Distortion and harmonic factor.

Solution : (a) RMS output voltage,

$$V_{o\,(RMS)} = V_{DC} = \mathbf{120\ V}$$

(b) Fundamental output voltage average

$$= V_{o\,(av)} = 0.707 \times m \times V_{DC}$$

$$= 0.707 \times 0.8 \times 120$$

$$= \mathbf{67.872\ V}$$

(c) Distortion factor $= 0.707 \times m$

$$= 0.707 \times 0.8$$

$$= \mathbf{0.5656}$$

Harmonic factor $= \sqrt{\dfrac{2}{(m)^2} - 1}$

$$= \sqrt{\dfrac{2}{(0.8)^2} - 1}$$

$$= \mathbf{1.457}$$

REVIEW QUESTIONS

1. What is a inverter ? Which devices are used for inverter ? Compare transistorized inverter with SCR inverter.
2. List out features and applications of inverter.
3. How inverters are classified ?

4. Compare voltage fed inverter with current fed inverter.
5. What is a series inverter ? Sketch circuit diagram and associated waveforms of a basic series inverter. State its operation and limitations.
6. Sketch circuit diagram of modified series inverter with coupled inductors and modified series inverter half bridge type.
7. Explain with circuit diagram three-phase series inverter.
8. With neat circuit diagram and waveform explain the operation of parallel inverter.
9. State the limitations of parallel inverter. How these limitations are overcome in modified parallel inverter ? Sketch its circuit diagram.
10. Sketch circuit diagram of McMurry Bedford half bridge inverter. What is the drawback of half bridge inverter ?
11. Along with waveforms explain full bridge inverter circuit operation. Sketch its circuit diagram.
12. Sketch circuit diagram of modified McMurry inverter and McMurry Bedford inverter.
13. Why output voltage control is necessary ? State methods for this operation.
14. Explain the method of output voltage control using external A.C. voltage control.
15. List out and sketch block diagram of four methods of input D.C. voltage.
16. With waveform explain single pulse PWM inverter.
17. How multiple pulse PWM operate ? Sketch its waveform.
18. Compare sinusoidal PWM and multiple pulse PWM inverter.
19. What is harmonic ? State drawbacks of presence of harmonic.
20. List out methods for harmonic reduction. Explain LC filter method.
21. How resonant filter is used to eliminate harmonics ?
22. What is OTT filter ? Sketch its circuit diagram.
23. Explain 3 phase bridge inverter.
24. Sketch waveform for 120° conduction of 3ϕ inverter.
25. Sketch and explain waveform for 180° conduction of 3ϕ inverter.
26. Compare 120° and 180° conduction of 3ϕ inverter.

Chapter 5

AC CONTROLLERS, UPS AND SIMULATION OF CONVERTERS

Weightage of Marks = 16, Teaching Hours = 09

Contents

- AC controller :
    - ON-OFF control
    - Phase angle control
- Single phase AC control
    - Half wave
    - Full wave
- UPS
    - Operating principle
    - Types
    - Battery charger
- Simulation

Objectives

After learning this chapter, reader will be able to :

- Describe various methods of AC controllers.
- Explain single phase half wave AC controller with R and RL load circuit.
- Explain single phase full wave AC controller with R and RL load.
- Sketch UPS configuration.
- State types and their comparison of UPS.
- Explain battery charger.
- State need of simulation, tools for simulation, features of good simulation and selection criteria.

5.1 INTRODUCTION

- To control D.C. power in load, unidirectional devices such as SCRs are used. By connecting a reverse parallel pair of thyristor or TRIAC between A.C. supply and load the voltage applied to the load can be controlled. This type of power controller is known as A.C. voltage controller or A.C. regulator. A.C. voltage controller converts fixed mains voltage directly to variable alternating voltage without the change in frequency. These types of controllers are widely used in speed control of polyphase induction motors, domestic and industrial heating on load transformer, light controls, static reactive power compensation.

- Thyristor and TRIAC based controllers are more efficient, compact and flexible in control. These are also suitable for closed loop control because of low control power and fast response. These are phase controlled controllers with line commutation. These circuits do not require any complex commutation circuits. The major drawback of such controller is the presence of harmonics in supply current and load voltage.

Two types of A.C. voltage controllers are :

(1) Unidirectional or half wave control.

(2) Bidirectional or full wave control.

5.2 HALF WAVE A.C. VOLTAGE REGULATOR

- In this circuit one SCR and one diode is used. These are connected in antiparallel. Power fed to the load is controlled by delaying triggering pulse applied to the SCR. Fig. 5.1 shows the circuit diagram for half wave A.C. voltage regulator. Due to the presence of diode the control voltage range is limited and the effective RMS output voltage varies between 70.7% to 100%. Positive half cycle is not identical to negative half cycle.

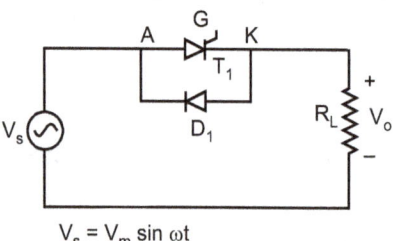

$V_s = V_m \sin \omega t$

Fig. 5.1 : Half wave A.C. controller

- Fig. 5.2 shows waveforms for half wave A.C. controller. As the waveforms in positive half cycle and negative half cycle are not identical, so D.C. component is introduced in the load circuit. As only positive cycle is controllable, so it is called as unidirectional controller.

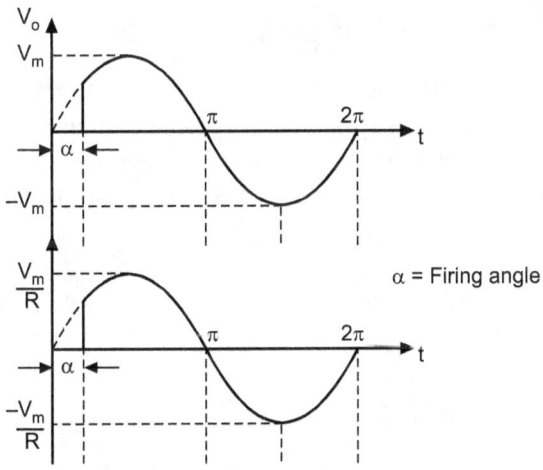

Fig. 5.2 : Half wave A.C. controller waveforms for R load

If
$$v_o = V_m \sin \omega t = \sqrt{2}\, V_s \sin \omega t$$
$$\alpha = \omega t \text{ firing angle}$$

$$V_o = \left\{ \frac{1}{2\pi} \left[\int_0^\pi 2V_s^2 \sin^2 \omega t\, d(\omega t) + \int_\pi^{2\pi} 2V_s^2 \sin^2 \omega t\, d(\omega t) \right] \right\}^{1/2}$$

$$= \left\{ \frac{2V_s^2}{4\pi} \left[\int_\alpha^\pi (1 - \cos 2\omega t)\, d(\omega t) + \int_\pi^{2\pi} (1 - \cos 2\omega t)\, d(\omega t) \right] \right\}^{1/2}$$

$$= V_s \left\{ \frac{1}{2\pi} \left(2\pi - \alpha + \frac{\sin 2\alpha}{2} \right) \right\}^{1/2}$$

$$V_{av} = \frac{1}{2\pi} \left[\int_\alpha^\pi \sqrt{2}\, V_s \sin \omega t\, d(\omega t) + \int_\pi^{2\pi} \sqrt{2}\, V_s \sin \omega t\, d(\omega t) \right]$$

$$= \frac{\sqrt{2}\, V_s}{2\pi} (\cos \alpha - 1)$$

- Switching device is so operated that load gets connected to AC source for a part of each half cycle or part of each cycle of the input voltage.
- For R-L load, during 0 to π, T_1 is forward biased. At $\omega t = \alpha$, T_1 is triggered and $i_o = i_{T_1}$. At π load and source voltages are zero but current is not zero because of the presence of inductance in the load circuit. At $\beta > \pi$, load current reduces to zero. β is called as extinction angle. After π, T_1 is reverse biased but does not turn OFF because i_o is not zero. At β when i_o is zero, T_1 is turned OFF as it is already reverse biased. During negative cycle diode conducts. Current flows in the reverse direction.
- Output voltage of half wave A.C. controller is limited to a lower range. So half wave controller are suitable only for resistive load such as heating and lighting.

5.3 FULL WAVE A.C. CONTROLLER

- For single phase full wave A.C. controller, various configurations are shown in Fig. 5.3 (a) is a full wave A.C. controller using antiparallel configuration of SCR. Fig. 5.3 (b) shows common cathode connection of full wave A.C. controller. Fig. 5.3 (c) shows single thyristor diode bridge connection for A.C. full wave controller and Fig. 5.3 (d) shows TRIAC based full wave A.C. controller.

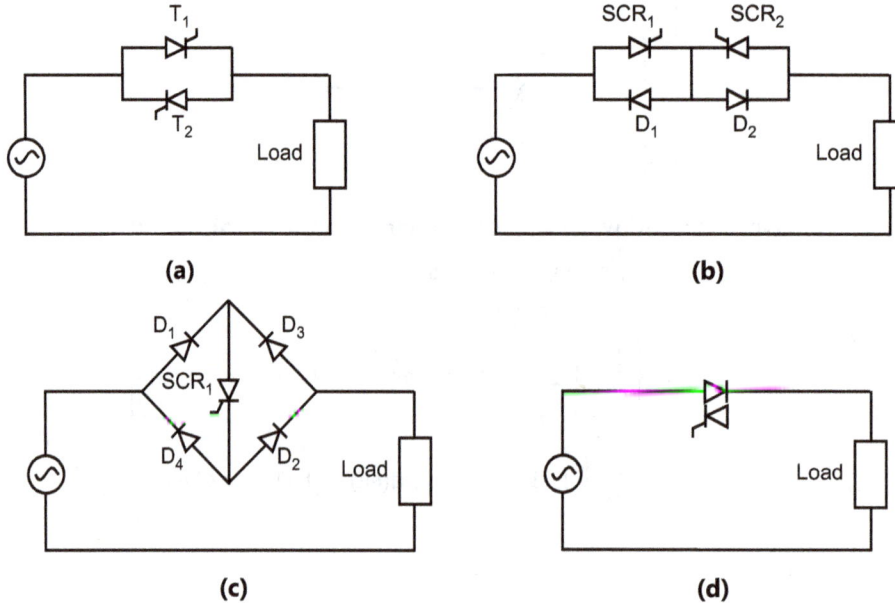

Fig. 5.3 : Full wave controller configurations

- Full wave A.C. controller (ACVC) based on antiparallel thyristor configuration is applied in applications which have a high mechanical inertia and high thermal constant such as in speed control of A.C. motors and induction heating.
- TRIAC based ACVC are suitable for low power applications. For these applications, isolation between control and power circuit may not be necessary.

5.3.1 Single Phase A.C. Controller with Pure Resistive Load (Full Wave)

- A single phase A.C. voltage bidirectional controller feeding a purely resistance is shown in Fig. 5.4. As the load is purely resistive the load current $i_o = \dfrac{V_o}{R}$ at any instant will be in phase with the load voltage (v_o).

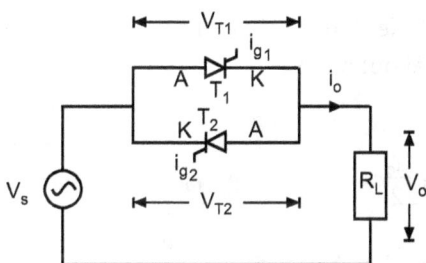

Fig. 5.4 : Full wave A.C. voltage controller with R load

- The thyristor T_1 forward bias during the positive half cycle is triggered at a firing angle α. The SCR_1 conducts from $\omega t = \alpha$ to $\omega t = \pi$. During this period, source voltage is applied to load. At $\omega t = \pi$, current through T_1 decreases and falls to zero and then T_1 reverse biases and turns OFF.
- Fig. 5.5 shows waveforms for full wave antiparallel bidirectional A.C. voltage controller with resistive load.

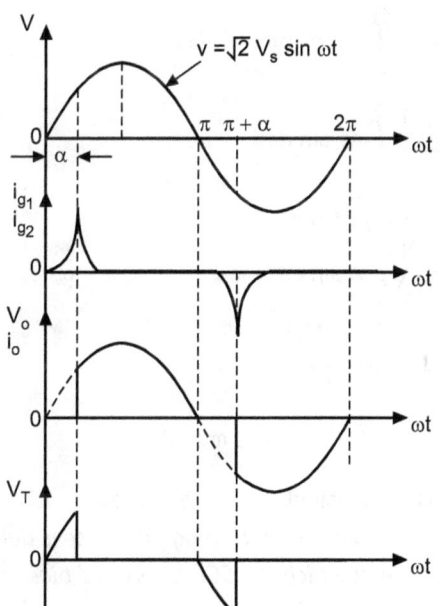

Fig. 5.5 : Single phase A.C. voltage controller with R load

- The SCR T_2 forward biased during negative half cycle is triggered at $\pi + \alpha$ and conducts upto 2π. The load is subjected to A.C. source voltage of negative half cycle during the period $\omega t = (\pi + \alpha)$ to $\omega = 2\pi$. Each SCR is reverse biased for the duration π. Firing angle α can be varied between $0 \leq \alpha \leq \pi$. RMS and fundamental component of the load voltage can be varied from a maximum to zero.

- Trigger pulse of amplitude 1 to 3 V is sufficient to switch ON the thyristor. Output voltage is non-sine signal but periodic.

  In Fourier series,

  $$V_o(\omega t) = \frac{a_o}{2} + \sum_{n=1}^{\infty} (a_n \cos n\omega t + b_n \sin n\omega t)$$

  $$= \frac{a_o}{2} + \sum_{n=1}^{\infty} c_n \sin(n\omega t + \phi_n)$$

  where,

  $c_n = \sqrt{a_n^2 + b_n^2}$ = Peak value of nth harmonic

  $\phi_n = \tan^{-1}\left(\dfrac{a_n}{b_n}\right)$ = Phase displacement of nth harmonic

  $$\frac{a_o}{2} = \frac{1}{2\pi} \int_0^{2\pi} V_o \, d(\omega t) = \text{D.C. value}$$

  $$a_n = \frac{1}{\pi} \int_0^{2\pi} V_o \cos n\omega t + d(\omega t)$$

  $$b_n = \frac{1}{\pi} \int_0^{2\pi} V_o \sin n\omega t + d(\omega t)$$

  $$v = V_s \sqrt{2} \sin \omega t$$

  $$V_o = \sqrt{2} V_s \sin \omega t \mid \pi, 2\pi, \ldots; \alpha, \pi + \alpha, \ldots$$

  $$V_T = \sqrt{2} V \sin \omega t \mid \alpha, \pi + \alpha; 0, \pi, \ldots$$

  where SCR_1 is ON load current, $i_o = i_{T_1}$.

  $$i_{T_1} = \frac{V_m \sin \omega t}{R} \quad . \quad \alpha \leq \omega t \leq \beta = \pi$$

- α is a delay angle. It is also called as angle of retard. It is defined *as the interval in electrical angular measure by which the turning ON pulse is delayed by phase control from the earliest instant in a cycle at which the SCR is forward biased.*

  $$I_R = \frac{V_R}{R}$$

  Output power, $P_o = I_R^2 R = V_R I_R$

- As the output current is same as load current, the input power factor,

  $$PF = \frac{P_o}{VI_R} = \frac{V_R}{V} = \sqrt{\frac{1}{\pi}(\pi - \alpha) + \frac{\sin 2\alpha}{2}}$$

- The average value of output current is given by,

$$I_{o\,ave} = \frac{1}{2\pi} \int_0^{2\pi} i_{T_1}\, dt(\omega t)$$

$$= \frac{V_m}{2\pi R} \int_0^{2\pi} \sin \omega t\, d(\omega t)$$

$$= \frac{V_m}{2\pi R}(1 - \cos \alpha)$$

- The RMS value of the thyristor,

$$I_{TR} = \sqrt{\frac{1}{2\pi} \int_0^{2\pi} i_{T_1}^2\, d(\omega t)}$$

$$= \sqrt{\frac{1}{2\pi R} \int_0^{\pi} (V_m \sin \omega t)^2\, d(\omega t)} = \frac{I_R}{\sqrt{2}}$$

- When A.C. voltage controller is used for the speed control of a single phase induction motor, only fundamental component is useful in producing the torque. The harmonics in the motor current merely increases the losses and therefore heating of the induction motor.
- For heating and lighting control both fundamental and harmonics are useful in producing the A.C. controlled power.
- The power factor is poor for low values of the load current and appreciable amount of harmonics is present.

5.3.2 Single Phase Full Wave A.C. Voltage Controller with RL Load

- Principle of working is same as in case of A.C. voltage controller with R load. Fig. 5.6 shows single phase A.C. voltage controller with RL load. Such type of load as very common in practice. In such loads, the load current will be lagging behind the applied voltage. Because of this the conduction angle β is $\pi < \beta < 2\pi$.
- SCR_1 and SCR_2 are triggered at a delay angle α during each positive and negative half cycle. Instantaneous output voltage is given by,

$$v_o = V \quad \text{for } T_1 \text{ or } T_2 \text{ is ON}$$

$$v_o = 0 \quad \text{for } T_1 \text{ and } T_2 \text{ OFF}$$

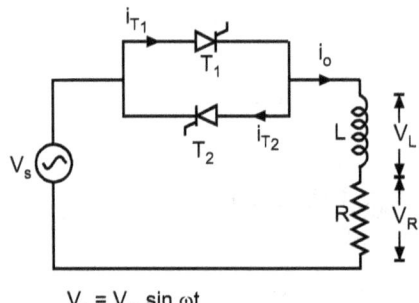

Fig. 5.6 : Single phase A.C. voltage controller with R-L load

Instantaneous current,

$$i_o = i_{T_1} \text{ when } T_1 \text{ is ON}$$
$$i_o = -i_{T_2} \text{ when } T_2 \text{ is ON}.$$

When T_1 is ON the load is connected to the supply and $i_{T_1} = i_o$ by KVL.

$$V_L + V_R = V$$

$$\frac{di_{T_1}}{dt} + \left(\frac{R}{L}\right) i_{T_1} = \left(\frac{V_m}{L}\right) \sin \omega t$$

$$i_N = K e^{-t/\tau}$$

where K = Arbitrary constant

$\tau = \dfrac{L}{R}$ is the time constant of the circuit

$$i_F = \frac{V_m}{|Z|} \sin(\omega t - \phi)$$

$$|Z| = \sqrt{R^2 + (\omega L)^2}$$

$\phi = \tan^{-1}\left(\dfrac{\omega L}{R}\right)$ is the phase angle of the load impedance

$$i_{T_1} = i_N + i_F = K e^{-t/\tau} + \frac{V_m}{|Z|} \sin(\omega t - \phi) \qquad \text{for } \alpha \leq \omega t \leq \beta$$

The SCR T_1 is triggered at $\omega t = \alpha$ or $t = (\alpha/\omega)$. At that instant, $i_{T_1} = 0$.

$$0 = K e^{-(\alpha/\omega)(L/R)} + \frac{V_m}{|Z|} \sin(\alpha - \phi)$$

$$K = -\frac{V_m}{|Z|} \sin(\alpha - \phi) e^{(R/L)(\alpha/\omega)}$$

$$i_{T_1} = \frac{V_m}{|Z|} \{\sin(\omega t - \phi) - \sin(\alpha - \phi) e^{(R/L)[(\alpha/\omega) - t]}\} \qquad \text{for } \alpha \leq \omega t \leq \beta$$

- Under the steady-state condition, current in R-L load excited by a sine supply lags behind the applied voltage by the phase angle of the load impedance. The conduction angle of the thyristor y is,

$$y = \beta - \alpha$$

When $\alpha = 0°$ then conduction angle is π.

- Fig. 5.7 shows waveforms for RL load operates by single phase full wave A.C. controller.

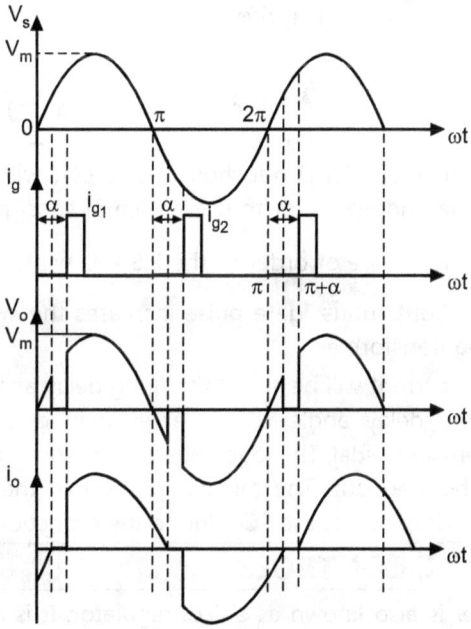

Fig. 5.7 : Singe phase A.C. controller with R-L load

- Once the β extinction angle is known the output RMS voltage is,

$$V_R = \sqrt{\frac{1}{2\pi}\int_0^{2\pi} v_o^2\, d(\omega t)} = \sqrt{\frac{2}{2\pi}\int_0^{\beta} (V_m \sin \omega t)^2\, d(\omega t)}$$

$$= \sqrt{\frac{V_m^2}{\pi}\int_0^{\beta}\left(\frac{1-\cos 2\omega t}{2}\right)d(\omega t)}$$

$$= V\sqrt{\frac{1}{\pi}\left[\beta - \alpha + \frac{\sin 2\alpha}{2} - \frac{\sin 2\beta}{2}\right]}$$

where $V = V_m/\sqrt{2}$ is the RMS value of the input voltage.

(Chap. 5.9)

RMS value of the SCR current,

$$I_{TR} = \sqrt{\frac{1}{2\pi} \int_{\alpha}^{\beta} i^2 \, I_1 \, d(\omega t)}$$

$$P_o = I_R^2 R$$

where P_o = Output power

Average value of the thyristor current can be found as,

$$I_{av} = \frac{1}{2\pi} \int_{\alpha}^{\beta} i_o \, d(\omega t)$$

$$= \frac{\sqrt{2} \, V_s}{2\pi 2} \int_{\alpha}^{\beta} [\sin(\omega t - \phi) - \sin(\alpha - \phi) \, e^{R/L \, p(\alpha/\omega) - t}] \, d(\omega t)$$

- In order to initiate and maintain conduction in a circuit with series inductance, it is necessary to sustain the firing pulse or to use a train of short pulses. Typical pulse train frequencies used in practice are of order of the 2.5 kHz with a mark space ratio $\frac{1}{10}$ for 50 Hz supply voltage. Continuous gate pulse increases the switching loss of SCR and requires large isolating transformer.
- Load voltage and load current will be sine if the firing delay angle α is less than the load power factor ϕ. If the delay angle α is greater than ϕ, the load current will be discontinuous and non-sinusoidal. The load voltage waveform has the shape of sine with a vertical segment chopped out. The missing portion of the load voltage waveform represents the voltage drop across the SCR during the extinction period.

5.4 INTEGRAL CYCLE CONTROL

- A.C. voltage controller is also known as a A.C. regulator. It is a converter which take a constant RMS voltage and frequency AC input and output variable RMS voltage A.C. at the same frequency as the input. These are naturally commutated converters. Major applications of A.C. controller are :
  (1) Transformer tap changing.
  (2) Illumination control.
  (3) Domestic and industrial heating.
  (4) Induction heating.
  (5) Static reactive power compensators in power system.
  (6) Speed control of induction motors in pumps and fans.
- These converters causes harmonic in supply current and load voltage. The harmonics become more at lower output voltages. Output voltage harmonics affect the performance of induction motor. Supply current harmonics adversely affect other equipments connected to the same power supply.

- In ON-OFF type of control the AC switch connects the load to the supply for an integral number of cycles n and disconnects the load for some integral number of cycle m. Therefore, this type of control is also called as integral cycle control, zero voltage switching, burst firing or cycle syncopation. Fig. 5.8 shows single phase AC voltage controller.

- In this circuit, i_{G_1} and i_{G_2} turn ON the thyristors SCR_1 and SCR_2 at zero voltage crossing of the supply voltage. The source is connected to the load for n (= 2) cycles. When gate pulses are removed, the supply is disconnected from the load for m = 1 cycle. In this manner, turn ON and turn OFF are repeated to control the power flow from source to the load.

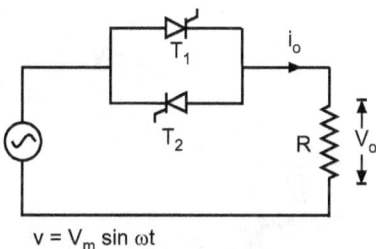

Fig. 5.8 : Single phase AC controller

- Power flow from source to the load can be varied by varying n and m. Fig. 5.9 shows the waveforms of output voltage and current.

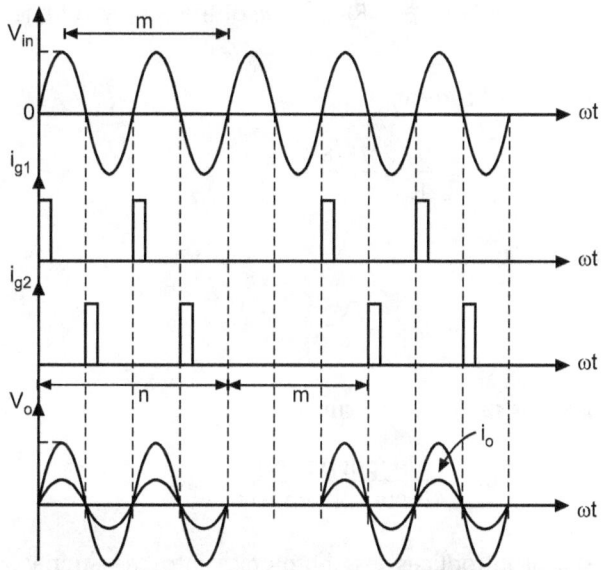

Fig. 5.9 : Waveforms for ON-OFF AC single phase voltage controller

- If input voltage $v = V_m \sin \omega t$ is connected to the load for n cycles and it is disconnected for m cycles then

$$\left. \begin{array}{l} v_o = V_m \sin \omega t \\ i_o = \dfrac{V_m \sin \omega t}{R} \end{array} \right\} \text{ for n cycles}$$

$$\left. \begin{array}{l} v_o = 0 \\ i_o = 0 \end{array} \right\} \text{ for m cycles}$$

The RMS voltage is given by,

$$V_R = \sqrt{\dfrac{\pi}{2\pi(n+m)} \int_0^{2\pi} (V_m \sin \omega t)^2}$$

$$= \dfrac{V_m}{\sqrt{2}} \sqrt{\dfrac{n}{n+m}}$$

$$= V\sqrt{\delta} \quad \text{where} \quad \delta = \dfrac{n}{n+m}.$$

It is called as duty cycle.

$$V = \dfrac{V_m}{\sqrt{2}} = \text{RMS value of the supply voltage}$$

The RMS value of the load current,

$$i_R = \dfrac{V_R}{R} = \dfrac{V\sqrt{\delta}}{R}$$

Power delivered to the load,

$$P_o = I_R^2 R = \dfrac{\delta V^2}{R}$$

The input line current is same as load current.

$$\text{Power factor, PF} = \dfrac{\text{Input power}}{\text{Input volt ampere}}$$

- Integral cycle control introduces less harmonics into the supply when compared to phase control. So it is suitable for heating loads and motor drive.

(Chap. 5.12)

5.5 UNINTERRUPTIBLE POWER SUPPLY (UPS)

- In many applications, interrupt free power is required. UPS can maintain the power supply under all conditions. Applications like computer system, ICU equipments, process plants, safety monitors require use of UPS. It provides interrupt free power to the load. A UPS system has following features :

    (1) It shall provide good quality power to the load at all conditions of supply power.

    (2) In shall regulate the load voltage when the line supply variation occurs.

    (3) It shall provide constant voltage and constant frequency supply to the critical load.

    (4) It shall provide complete isolation between load and line supply.

    (5) It must suppress the line transient and minimize EMI.

- A typical UPS consists of rectifier, charger, inverter, filter, battery bank. Fig. 5.10 shows the block diagram of typical UPS. A rectifier converts a single phase or three phase A.C. voltage into D.C. It gives power to the inverter as well as to the battery bank. It charges the battery. The inverter gets a d.c. input voltage from the rectifier when the A.C. mains is ON and from the battery bank when the A.C. mains is OFF. Inverter converts this D.C. voltage into A.C. voltage. This A.C. is filtered and supplied to the load. A static switch is used to connect inverter to the line supply or to the battery depending on the line supply status.

- If T is the period of the input voltage, which is typically 20 msec at 50 Hz, (m + n) T is the period of ON-OFF control. In practical applications, (m + n) T should be less than the mechanical or thermal time constant of the load and it is less than 1 sec. Typically m + n is around 100 cycles. Integral cycle control is employed in heating applications where the time constant of the load is very large.

$$\text{Duty cycle} = \frac{T_{ON}}{T_{ON} + T_{OFF}} = \frac{n}{m + n}$$

- When the load is resistive, it is advisable to have a zero crossing switch built into the integral cycle control scheme so that ON time always starts at the zero point of the applied A.C. cycle voltage to avoid high di/dt.

- For motor control the duration of ON period must be an integral multiple of the period of the applied voltage. This is used for avoiding magnetic saturation resulting from an unequal number of positive and negative half cycles during ON time.

- Three types of UPS are :

    (1) ON-line UPS.

    (2) OFF-line UPS.

    (3) Line interactive UPS.

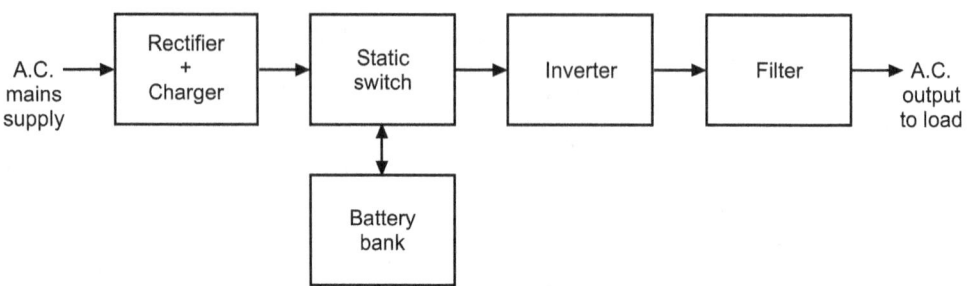

Fig. 5.10 : Block diagram of UPS

- In ON-line UPS, load is always connected to the inverter through the UPS static switch. This UPS static switch is normally 'ON'. It turns OFF when UPS system fails. Fig. 5.11 shows the block diagram for ON-line UPS.

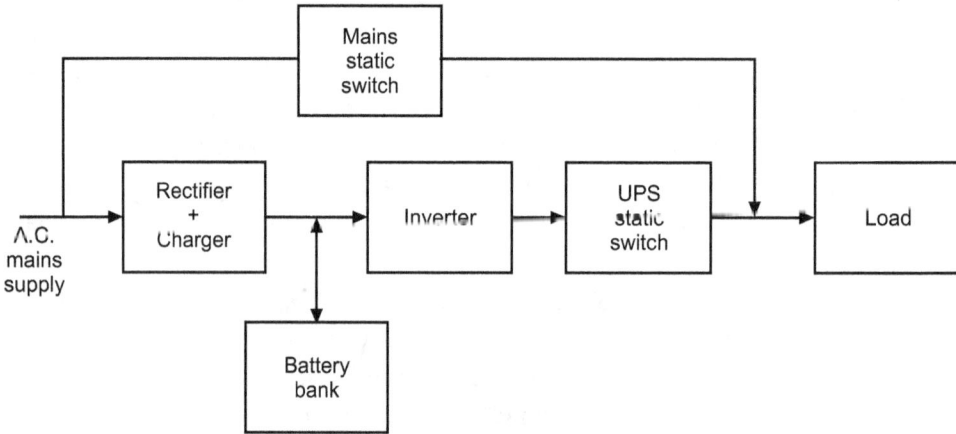

Fig. 5.11 : Block diagram of ON-line UPS

- ON-line UPS has three operating modes.

  Mode I : When A.C. line supply is ON, the rectifier circuit will supply the power to the inverter as well as to the battery. It charges the battery. Its ratings are larger. The inverter output is connected to the load through the UPS static switch.

  Mode II : If the line supply power fails suddenly, the rectifier output will be zero and hence the battery bank gives power to the inverter. There will not be any change in the inverter output. In this mode, battery discharges and no charging occurs. When assigned A.C. line supply is available, the charger supplies power to the battery bank. Battery charging occurs in constant current mode and then in constant potential mode.

  Mode III : In case of failure of inverter, the normally OFF mains static switch is turned ON which connects line supply to the load in less than 0.25 cycles period with no phase discontinuity. It activates inverter failure alarm.

- This ON-line UPS provides the complete isolation of critical load from A.C. mains and also provides power conditioning. Its changeover time is very less. This system protects the load against transient, spikes, surges, line noise, frequency and voltage variations, blown out.

Major specifications of ON-line UPS :

- Power rating   500 VA, 1 kVA to 50 kVA
- Output voltage   230 V ± 0.1%
- Output frequency   50 Hz ± 0.1%
- Input voltage   230 V ± 15%
- Output voltage waveform   Sine wave
- Power factor   70.8 lagging
- Back-up time   30 min to 4 hrs
- Total harmonic distortion   < 3%
- Efficiency   > 85%
- Protection   Over voltage
                                    Under voltage
                                    Over current

- In OFF-line UPS, mains static switch is normally ON switch. It directly connects the A.C. mains supply to the load when mains is ON. From block diagram point of view, there is no difference but only static switch condition is different. Fig. 5.12 shows the block diagram of OFF-line UPS.

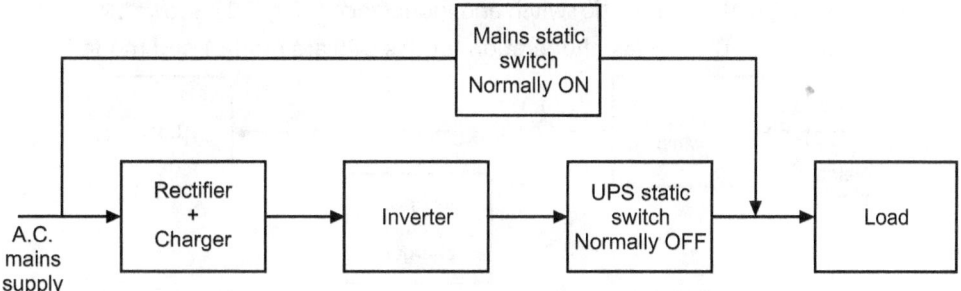

Fig. 5.12 : OFF-line UPS

- Battery charger is a stabilized one which maintains the battery on float at fully charged condition. It provides stabilized power to the inverter. The UPS static switch is normally OFF. It is closed only when the mains is failed. In OFF line UPS, the inverter comes into the circuit only when the mains is OFF. The rectifier and charger has to only charge the battery bank. So its power rating and size is lower than ON-line UPS. When mains supply fails, the static switch operate to disconnect mains from the load and connect the load to the UPS system. The battery will supply the power to the load via inverter. Normally 5 msec time is required for switchover.

Specifications of OFF-line UPS :

• Power rating	500 VA to 2 kVA
• Input voltage	230 V ± 25%
• Battery voltage	24 V/6.5 VA, 48 V/6.5 AH
• Output voltage	For mains 230 V ± 5%
	For UPS 230 V ± 0.5%
• Output voltage waveform	Sine
• Output frequency	50 Hz ± 3%
• Battery charging time	4 hrs
• Back-up time	30 min or more
• Transfer time	6 msec
• Efficiency	> 85%
• Protection	Output overload
	Mains over voltage
	Low battery

- Interactive UPS or line interactive UPS block diagram is same as OFF-line UPS. The main block of this system is battery charger cum inverter. Normally load is supplied power from mains supply through static switch and inductance L. Fig. 5.12 shows block diagram for interactive UPS. The modes of operation for this UPS are mode 1 and mode 2.

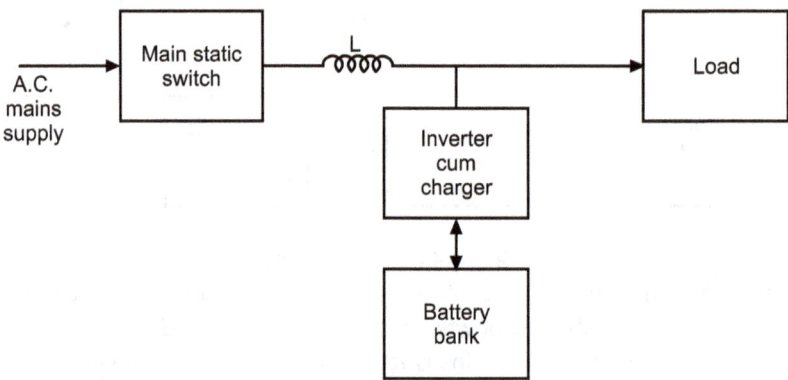

Fig. 5.13 : Interactive UPS

- In mode 1 mains supply is ON. The static switch is closed and load gets connected directly to the A.C. mains through the inductance L. The inverter cum charger block operates as charger and chargers the battery bank.

- In mode 2 mains is OFF. As soon as mains supply fails, the static switch is turned OFF and inverter cum charger operates as an inverter. Now battery supplies power to the load through the inverter. It takes 5 msec time for change over. It does not provide isolation between load and A.C. mains supply. It gives good voltage regulation by using power conditioning like stabilizer or constant voltage transformer (CVT).

- Reliability is measured in terms of MTTF (mean time to failure). Reliability can be improved by providing redundancy i.e. use of two UPS with circuit breaker. Redundancy may be parallel redundancy or dual and isolated redundancy.

5.6 BATTERY BANK

- The operation of UPS depends on the battery. If battery is not properly selected then overall life and reliability decreases. Different types of battery are (a) Lead-acid, (b) Ni-Cd, (c) Sealed maintenance free (SMF). Normally lead acid batteries are used.

- Battery capacity is expressed in terms of AH. This rating tells us about how much amount of current that battery can supply for 1 hour. For example, battery of 4 AH means 4 A current for 1 hr. Capacity of battery depends on :

    (1) Rate of discharge.

    (2) Temperature.

    (3) Density of electrolyte.

- Battery capacity can be calculated from :

    (1) $\text{Battery (kW)} = \dfrac{\text{Load kVA} \times \text{Power factor}}{\text{Inverter efficiency}}$

    (2) $\text{Number of cells} = \dfrac{\text{Minimum allowable battery voltage}}{\text{Final voltage per cell}}$

    (3) $\text{Cell capacity (kW/cell)} = \dfrac{\text{Battery kW}}{\text{Number of cells}}$

    (4) $\text{AH efficiency} = \dfrac{\text{A.H. during discharge}}{\text{A.H. input while charging}}$

Typically, it is 90 to 95%.

$$\text{Watt hour efficiency} = \text{AH efficiency} \times \dfrac{\text{Average cell volt at discharging}}{\text{Average cell voltage at charging}}$$

$$= 70 \text{ to } 80\%.$$

(Chap. 5.17)

5.7 SIMULATION

- Simulation is a process of creating various conditions for a particular circuit by using software tools. For simulation components in real form are not used but they are selected from component library available in simulation software. Before actually conducting practicals using real components, simulation is done and tested. Simulation is helpful in practical design, project work as well as in industry for product design. Simulations are also helpful for analysis under various input signal and noise signal conditions. Computer hardware and software provides a method for circuit design and analysis. Computers are well capable of performing the complex, large and repetitive computations. From industry point of view, simulation allows investigation of the circuit behaviour before actual fabrication. It helps in saving of material, labour and time. Simulation provides waveform based analysis so that user get better understanding of circuit operation.

- Simulation tools are useful for wide variety of circuits from basic circuit analysis to advance topics such as Fourier analysis, active filter design, switch mode and resonant mode power electronic circuit. Simulation software does not require any special hardware requirement for computers. Normal computer hardware are sufficient to run simulation. Simulation allows user to create circuit topology and its modifications, design of the required circuit condition with control circuit, making simulated fault measurement in a state environment and interpreting the resulting waveform.

  Following are advantages of simulation for power electronics circuit :

  - Fast optimisation of system and control.
  - Better understanding of component and circuit functions.
  - Saving of circuit and system development time and cost.
  - Easy testing and finding critical states, regions and condition for operation.
  - Easy waveform analysis.
  - No need of expensive testing and measuring equipments.

- Now-a-days many simulation tools are available. Each simulation tool has few advantages and drawbacks. Three methods to enter the circuit details for simulation are :

- **Mathematical input :** As in the case of MATLAB, mathematical model of circuit and signals are entered using MATLAB coding.

- **Netlist input :** It is used in spice. The circuit elements are entered using description with keyboard. This method is not normally used in advance simulation tools.

- **Graphical input :** Most of the recent simulation tools provide graphical method to enter component, signal source and output meters, scopes etc. It is more user friendly and fast method for circuit simulation.

Following are the requirement of good simulation software tool :

- Easy use and user friendly operation.
- Accuracy in result calculations.
- Comfortable input of the circuit.
- Correct models of the elements with all technical specifications.
- Correct error messages with easy interpretative.
- Robust execution.
- Facility to integrate various algorithms.
- Good and compatible output for other programs.
- Upgradation for new components.
- Portability of models.
- Size of software.
- Run time requirement.
- Component library.
- Output tools, CRO, DSO, logic analyser, etc.

- Power electronic simulation tool must incorporate the ability to simulate the elements of power electronic system such as power diode, power BJT, thyristor, GTO, IGBT as well as complex control and protection system. Simulation tool provides waveform oriented solution for circuit analysis. This allows including and testing of any additional circuit for harmonic suppression. It facilitates to look resulting waveform and post processing manipulation.

- Various simulation tools are available for power electronic circuits such as PSpice, MATLAB, Simulink, Simpower system, PLECS, PSIM, Simpower, CASPOC, Saber.

- PSpice is a most popular simulation tool used for analog and digital circuit. It is intended for low power analog electronic and digital circuits. It has large library with PSpice models for various electronic components. This library can be expanded. PSpice is very powerful and flexible tool.
- MATLAB is a mathematical tool with various toolboxes suitable for variety of applications. Simulink toolbox is a graphical tool for entering of functions. Simpower system is a toolbox useful for simulation of electrical power system including power electronics. Elements of various toolboxes can be used together. Analysis of new converter circuits, large rating converter, multiconverter system, line commutated converter and electrical drive system require an appropriate global simulation tool. Simulation tool shall support modulator simulation. The built-in function and toolboxes of SIMULINK facilitates the design and the analysis of high performance A.C. and D.C. drive. For power electronic simulation, another toolbox of MATLAB is PLECS.
- PLECS is a fast and reliable toolbox for MATLAB PSIM is a specifically developed toolbox for power electronics. It is optimized as per the need of power electronics. It can be interfaces to MATLAB SIMULINK.
- Sim power system is suitable to know behaviour of electrical network. It is useful for large and complex electrical system simulation. It provides component library and analysis tool for simulation of electrical power system. The library provides models of electrical power components including three phase machines, drives and components for applications such as FACTS (Flexible A.C. transmission system) and renewable energy system. Harmonic analysis, calculations of total harmonic distortion (THD), load flow and other electrical power system analysis are automated.
- Sim power system models can be used to develop control system and test system level performance. Models can be parameterized using MATLAB variables and expressions. It is possible to add mechanical, hydraulic, pneumatic and other components to the model using simscape and test them together in a single simulation environment. It supports model based design methodology.
- Few basic examples for simulation using sim power system are explained.

    (1) Single phase rectifier.

    (2) Single phase inverter.

    (3) Copper and DC/AC PWM converter.

    (4) AC-DC-AC converter.

1. Single-Phase Rectifier :

- This example shows how to build a single-phase rectifier using the Universal Bridge, Multimeter, and Discrete System blocks

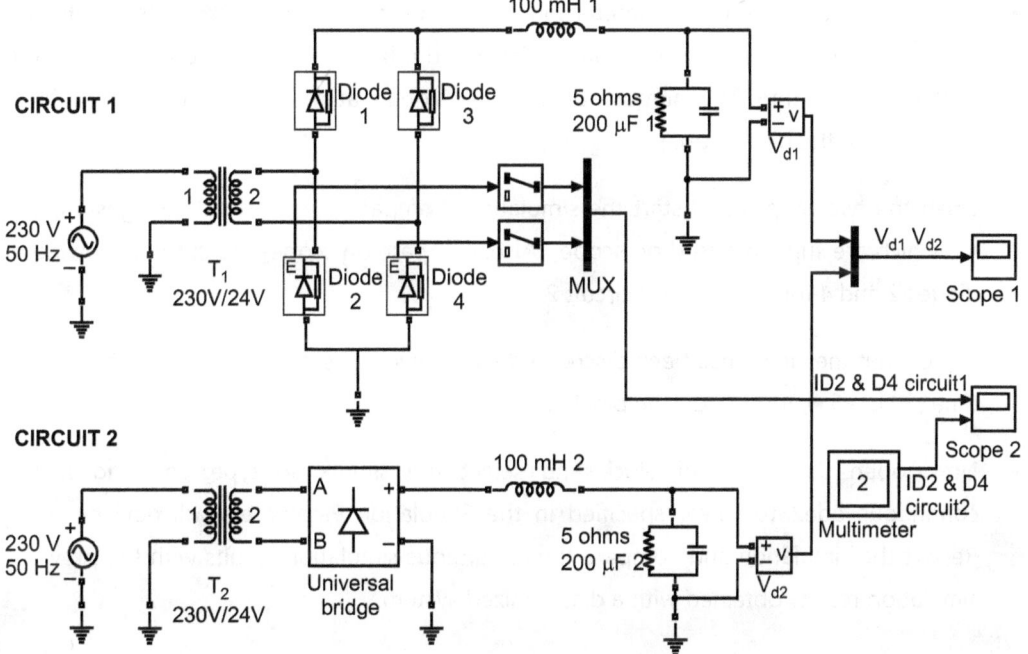

Fig. 5.14 : Screen view for simulation of single phase rectifier

Description :

- This system contains two identical circuits showing the operation of a single phase rectifier.
- The rectifiers are fed by a 130 V/ 24 V linear transformer. The rectified voltage is filtered by a 100 mH / 200 uF filter and applied to a 5 ohm resistive load. The load voltages are measured by two Voltage Measurement blocks V_{d1} and V_{d2}.
- The top circuit (circuit 1) uses four individual diodes connected in a bridge configuration. The currents of diodes 2 and 4 are obtained at the measurement 'm' output of the diode blocks and sent to input 1 of Scope 2 through Selector and Multiplex blocks.
- The bottom circuit (circuit 2) is functionally identical to circuit 1, but the circuit assembly is considerably simplified by the use of the Universal Bridge.

Simulation :

- Open the Universal Bridge dialog box and notice that in order to obtain a four-diode bridge configuration, the **power electronic device** field has been set to diodes and that the number of arms has been set to 2. Also, observe that the **measurements** field has been set to device currents, thus allowing measurement of diode currents through the multimeter block.

- Now, double click on the multimeter block. The four diode currents are listed in the left column. Notice that only currents in diodes 2 and 4 have been selected and transferred in the right column. The number of available signals at the multimeter output (2) is displayed on the block icon.

- Open the two scopes and start the simulation. Compare the two load voltages V_{d1} and V_{d2} which are superimposed on scope$_1$. Also, compare on scope$_2$ the currents flowing in diodes 2 and 4 for circuit 1 and circuit 2.

- Notice that the circuit has been discretized by means of the powergui block. The sample time (50 e – 6 s) appears on the block icon.

- Now, open the Powergui block and select the simulation type Continuous. The continuous ode23tb solver specified in the Simulation Parameters will now be used. Restart the simulation and compare the continuous simulation results with the previous simulation results obtained with a discretized system.

- The system can be modified for single phase controlled converter by selecting SCR instead of diode along with trigger signal generator.

2. **Single-Phase PWM Inverter :**

- This example shows the harmonic analysis of PWM waveforms using the powergui/FFT tool.

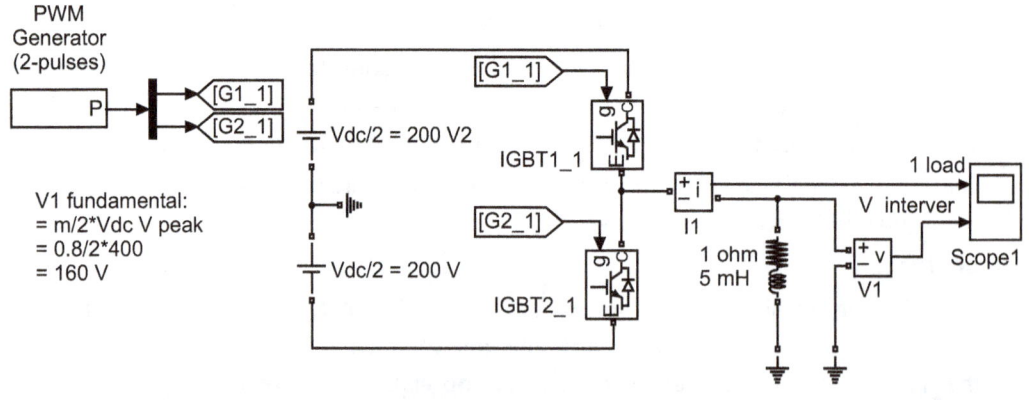

(a) DC/AC half-bridge inverter

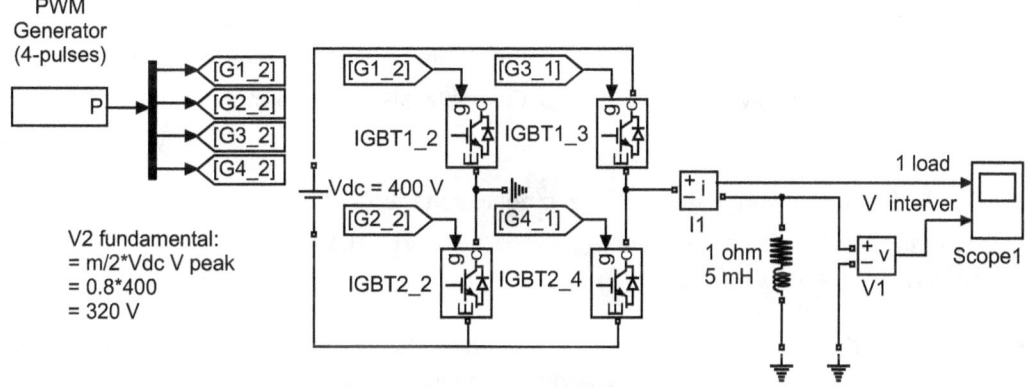

(b) DC/AC full-bridge inverter

Fig. 5.15 : Single-phase PWM inverter

Description :

- The system consists of two independent circuits illustrating single-phase PWM voltage-sourced converters (VSC).
    1. Half-bridge converter.
    2. Full-bridge converter.
- The converters are built with the IGBT/Diode block which is the basic building block of all VSCs. The IGBT/Diode block is a simplified model of an IGBT (or GTO or MOSFET)/Diode pair where the forward voltages of the forced-commutated device and diode are ignored. You may replace these blocks by individual IGBT and diode blocks for a more detailed representation. VSCs are controlled in open loop with the PWM Generator block. The two circuits use the same DC voltage (V_{dc} = 400 V), carrier frequency (1080 Hz) and modulation index (m = 0.8).
- In order to allow further signal processing, signals displayed on the two Scope blocks (sampled at simulation sampling rate of 3240 samples/cycle) are stored in two variables named sps1phPWM1_str and sps1phPWM2_str (structures with time).

Simulation :

- Run the simulation and observe the following two waveforms on the two Scope blocks: Current into the load (trace 1), Voltage generated by the PWM inverter (trace 2).
- Once the simulation is completed, open the Powergui and select FFT Analysis to display the 0 – 5000 Hz frequency spectrum of signals saved in the three sps1phPWMx_str structures. The FFT will be performed on a 2-cycle window starting at t = 0.1 – 2/60 (last 2 cycles of recording). For each circuit, select Input labeled 'V inverter'. Click on Display and observe the frequency spectrum of last 2 cycles.

- The fundamental component of V inverter is displayed above the spectrum window. Compare the magnitude of the fundamental component of the inverter voltage with the theoretical values given in the circuit. Compare also the harmonic contents in the inverter voltage.

  The half-bridge inverter generates a bipolar voltage (–200 V or +200 V). Harmonics occur around the carrier frequency (1080 Hz + – k × 60 Hz), with a maximum of 103% at 1080 Hz.

- The full-bridge inverter generates a monopolar voltage varying between 0 and +400V for one half cycle and then between 0 and –400V for the next half cycle. For the same DC voltage and modulation index, the fundamental component magnitude is twice the value obtained with the half-bridge. Harmonics generated by the full-bridge are lower and they appear at double of the carrier frequency (maximum of 40% at 2 × 1080 + –60 Hz) As a result, the current obtained with the full-bridge is smoother.

- If you now perform a FFT on the signal I load you will notice that the THD of load current is 7.3% for the half-bridge inverter as compared to only 2% for the full-bridge inverter.

3. DC/DC and DC/AC PWM Converters :

- This example shows the harmonic analysis of PWM waveforms using the Powergui/FFT tool.

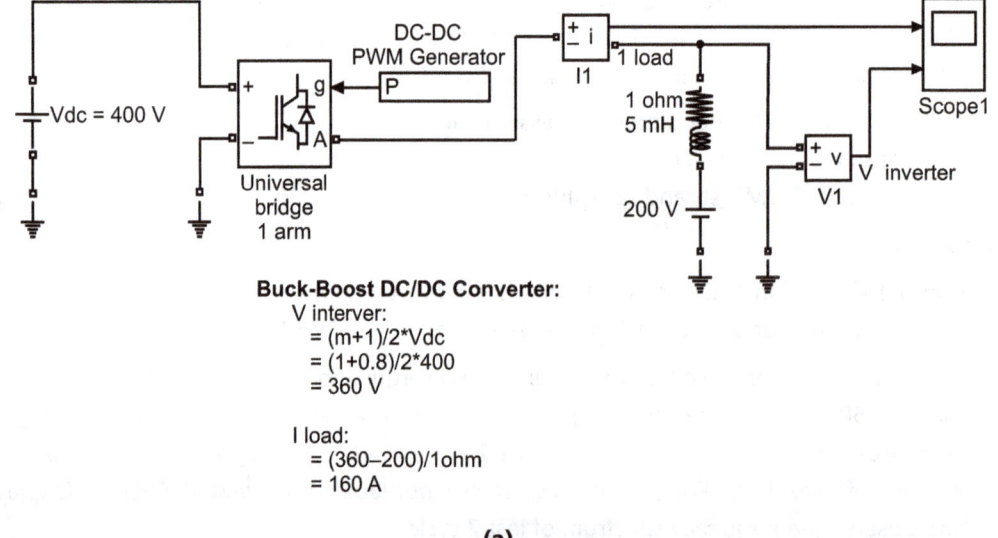

(a)

(Chap. 5.24)

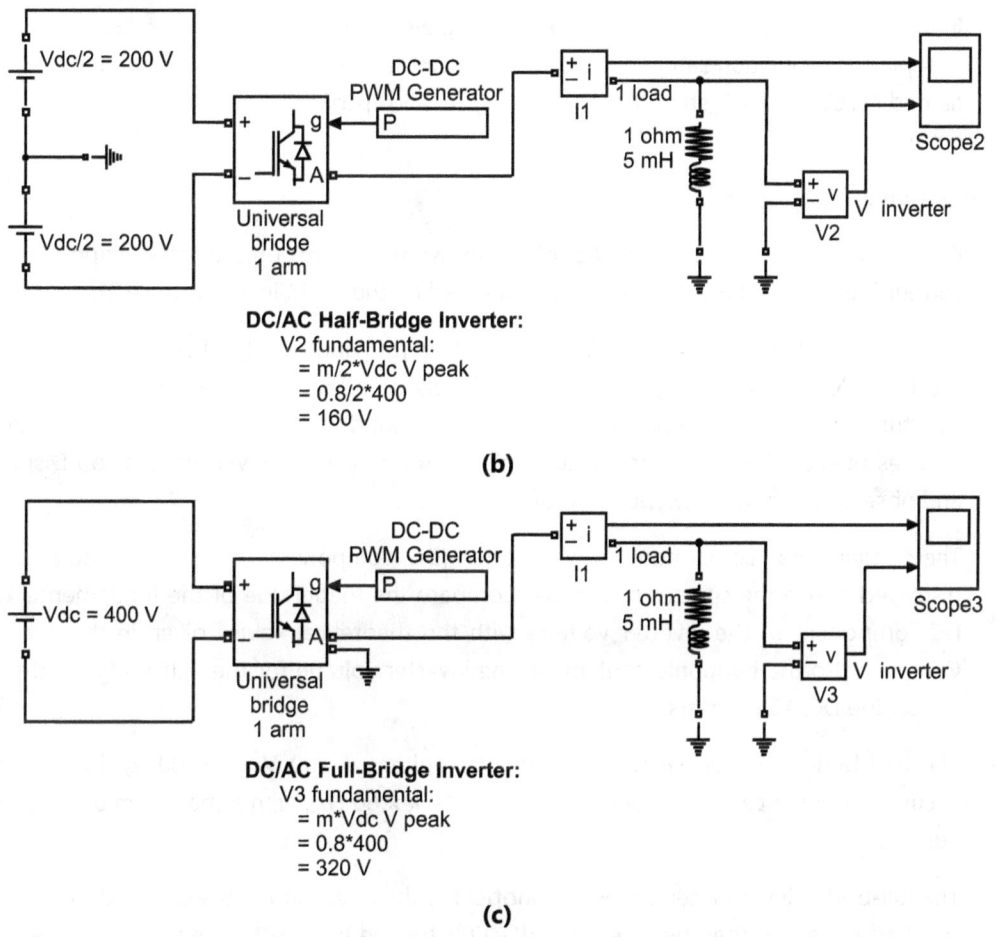

(b)

(c)

Fig. 5.16 : Screen view for simulation of 1φ chopper 2, half bridge inverter 3, full bridge inverter

Description :

- The system consists of three independent circuits illustrating various PWM DC/DC and DC/AC inverters. All converters are controlled in open loop with the PWM Generator block. The three circuits use the same DC voltage (V_{dc} = 400V), carrier frequency (1080 Hz) and modulation index (m = 0.8). From top to bottom, the three circuits are :

1. DC/DC, two-quadrant converter (one-arm; two-switches).
2. DC/AC, half-bridge, bipolar converter (one-arm; two-switches).
3. DC/AC, full-bridge, monopolar converter (two-arms; four-switches).

- In order to allow further signal processing, signals displayed on the three Scope blocks (sampled at simulation sampling rate of 3240 samples/cycle) are stored in three variables named 'psb1phPWM1_str' , 'psb1phPWM2_str' and 'psb1phPWM3_str' (structures with time).

Simulation :

- Run the simulation and observe the following two waveforms on the three Scope blocks: current into the load (trace 1), voltage generated by the PWM inverter (trace 2).

- Once the simulation is completed, open the Powergui and select FFT Analysis to display the 0 - 5000 Hz frequency spectrum of signals saved in the three psb1phPWMx_str structures. The FFT will be performed on a 2-cycle window starting at t = 0.1 - 2/60 (last 2 cycles of recording). For each circuit, select Input labeled 'V inverter'. Click on Display and observe the frequency spectrum of last 2 cycles.

- The fundamental component of V inverter (DC component in case of circuit 1) is displayed above the spectrum window. Compare the magnitude of the fundamental or DC component of the inverter voltage with the theoretical values given in the circuit. Compare also the harmonic contents in the inverter voltage for the half-bridge and the full-bridge DC/AC inverters.

- The half-bridge inverter generates a bipolar voltage (−200 V or +200 V). Harmonics occur around the carrier frequency (1080 Hz + − k × 60 Hz), with a maximum of 103% at 1080 Hz.

- The full-bridge inverter generates a monopolar voltage varying between 0 and +400V for one half cycle and then between 0 and -400V for the next half cycle. For the same DC voltage and modulation index, the fundamental component magnitude is twice the value obtained with the half-bridge. Harmonics generated by the full-bridge are lower and they appear at double of the carrier frequency (maximum of 40% at 2 × 1080 + −60 Hz) As a result, the current obtained with the full-bridge is cleaner.

- If you now perform a FFT on the signal Iload you will notice that the THD of load current is 7.3% for the half-bridge inverter as compared to only 2% for the full-bridge inverter.

- These circuit models consists of IGBT. It can be replaced by SCR. But now-a-days in practice instead of SCR, IGBTs are more commonly used.

4. AC-DC-AC PWM Converter :

- This example shows how to model an AC-DC-AC PMW converter.

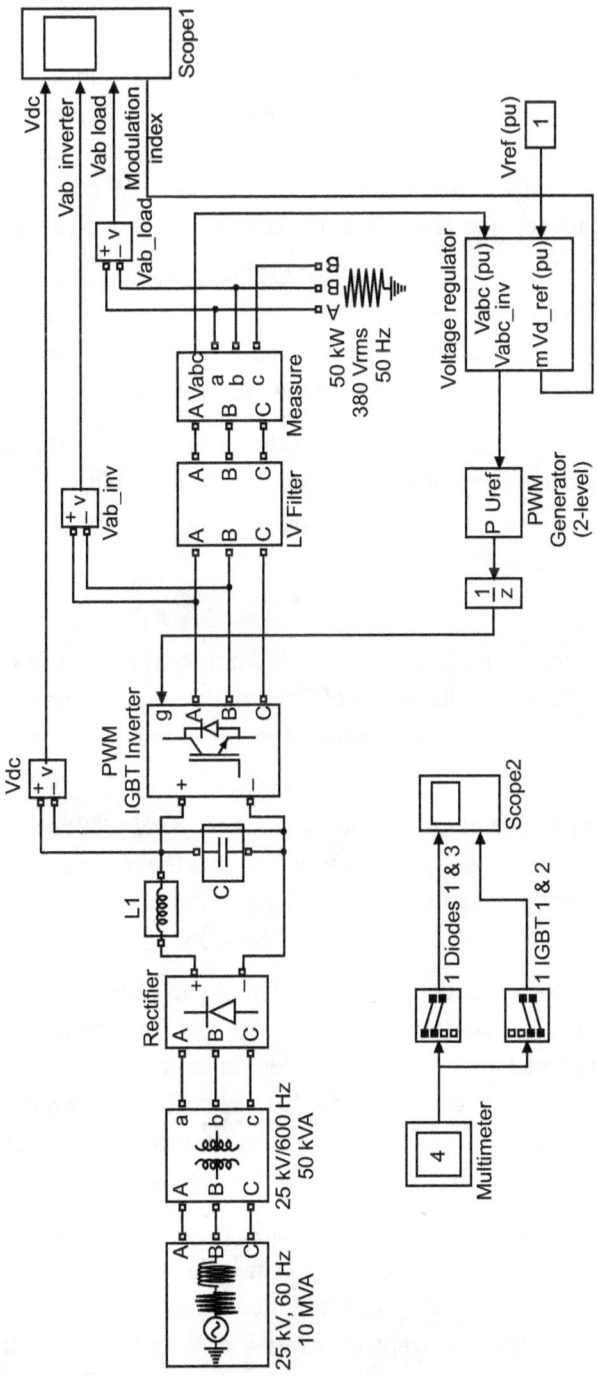

Fig. 5.17 : Screen view for simulation of cycloconverter (converter and inverter)
(Chap. 5.27)

Description :

- A 60 Hz, voltage source feeds a 50 Hz, 50 kW load through an AC-DC-AC converter. The 600V, 60 Hz voltage obtained at secondary of the Wye/Delta transformer is first rectified by a six pulse diode bridge. The filtered DC voltage is applied to an IGBT two-level inverter generating 50 Hz. The IGBT inverter uses Pulse Width Modulation (PWM) at a 2 kHz carrier frequency. The circuit is discretized at a sample time of 2 us

- The load voltage is regulated at 1 pu (380 V_{rms}) by a PI voltage regulator using abc_to_dq and dq_to_abc transfomations. The first output of the voltage regulator is a vector containing the three modulating signals used by the PMW Generator to generate the 6 IGBT pulses. The second output returns the modulation index.

- The Multimeter block is used to observe diode and IGBT currents. In order to allow further signal processing, signals displayed on Scope1 block (sampled at simulation sampling rate of 2 us) are stored in a variable named 'psbbridges_str' (structure with time).

Simulation :

- Start the simulation. After a transient period of approximately 50 ms, the system reaches a steady state. Observe voltage waveforms at DC bus, inverter output and load on Scope1. The harmonics generated by the inverter around multiples of 2 kHz are filtered by the LC filter.

- As expected the peak value of the load voltage is 537 V (380 V_{rms}). In steady state, the mean value of the modulation index is m = 0.80 and the mean value of the DC voltage is 778 V. The fundamental component of 50 Hz voltage buried in the chopped inverter voltage is therefore : V_{ab} = 778 V × 0.612 × 0.80 = 381 V_{rms}.

- Once simulation is completed, open the Powergui and select 'FFT Analysis' to display the 0 - 7000 Hz frequency spectrum of signals saved in the 'psbbridges_str' structure. The FFT will be performed on a 2-cycle window starting at t=0.1-2/50 (last 2 cycles of recording). Select input labeled 'Vab Load' . Click on Display and observe the frequency spectrum of last 2 cycles. Notice harmonics around multiples of the 2 kHz carrier frequency. Maximum harmonic is 1.4% of fundamental and THD is 2%.

- Observe diode currents on trace 1 of Scope2, showing commutation from diode 1 to diode 3. Also observe on trace 2 currents in switches 1 and 2 of the IGBT/Diode bridge (upper and lower switches connected to phase A). These two currents are complementary. A positive current indicates a current flowing in the IGBT, whereas a negative current indicates a current flowing in the antiparallel diode.

SOLVED EXAMPLES

Example 5.1 : *A single phase ON-OFF type AC voltage controller with an input 230 V, 50 Hz is connected to a resistive load of 20 Ω. The circuit is operating with the switch ON for 30 cycles and OFF for 30 cycles. Determine : (i) the RMS output current, (ii) The power factor.*

Solution : Given data :

Input voltage = 230 V, T_{ON} = 30 cycles, T_{OFF} = 30 cycles.

Load resistance = 20 Ω

$$\text{Duty cycle } \delta\% = \frac{T_{ON}}{T_{ON} + T_{OFF}} \times 100 = \frac{30}{30+30} \times 100$$

$$= \frac{30}{60} \times 100 = 50\%$$

Output voltage, $V_R = V_{in} \times \sqrt{\delta}$

$= 230\sqrt{0.5}$

$= 162.63$ V

RMS output current, $I_R = \dfrac{V_R}{R} = \dfrac{162.63}{20}$ = **8.13 A**

Power factor, PF $= \sqrt{\delta} = \sqrt{0.5} =$ **0.707 (Lagging)**

Example 5.2 : *The A.C. voltage controller has R_L = 20 Ω with input 230 V, 50 Hz. If ON-OFF control is adopted with T_{ON} = 50 cycles and T_{OFF} = 150 cycles, calculate RMS output voltage, power factor, average and RMS values of SCR currents.*

Solution : Given data : ON-OFF control

T_{ON} = 50 cycles

T_{OFF} = 150 cycles

Input voltages = 230 V, 50 Hz

$$\text{Duty cycle } \delta\% = \frac{T_{ON}}{T_{ON} + T_{OFF}} \times 100$$

$$= \frac{50}{50+150} \times 100 = \frac{50}{200} \times 100$$

$= $ **25%**

RMS voltage $= V_{in} \sqrt{\delta}$

$= 230\sqrt{0.25} =$ **115 V**

Output power, $P_o = \dfrac{\delta \times V_{in}^2}{R_L} = \dfrac{0.25 \times (230)^2}{20}$

$= \mathbf{661.25\ watts}$

Power factor $= \sqrt{\delta} = \sqrt{0.25} = \mathbf{0.5\ (lagging)}$

Average current through SCR,

$$I_{TO} = \dfrac{V_m \delta}{\pi R} = \dfrac{230\sqrt{2} \times 0.25}{\pi \times 20}$$

RMS current $= \mathbf{1.29\ A}$

$$I_R = \dfrac{V_m \sqrt{\delta}}{2R} = \dfrac{230\sqrt{2} \times \sqrt{0.25}}{2 \times 20}$$

$= \mathbf{4.065\ A}$

Example 5.3 : *A single-phase AC voltage controller employing two SCRs in anti-parallel supplies power to a 2 kW, 230 V heater element from an AC source of 230 V 50 Hz. If the SCRs are triggered symmetrically with a delay angle $\alpha = 30°$, calculate RMS current flowing through the heater element.*

Solution : Given data : Input voltage = 230 V, Power rating = 2 kW = 2000 watt

$\therefore$ R of heater $= \dfrac{(\text{Voltage rating})^2}{\text{Power rating}}$

$= \dfrac{230^2}{2000} = 26.45\ \Omega$

RMS current flowing through the heater element,

$$I_R = \dfrac{V_R}{R}$$

Firing angle, $\alpha = 30° = \dfrac{\pi}{6}$

V_R = RMS load voltage

$$V_R = 230\sqrt{\dfrac{1}{\pi}\left(\pi - \dfrac{\pi}{6} + \dfrac{\sin 2\,(\pi/6)}{2}\right)}$$

$= 226.66\ V$

$\therefore\quad I_R = \dfrac{226.66}{26.45} = \mathbf{8.57\ A}$

Example 5.4 : *The single-phase full wave AC voltage controller supplies a purely resistive load of R = 10 Ω from an AC source of 230 V 50 Hz. If the delay angles of SCR are equal to $\alpha_1 = \alpha_2 = \pi/2$, calculate the RMS output voltage and current, power factor, the average and RMS values of SCR circuit.*

Solution : Given data : AC source = 230 V 50 Hz, $R_L = 10\ \Omega$, $\alpha_1 = \alpha_2 = \pi/2$

RMS output voltage, $V_R = 230 \sqrt{\dfrac{1}{\pi}\left(\pi - \dfrac{\pi}{2} + \dfrac{\sin 2\dfrac{\pi}{2}}{2}\right)}$

$= \mathbf{162.63\ V}$

RMS value of load current,

$$I_R = \dfrac{V_R}{R} = \dfrac{162.63}{10} = \mathbf{16.26\ A}$$

Output power, $P_o = V_R I_R = 162.63 \times 16.26 = \mathbf{2644.36\ watts}$

The input volt-ampere $= 230 \times 16.26$

$= \mathbf{3739.8\ VA}$

Power factor PF $= \dfrac{P_o}{VA} = \dfrac{2644.36}{3739.8} = \mathbf{0.707\ (lagging)}$

The average value of SCR current,

$$I_{T\ av} = \dfrac{230\sqrt{2}\left(1 + \cos\dfrac{\pi}{2}\right)}{2\pi \times 10} = \mathbf{5.18\ A}$$

RMS SCR current, $I_{T\ RMS} = \dfrac{I_R}{\sqrt{2}} = \dfrac{16.26}{\sqrt{2}} = \mathbf{11.5\ A}$

Example 5.5 : *A single phase ACVC supplies an inductive load with a resistance of 20 Ω and load inductance angle of 45°. The input A.C. voltage is 230 V, 50 Hz. Determine : (a) control range of delay angle, (b) the range of delay angle for which RMS load voltage remains constant, (c) the maximum RMS load voltage, (d) the maximum RMS load current.*

Solution : (a) The control range of delay angle α is,

$$\phi \leq \alpha \leq 180°$$

ϕ = Impedance angle

$$\mathbf{45° \leq \alpha \leq 180°}$$

(b) The range of delay angle for which the RMS load voltage remains constant = 230 V is,

$$0 \leq \alpha \leq \phi$$

∴ $\mathbf{0 \leq \alpha \leq 45°}$

(Chap. 5.31)

(c) The maximum load voltage is equal to supply voltage = 230 V and occurs for delay angle in the range,

$$0 \leq \alpha \leq 45°$$

(d) The load has $X_L = 20 \tan 45° = 20$ and the load impedance is $|Z|$

$$= \sqrt{R^2 + X_L^2} = 20\sqrt{2}\ \Omega$$

RMS load current, $\quad I_R = \dfrac{V_{R\ (max)}}{|Z|} = \dfrac{230}{20\sqrt{2}} = \mathbf{8.13\ A}$

Example 5.6 : *A 1φ ACVC control the power input to a load circuit consisting of R = 3 Ω an ωL = 4 Ω if the supply voltage is 230 V, 50 Hz. Calculate :*

(a) Control range of firing angle.
(b) Maximum value of RMS load current.
(c) Maximum power input to the load.
(d) Maximum power factor.
(e) Maximum value of average and RMS thyristor current.

Solution : (a) Control range of firing angle is φ to π.

$$\psi = \text{Load phase angle} = \tan^{-1}\dfrac{\omega L}{R} = \tan^{-1}\dfrac{4}{3}$$

$$= \tan^{-1} 1.333 = 53.13°$$

$$\therefore \quad \mathbf{53.13° \leq \alpha \leq \pi}$$

(b) The maximum value of RMS load current occurs when $\alpha = \phi = 53.13°$. But at this value of firing angle, the power circuit of the AC voltage controller behaves as if the load is directly connected to the AC source.

The maximum of RMS load current $= \dfrac{230}{\sqrt{R^2 + \omega^2 L^2}} = \dfrac{230}{\sqrt{3^2 + 4^2}} = \mathbf{46\ A}$

(c) Maximum power input to the load $= I_o^2 R = (46)^2 \times 3 = \mathbf{6348\ watts}$

(d) Maximum power factor $= \dfrac{6348}{230 \times 46} = 0.6 = \cos \phi$

(e) Maximum value of SCR RMS current,

$$I_{T\ RMS} = \dfrac{I_o}{\sqrt{2}} = \dfrac{46}{\sqrt{2}} = \mathbf{32.527\ A}$$

Average value of SCR current,

$$I_{av\ SCR} = \dfrac{I_{T\ RMS}}{1.57} = \dfrac{32.527}{1.57} = \mathbf{20.707\ A}$$

Example 5.7 : *A 2.0 V lead acid cell is discharged at a uniform rate of 30 A for 3 hours at an average e.m.f. 1.95 V. If then charged at a rate of 40 A for 4 hours to restore its voltage, determine : (a) A-H efficiency, (b) W-H efficiency.*

Solution : AH efficiency of battery $= \dfrac{\text{Discharging current rate} \times \text{Time}}{\text{Charging current rate} \times \text{Time}}$

$$= \dfrac{30 \times 3}{40 \times 4} = \dfrac{90}{160} = \textbf{56.25\%}$$

W.H. efficiency $= \dfrac{56.25 \times 1.95}{2} = \textbf{54.85\%}$

Example 5.8 : *For a UPS system select a suitable battery for following specifications :*

(i) UPS rating = 20 kVA.
(ii) Back-up time 20 min.
(iii) Inverter efficiency at full load = 85%.
(iv) Type of load – Induction with lagging PF = 0.8.
(v) Type of battery load acid.
(vi) Battery voltage range = 147 – 190 V.
(vii) Final voltage on cell = 1.80 V/cell.
(viii) Cell per jar = 6.

Solution : (i) Battery kW $= \dfrac{\text{Load kVA} \times \text{PF}}{\text{Efficiency}}$

$$= \dfrac{20 \times 0.8}{0.85} = \textbf{18.82 kW}$$

(ii) $\dfrac{\text{Number of cells in}}{\text{battery bank}} = \dfrac{\text{Minimum allowable battery voltage}}{\text{Final voltage per cell}}$

$$= \dfrac{147 \text{ V}}{1.80} - 81.6 = \textbf{82 cells}$$

(iii) Number of jars $= \dfrac{\text{Number of cells}}{\text{Number of cells per jar}}$

$$= \dfrac{82}{0.6} = 13.6 \approx \textbf{14}$$

(iv) Per cell kW rating $= \dfrac{\text{Total battery kW}}{\text{Number of cells}}$

$$= \dfrac{18.82}{82} = \textbf{0.22951 kW}$$

For 20 min back up, battery must be selected having discharge rate above 0.22951 kW.

REVIEW QUESTIONS

1. State types of AC voltage controller and state their principles.
2. With neat circuit diagram and waveform explain operation of half wave A.C. voltage controller. State its output voltage equation.
3. What is full wave A.C voltage controller ? Sketch circuit diagrams of four different configurations suitable for A.C. full wave voltage controller.
4. Explain single phase full wave A.C. voltage controller for R load. State the effect of change in firing angle. State output voltage, thyristor current and power factor equation.
5. With mathematical equation, waveform and circuit diagram, explain single phase AC controller for RL load.
6. What is integral cycle control ? With circuit diagram and waveform explain its operation. State effect of duty cycle.
7. State essential features of UPS. State types of UPS. Sketch their block diagram and list out specifications for each type.
8. What is battery bank ? State how to calculate battery bank capacity.
9. Compare ON line, OFF line and interactive UPS system.
10. What is simulation ? State various simulation tools for power electronics. List advantages, requirement of simulation tools. Explain any one power electronic circuit simulation.
11. Explain following terms :
    (a) Capacity of the battery.
    (b) Efficiency of the battery.
    (c) Redundancy of UPS.
12. Explain with block diagram solid state UPS.
13. Why ON-line UPS is more expensive ?
14. List out merits and demerits of ON-line and OFF-line UPS.
15. For a single-phase AC voltage controller explain how pulse gating is suitable for R load and not for RL load. How high frequency carrier gating is essential for RL load ?
16. For a single-phase AC voltage regulator develop a relation between conduction angle Y and firing and α and plot their variation as a function of load phase angle ϕ.
17. Explain why the single phase AC regulator using two SCRs must have its trigger sources isolated from each other.
18. What are the advantages and disadvantages of ON-OFF control ? Compare it with phase control.
19. Define the terms delay angle, extinction angle and conduction angle.
20. Explain how we can determine the angle of extinction of SCR in a single phase, phase control type ACVC connected to RL load.

...

APPENDIX A

ABBREVIATIONS

A	B
AC	Alternating Current
AH	Ampere Hour
AM	Amplitude Modulation
BJT	Bi Junction Transistor
CB	Common Base
CC	Common Collector
CE	Common Emitter
CSI	Current Source Inverter
DC	Direct Current
DIAC	Diode AC Switch
ELCB	Earth Leakage Circuit Breaker
FCT	Field Controlled Thyristor
FM	Frequency Modulation
FWE	Full Wave Rectifier
Ge	Germanium
GTO	Gate Turn Off Thyristor
HVDC	High Voltage Direct Current
HWR	Half Wave Rectifier
HWCR	Half Wave Controlled Rectifier
IC	Integrated Circuits
IGBT	Insulated Gate Bipolar Transistor
IGR	Inter Group Reactor
KCL	Kirchoff Current Law
KVL	Kirchoff Voltage Law
LASCR	Light Activated Silicon Control Rectifier
LC	Inductor Capacitor
LCD	Liquid Crystal Display
LED	Light Emitting Diode
MCB	Mains Circuit Breaker
MCT	Mos Controlled Thyristor
MOSFET	Metal Oxide Semiconductor Field Effect Transistor
PHC	Power Handling Capacitor
PIV	Peak Inverse Voltage
PRV	Peak Reverse Voltage
PUT	Programmable Unijunction Transistor

A	B
PWM	Pulse Width Modulation
RCT	Reverse Conducting Thyristor
RFI	Radio Frequency Interferance
RL	Resistor Inductor
RMS	Root Mean Square
SBS	Silicon Bilateral Switch
SCR	Silicon Control Rectifier
SCS	Silicon Control Switch
Si	Silicon
SMPS	Switch Mode Power Supply
SOA	Safe Operation Area
SSR	Solid State Relay
SUS	Silicon Unilateral Switch
SVC	Static Var Compancitor
TCR	Thyristor Controlled Reactor
TRC	Time Ratio Control
TRIAC	Triode AC Control Switch
TSC	Thyristor Switched Capacitor
TVM	Transistor Volt Meter
UJT	Uni Junction Transistor
UPS	Uninterrupted Power Supply
VBO	Break Over Voltage
VP	Peak Voltage
VSI	Voltage Source Inverter
VV	Valley Voltage
VZ	Zener Breakdown Voltage

LIST OF SEMINAR TOPICS RELATED TO POWER ELECTRONICS

- Advance Thyristor Devices
- SCR Selection according to applications
- Polyphase Rectifier
- Power BJT
- A.C. Voltage Controllers 1ϕ
- Static Induction Transistor
- Series Operation of SCR
- Parallel Operation of SCR
- SCR Protection Circuits
- Safe Operation Area
- Thermal Model of Thyristor
- Dual Converter

- A.C. Voltage Controller 3 φ
- Industrial Applications of Cycloconverter
- Cycloinverter
- Selection of Battery Charger Circuits
- Heat Sink
- Mounting of Mesa SCR
- HVDC System
- Servo Stabiliser
- Stepper Motor Operation
- Drives in Textile Mill
- Drives in Rolling Mill
- Use of Thyristors in Traction
- Use of Thyristors in Signaling
- ELCB (Earth Leakage Circuit Breaker)
- Optoelectronic Devices
- Microcontroller Base Phase Control
- RFI
- Temperature Controller using SCR
- Servomotor
- Stepper Motor Application

QUESTIONS FOR ORAL EXAMINATION

- How to test SCR ?
- How to identify terminals of SCR ?
- State difference between P-N junction diode and SCR.
- State function of gate terminal of SCR.
- What is negative resistance ?
- State the significance of holding current, latching current and breakover voltage.
- Define turn-on time, turn-off time, firing angle, conduction angle.
- State function of free wheeling diode.
- State working principle of phase control.
- Define uncontrolled rectifier, controlled rectifier, line commutation, force commutation.
- What is M-2, M-6 connection ?
- How output voltage waveform differ due to type of load R and RL ?
- State the principle of phase control.
- State the meaning of source impedance.
- How source impedance affect the performance of converter ?
- State the principle of inverter.
- State selection factors for inverter.
- List the requirements of inverter.
- What do you mean by inverter grade SCR ?
- State the function of inductor in inverter circuit.
- List performance parameters of chopper.
- How static switch is different from electromechanical switch ?
- Which components are suitable for static switch ?
- State advantages of static switch.

- State difference between fuse and circuit breaker.
- List the specifications of circuit breaker.
- State difference between A.C. and D.C. switches.
- Define AH rating of battery.
- How protection occur in battery charger circuit ?
- State factors affecting life of battery.
- State specifications of cell phone charger.
- Define the term base speed of D.C. motor.
- What is back e.m.f. ?
- How torque and speed are related for induction motor ?
- State advantages of stepper motor.
- State how to increase step resolution.
- State the function of transistor in stepper motor.
- What is 8 pole stepper motor ?
- Why high step resolution is possible in hybrid stepper motor ?
- State advantages of D.C. servomotor.
- State function of rate generator.
- Compare A.C. and D.C. servomotors.
- List out specifications of D.C. servomotor.
- What is servo amplifier ?
- Compare induction heating with dielectric heating.
- State role of thyristors in weld control system.
- How circuit breaker operate ?

Major manufacturers of power electronics components :
- ABB
- Advanced Power Technology
- Fairchild Semiconductor
- Hitachi Ltd.
- International Rectifier
- IXYS semiconductor GmbH
- Mitsubishi Electric
- National Semiconductor INC
- Philips Semiconductors
- Powerex INC
- Powertech Inc.
- Samsung Ltd.
- Semicron I International
- Toshiba Crop.
- Unitrode Integrated Circuits
- Vishay Siliconix Inc.
- Westcode Semiconductor Ltd.

APPENDIX B

IMPORTANT TERMS AND THEIR DEFINITIONS

- **Acceptor Impurity :** Also called acceptor, an impurity that has too few valence electrons to complete the crystalline structure when covalent bonded with silicon or germanium. P-type material results.
- **Active :** (1) The conducting state of a control device. (2) Controlling power from a separate supply. (3) Requiring a power supply separate from the controls.
- **Active Filter :** A filter which is switched in response to demand to attenuate or eliminate harmonic components and compensate for active power.
- **Advance, Firing Angle :** The angle at which a thyristor starts conduction in advance of, and relative to, the instant when the thyristor forward voltage falls to zero in a converter. Used in relation to the inverting mode of operation.
- **Alpha (α) :** In a transistor, the ratio that exists between emitter and collector gain. Symbol for current gain in a common base amplifier. In a junction transistor, alpha is always less than unity (1).
- **Ambient :** The temperature of the general mass of air or cooling medium into which heat is finally transferred from a hot body.
- **Anode :** The positive point of an active device to which electrons are attracted.
- **Anode Gate :** One of the gate electrodes of a silicon bilateral switch.
- **Anti-parallel :** The parallel connection of two unidirectional devices or converters, so making the overall characteristic bidirectional.
- **Approximation Method :** A method is used to analyze transistor circuits where small amount of current and/or resistance are ignored in order to simplify the analysis.
- **Astable Multivibrator :** A circuit which has two momentarily stable states, between which it continually alternates. Time spent in each fixed state and switching time are controlled by circuit parameters.
- **Asymmetrical :** Not uniform in characteristics or construction.
- **Auxiliary Thyristor :** A second or further thyristor, probably linked to the communication capacitor, used to initiate and execute the turn off of a main load current carrying thyristor.
- **Avalanche :** A chain reaction which occurs when minority carriers are accelerated by a high electrical field, so liberating further carriers leading to a sharp increase in reverse current and break-down.
- **Back e.m.f. :** An expression commonly used for the voltage internally generated in a machine as a consequence of its rotation.
- **Back-to-Back :** See anti-parallel.
- **Barrier Region :** See depletion region.

- **Base :** (1) The region between the emitter and collector of a transistor which receives minority carriers injected from emitter. (2) On a printed circuit board, the base is the material that supports the printed pattern.
- **Base Current :** The current that flows in the base of a transistor. Base current will normally range between 2% and 8% of emitter current.
- **Base Drive :** The source of base current to fully turn on (saturate) a transistor.
- **Beta (β) :** Also called current transfer ratio. Current gain within a common emitter amplifier. Current gain is calculated by comparison of the change in the collector current to the change in the emitter current. The formula for beta is

$$\text{Beta } (\beta) = \frac{I_c}{I_b}$$

- **Bias :** D.C. voltage or current applied to a solid state device that establishes the operating (Q) point.
- **Bidirectional :** (1) Responsive in opposite directions. (2) Capable of supporting current in two directions, for example, a triac.
- **Braking :** Reversing the power flow in a motor, so reversing the shaft torque and causing it to generate.
- **Bi-FET Circuitry :** Circuitry that contains both bipolar and field effect transistor devices.
- **Bilateral :** See Bi-directional.
- **Bipolar Transistor :** A transistor in which both positive and negative current carriers are used to support current flow. All NPN and PNP transistors are of this type.
- **Bipolar Junction Transistor :** See Bipolar Transistor.
- **Bistable Multivibrator :** A circuitry having two stable states; it will remain in either state indefinitely unless triggered by a voltage of correct polarity and amplitude at which time it will immediately switch states.
- **Break Down :** The phenomenon that occurs in a reversed biased diode where current behaves as if the circuit contained negative resistance.
- **Breakdown Point :** The point at which conduction of a semiconductor device enters the negative resistance region.
- **Breakdown Potential :** See Breakdown Voltage.
- **Breakdown Voltage :** (1) The voltage that causes conduction within a semiconductor device when it enters the negative resistance region. (2) The reverse voltage level at which the reverse current increases rapidly in a device (say diode).
- **Breakover :** (1) The start of current flow in a silicon controlled rectifier. (2) The change from the non-conducting state to the conducting state in a forward-biased device (say thyristors) if breakover voltage exceeded.
- **Breakover Point :** The point at which current begins to flow in a silicon controlled rectifier.

- **Bridge :** Full wave converter.
- **Brushless D.C. Motor :** A term often used for an inverter fed synchronous motor.
- **Burst Firing :** See Integral Cycle.
- **Bypass Diode :** See Commutating Diode.
- **Cathode :** General name used to denote the negative electrode of an active device.
- **Cathode Gate :** One of the gate electrodes of a silicon bilateral switch.
- **C.B. Amplifier :** See Common Base Amplifier.
- **C.B. Junction :** The collector-base junction of a bipolar transistor.
- **C.C. Amplifier :** See Common-Collector Amplifier.
- **C.E. Amplifier :** See Common-Emitter Amplifier.
- **Celsius Temperature :** Also called centigrade temperature. A temperature scale based on freezing = 0° and boiling = 100° when both exist under normal conditions.
- **Channel Pinch-off :** The reduction of channel current in a field effect transistor to its smallest amount possible.
- **Characteristic Curve :** A graph plotted to show the relationship that exists between changing values. For example, collector current change as compared to collector voltage change.
- **Chopping :** A technique of rapidly switching on and off a source of voltage.
- **Clamping Voltage :** Introduction of a voltage reference level to a pulsed or a transient waveform to limit the peak value.
- **Closed Loop :** A system in which information regarding the state of the controlled quantity is fed back to the controlling element.
- **Closed Loop Circuit :** A circuit in which the output is continuously fed back to the input for constant comparison.
- **CMOS :** See Complementary MOS.
- **Collector :** The element of a transistor in which the majority of emitter current flows.
- **Collector Current :** The amount of total transistor current that flows in the collector element. Collector current ranges between 92% and 98% of total (emitter) current.
- **Common Base Amplifier :** Also called grounded base amplifier. A transistor amplifier in which the base element is common to both the input and the output circuit.
- **Common Base Configuration :** See Common Base Amplifier.
- **Common Collector Amplifier :** Also called an emitter follower. A transistor in which the collector element is common to both input and output circuit.
- **Common Collector Configuration :** See Common Collector Amplifier.
- **Common Drain Amplifier :** An amplifier configuration used with field effect transistors whose operation is similar to that of the bipolar transistor common emitter amplifier.

- **Common Drain Configuration :** See Common Drain Amplifier.
- **Common Emitter Amplifier :** Also called grounded emitter amplifier. An amplifier in which the emitter element is common to both input and output circuit.
- **Common Emitter Configuration :** See Common Emitter Amplifier.
- **Common Gate Amplifier :** An amplifier configuration used with field effect transistors whose operation is similar to that of the bipolar common base amplifier.
- **Common Gate Configuration :** See Common Gate Amplifier.
- **Common Mode Rejection :** Also called 'In Phase Rejection'. A measure of how well a differential amplifier ignores a signal which appears simultaneously and in phase at both the input terminals.
- **Common Source Amplifier :** An amplifier configuration used with field effect transistors whose operation is similar to that of the bipolar transistor common base amplifier.
- **Common Source Configuration :** See Common Source Amplifier.
- **Commutating Diode :** A diode placed across a D.C. load to permit transfer of load current away from the source, and to allow the thyristors in the D.C. source to turn off. In addition to permitting commutation of source thyristors, the diode will prevent reversal of load voltage.
- **Commutating Reactance :** The value of the reactance delaying the commutation of current from one device to another in a converter.
- **Commutation Angle :** See overlap angle.
- **Complementary MOS :** Pertaining to N and P channel enhancement mode devices fabricated compatibly on a silicon chip and connected into push pull complementary circuits.
- **Complementary SCR :** See Programmable UJT.
- **Complementary Thyristor :** The other series connected thyristor in an arm of a bridge circuit.
- **Conduction Angle :** The angle over which the device conducts.
- **Conduction Band :** A partly filled energy band in which electrons can move freely, allowing the material to act as a conductor of electron current.
- **Conduction Loss :** The energy dissipated within a device during its on-state conduction.
- **Conductor :** A material that has been designed to act as a carrier for electron flow.
- **Constant Current Inverter :** An inverter fed from a d.c. source with a large series inductor, so that over each inverter cycle the source current is almost constant.
- **Constant Voltage Inverter :** An inverter fed from a d.c. source with a large parallel capacitor, so that over each inverter cycle the source voltage remains almost constant.

- **Conventional Flow :** An explanation of current based on the belief that current in an external circuit will flow from positive pole of a battery to the negative pole of a battery.
- **Converter :** A circuit which converts d.c. to a.c. or vice versa.
- **Critical Damping :** (1) The value of damping that provides the most rapid transient response with minimum overshoot. (2) Damping which gives most rapid transient response without overshoot or oscillation.
- **Crowbar :** A device or action that places a high overload on the supply, so actuating protective devices. An expression that arises from placing a crowbar across power lines to short circuit them.
- **Crystal :** A solid in which the available atoms are arranged with some degree of geometric regularity.
- **Current Gain :** The ratio of change in output current to change in input current.
- **Cutoff :** Minimum value of bias which stops all current flow in an active device. An operating condition that is called cutoff and during which zero current flows.
- **Cycloconverter :** Frequency converter in which no intermediate d.c. state.
- **Cycloinverter :** A cycloconverter which is capable of converting power to higher frequency.
- **Damping :** (1) The reduction of an oscillator's output power that results from the dissipation that occurs because of internal resistance. (2) Extraction of energy from an oscillating system.
- **Darlington :** A power transistor incorporating a driver transistor on the same chip, or two separate transistors mounted in a single housing, giving high current amplification.
- **D.C. Load Line :** A line that is plotted on a device's characteristic curves that represents infinite number of Q points ranging from cutoff to saturation.
- **D.C. Link :** Intermediate d.c. stage between two systems of differing frequency.
- **Degeneration :** Also called negative feedback. A process by which a portion of the output signal of an amplifier is fed back to the input circuit 180° out of phase, thereby decreasing the amplification of the circuit.
- **Delay, Firing Angle :** The retarded angle at which a thyristor starts conduction relative to that instant when the thyristor forward voltage becomes positive, that is the angle by which the thyristor conduction is delayed to if it were a diode.
- **DE-MOSFET :** A MOSFET device that can operate in both the depletion and enhancement modes depending on the polarity of the bias applied to the device.
- **Depletion Layer :** Also called barrier layer. In a semiconductor, the region in which the mobile carrier charge density is insufficient to neutralize the net fixed charge density of donors or acceptors.
- **Depletion Mode :** A MOSFET device that operates in the mode where bias is used to 'deplete' the number of carriers present in the channel.

- **Depletion Region :** The region extending on both sides of a reversed biased semiconductor junction, in which all carriers are swept away from the vicinity of the junction; that is the area depleted of carriers.
- **Deposition Process :** The application of a material to a substrate through the use of chemical, vapour, electrical, vacuum or other processes.
- **Diac :** A four layered, two lead device that is used as a switch for control of electrical circuitry.
- $\frac{di}{dt}$ **= Rate of Rise of Current :** A device has a critical di/dt rating which if exceeded can cause overheating during turn-on.
- **Differentiator :** Also called differentiating circuit. A circuit in which the output voltage is substantially in proportion to the rate of change of the input voltage or current.
- **Diffusion :** A thermally induced process in which one type of material permeates the another.
- **Diode :** A two element semiconductor device that makes use of the rectifying characteristics of a P-N junction (junction diode).
- **Dip :** See Dual-in-line.
- **Discrete Circuitry :** Circuits build from separate components.
- **Displacement Current :** Displacement of electrons in a dielectric, which sets up a magnetic field as if a current is flowing.
- **Displacement Factor :** The cosine of displacement angle. With a sinusoidal voltage and harmonics present in the current, it is the cosine of the delay angle of the fundamental component.
- **Distortion Factor :** Ratio of fundamental r.m.s. current to the total r.m.s. current.
- **Donor Impurity :** Also called donor. An impurity which tends to release a free electron and thereby affects the conductivity of the crystal.
- **Doping :** (1) The addition of impurities to a semiconductor crystal in order to control its resistivity and to determine whether a P or N type material results. (2) The addition of impurities to a semiconductor to achieve a desired characteristic such as to produce N or P type material.
- **Double-way :** See full-wave.
- **Drain :** The element of field effect transistors that performs the same function as the collector in a bipolar transistor.
- **Drain Current :** Current that flows in the drain circuit of a field effect transistor that compares to the collector current in a bipolar transistor.
- **Drain-Source Saturation Current :** Amount of current that is required to saturate the drain element of a field effect transistor, when gate source voltage (V_{gs}) is equal to zero volts.

- **Dual-in-line (DIP) :** A type of package used to contain integrated circuits.
- **Duty Cycle :** The ratio of the on time to the cycle time in a chopper.
- $\frac{dv}{dt}$ **: Rate of Rise of Voltage :** A thyristor has a rated forward limit which, if exceeded may breakover the junction without the injection of gate current.
- **Emitter-Base Junction :** Emitter-Base junction within a bipolar transistor.
- **Electron :** (1) The negative particle contained in all atoms that orbits the nucleons in specific energy levels. (2) The elementary negative particle.
- **Electron Flow :** The movement of electrons from the negative pole of a power source to the positive pole of the source.
- **Electron-Hole Pair :** A positive current carrier (hole) and a negative carrier (electron), considered together as one entity.
- **EMC (Electromagnetic Compatibility) :** Relates to the ability of equipment not to cause interference and to its immunity from EMI.
- **EMI (Electromagnetic Interference) :** See EMC.
- **Emitter :** The transistor element through which 100% of current flows.
- **Emitter Current :** The direct current flowing in the emitter of a bipolar transistor. Emitter current = 100% of transistor current.
- **Emitter Follower :** See common collector amplifier.
- **E-MOSFET :** A MOSFET that operates because of the increase in the (enhancement) number of carriers available in the channel resulting from correct biasing.
- **End-Stop Pulse :** Delivered automatically by the firing circuit at an angle of firing advance which is just sufficient to ensure commutation.
- **Energy Level :** The electrical power contained in a orbiting electron.
- **Enhancement Mode :** See E-MOSFET.
- **Epitaxy :** The controlled growth of a layer of semiconductor material in a suitable substrate.
- **Epitaxial Growth :** A semiconductor fabrication process in which single crystal N or P material is deposited and grows on the surface of the substrate.
- **Error Signal :** Difference between the controlled (output) quantity and desired (input) quantity in a closed loop system.
- **Extrinsic :** Not perfect, contains impurities.
- **Extrinsic Semiconductor :** A doped material of high conductivity.
- **Fall Time :** The amount of time required for a pulse to drop from 90% of peak to 10% of its maximum amplitude.
- **Feedback :** (1) The return of a portion of the output signal to the input of the same stage. (2) Information on the state of the controlled quantity conveyed back to the controlling element.

- **Feedback Diode :** In an inverter to permit reverse power flow.
- **FET :** See Field Effect Transistor.
- **Field Effect Transistor :** A semiconductor device that operates using the electrostatic effect caused by bias changes to control the amount of current that flows.
- **Filter :** Attenuates currents of selected frequencies.
- **Firing :** Injection of gate current to turn on a forward biased thyristor or triac.
- **Firing Angle :** See Delay and Advance, Firing Angle.
- **Fixed Bias :** A constant value of D.C. bias voltage.
- **Flat Top :** The horizontal portion of a square or rectangular wave that results from the low frequency components that make up the wave.
- **Flip-Flop :** See Bistable Multivibrator.
- **Flywheel Diode :** See commutating Diode
- **Fly Wheel Effect :** The maintaining of oscillations in an LC resonant tank circuit during intervals between pulses of excitation energy.
- **Forbidden Band :** The region that exists between the valence band and conduction band of an element.
- **Forbidden Region :** See Forbidden Band.
- **Forward Bias :** An external voltage applied in the conducting direction of a PN junction.
- **Forward Breakover Potential :** Voltage required to cause breakover of an SCR.
- **Forward Current :** Current that flows across a PN junction that has forward bias applied.
- **Forward Voltage Drop :** Value at rated current.
- **Gain :** Any increase in signal power that results from being processed by an amplifier.
- **Gate Trigger Current / Voltage :** Amount of current, voltage required to start gate current flow in a four-layer devices such as an SCR.
- **Germanium :** A brittle, grayish-white metallic element having semiconductor properties that is used in the fabrication of transistors and PN junction diodes. Atomic number - 32, valency - 4, symbol - Ge.
- **GTO : Gate Turn Off Thyristor :** A thyristor which can be turned on or off by control of its gate current.
- **Half Controlled :** Unidirectional converter, reverse power flow not possible.
- **Half Wave :** A converter in which the a.c. input current (transformer secondary) is unidirectional.
- **Hand Capacitance Effect :** The capacitance introduced when one's hand is brought near a tuning capacitor or other insufficient part of a circuit or receiver.

- **Harmonic :** A component at an exact multiple of the fundamental.
- **Heat Sink :** A mass of metal that is added to a device for the purpose of absorbing and dissipating heat.
- **High Order Harmonics :** Components of a non-sinusoidal waveform which are at a higher multiple of the fundamental.
- **Holding Current :** (1) The value of average forward current (with the gate open) below which a silicon controlled rectifier will cutoff after having been conducting in the forward direction. (2) The value below which thyristor current will cause when the reduction rate is slow.
- **Hole :** A mobile vacancy in the electronic valence structure of a semiconductor. A hole exists when an atom has less than its normal number of electrons. A hole is equivalent to a positive charge.
- **Hole Flow :** Conduction in a semiconductor where electrons move into holes and thereby create new holes. The holes appear to flow towards the negative terminal of the battery, giving the equivalent of current movement from positive to negative.
- **Holes :** In the electronic valence structure of a semiconductor a mobile vacancy which acts like a positive electronic charge with a positive mass.
- **Hot Carrier Diode :** A diode in which a closely controlled, metal semiconductor junction provides virtual elimination of charge storage. This device has excellent diode forward and reverse characteristics, extremely fast turn on and turn off times, low noise characteristics and a wide dynamic range. Abbreviation - HCD.
- **Hybrid Circuitry :** (1) A circuit which combines thin film and semiconductor technologies. (2) An integrated circuit combining part made by a number of techniques such as diffused monolithic portions, thin film elements, and discrete devices.
- I_B : See Base Current.
- **I.C. :** See Integrated Circuits.
- I_C : See Collector Current.
- I_E : See Emitter Current.
- **IGBT :** Insulated Gate Bipolar Junction Transistor. A bipolar power transistor whose gate is voltage charge controlled in a similar manner to the MOSFET.
- **Impurity :** A material such as boron, phosphorous, or arsenic that is added to a semiconductor such as germanium or silicon to produce either P-type or N-type material.
- **Infinite Load Inductance :** A load in which the cyclic variation in current is negligibly small.
- **Input Signal :** The current, voltage or power or other driving force that is applied to a circuit or device.

- **i² t or ∫ i² t dt :** A measure of maximum possible surge energy a device can safely pass or at which a fuse will clear.
- **Insulated Gate Field Effect Transistor :** In general, any field effect transistor that has an insulated gate regardless of the fabrication process. Abbreviation : IGFET.
- **Insulator :** A material which has its valence electrons tightly bound to the atom and they are not free to move.
- **Integral Cycle :** A.C. load control in which regulation is by alternating a continuous whole number of half cycles on and off.
- **Integrated Circuit :** A combination of interconnected circuit elements inseparably associated on or within a substrate.
- **Integrator :** A device or circuit whose output is proportionate to the integral of the input signal.
- **Interbase Resistance :** Resistance that is arranged between base 1 and base 2 of unijunction transistor.
- **Interphase Transformer :** Centre-tapped reactor placed between parallel groups of a converter to permit independent commutation of the devices in each group.
- **Intrinsic Material :** A semiconductor material in which there are equal number of holes and electrons (no impurities).
- **Intrinsic Semiconductor :** A chemically pure material of poor conductivity.
- **Inverse Parallel :** See Anti-parallel.
- **Inversion :** Reverse power flow in a fully controlled converter occurs when the firing delay angle exceeds 90°.
- **Intrinsic Stand-off Voltage :** The voltage drop that exists across the bottom portion (tap to ground) of the interbase resistance of a UJT.
- **Inverting Amplifier :** An opamp whose output signal is 180° out of phase with the input signal.
- **Inverter :** A circuit which converts d.c. power to a.c. power by sequentially switching devices within the circuit.
- **JFET :** See Junction Field Effect Transistor.
- **Jitter :** Small rapid variations in a waveform due to fluctuations in the firing angle, supply voltage or other causes.
- **Junction :** (1) A contact between two sections of semiconductor material as in a diode. (2) A region of a transistor P and N type semiconductor material.
- **Junction Barrier :** The opposition to the diffusion of majority carriers across a PN junction due to the charge of the fixed donor and acceptor ions.
- **Junction Capacitance :** Capacitance that exists within the junction region of a semiconductor device.

- **Junction Field Effect Transistor :** A transistor made up of a gate region that is diffused into the channel region. When a control voltage is applied to the gate the channel is depleted or enhanced, and the current between the source and the drain is "pinched off".
- **Junction Resistance :** Resistance that exists within the junction region of a semiconductor device.
- **Junction Transistor :** A transistor having three alternate sections of P type and N type semiconductor material.
- **Kinetic Energy :** Energy which a system possesses by virtue of its motion.
- **Latched :** Locked into a condition awaiting an opposite signal to turn it off.
- **Latching Current :** The minimum forward current to maintain conduction in a thyristor after removal of gate current.
- **LC Tank :** A parallelly connected inductance and capacitance that, through its resonance, controls the frequency of operation of an LC oscillator.
- **Leading Edge :** The transition of a pulse which occurs first.
- **Leakage Current :** (1) A current that flows in a reverse biased semiconductor junction that is supported by minority carriers. (2) Undesirable flow of current through a device. That component of alternating current that pass through the rectifier without being rectified.
- **LED :** See Light Emitting Diode.
- **Light Emitting Diode :** A PN junction that emits light when biased in the forward direction.
- **Line Conditioner :** See Power Line Conditioner.
- **Load Line :** A line that is drawn on the collector characteristic curves of a transistor which represents infinite number of operating points for that transistor with specific collector resistance and collector voltage.
- **Losses :** Unwanted power dissipation.
- **Low-Order Harmonics :** Components of non-sinusoidal waveform which are at a low multiple of the fundamental.
- **Majority Carriers :** (1) The type of carriers that constitute more than half the total number of carriers in a semiconductor device. Electrons in N type and holes in P type. (2) The predominant carrier in a semiconductor; electrons in N type and holes in P type.
- **Majority Current :** Current in a semiconductor that is supported by the predominant carriers.
- **Maximum Average Forward Current :** Maximum average forward current that a diode can conduct without damage at an operating temperature of 25°C or 77°F.
- **Maximum Average Reverse Current :** Maximum average reverse current that a diode can conduct without damage at an operating temperature of 25°C or 77°F.

- **Maximum Power Dissipation :** The maximum power that the diode is capable of dissipating when operating at a temperature of 25°C or 77°F.
- **Maximum Reverse Current :** Rated value of small current that flows in a reverse biased diode or thyristor.
- **Maximum Surge Current :** Maximum current that can be allowed to flow in a diode without damage at an operating temperature of 25°C or 77°F.
- **MCT :** MOS (Metal Oxide Semiconductor) controlled thyristor. A thyristor with voltage charge controlled gate similar to the MOSFET.
- **Mean Current Rating :** Device forward current rating that is based on the mean value of a half sine wave of (say) 40 to 400 Hz, which the device can carry without overheating.
- **Metal Oxide Semiconductor Field Effect Transistor :** Abbreviated : MOSFET - A device consisting of diffused source and drain regions on either side of a P and N channel region, and a gate electrode insulated from the channel by silicon oxide layer.
- **Minority Carrier :** (1) The less predominant carrier in a semiconductor; electrons in P type and holes in N type materials. (2) The type of the carrier that constitute less than half the total number of carriers in a semiconductor device.
- **Minority Current :** Current in a semiconductor that is supported by the less predominant carriers.
- **Modulation Index :** The ratio of the reference magnitude to its maximum possible magnitude in a PWM waveform.
- **Monolithic I.C. :** An integrated circuit that is fabricated on a substrate made from a single semiconductor material.
- **Monostable Multivibrator :** Also called one shot multivibrator. A circuit having only one stable state, from which it can be triggered to change state, but only a predetermined interval, after which it returns to the original state.
- **MOSFET :** Abbreviation for Metal Oxide Semiconductor Field Effect Transistor. A device in which the gate voltage controls the ability to conduct or block the current flows.
- **Multivibrator :** A relaxation oscillator in which the inphase feedback voltage is obtained from two transistors and whose operating frequency and pulse durations are controlled by RC networks.
- **N-channel :** The resistive bar (channel) in a FET that is constructed from N type material.
- **Negative Carrier :** Electrons.
- **Negative Ions :** Ions that have an excess of electrons.
- **Negative Resistance Region :** The operating region within which an increase in applied voltage results in a decrease in current.

- **Negative Temperature Coefficient :** The amount of reduction in the value of the quantity, such as capacitance or resistance, for each degree of increase in operating temperature.
- **Neutron :** One of the three major particles that exist within an atom. The neutron possesses a neutral electrical charge and is found in the nucleus of the atom.
- **NMOS :** MOSFET devices that have an N-channel.
- **Non-Inverting Amplifier :** An operational amplifier whose output is in phase with the input.
- **NPN Transistor :** A junction transistor formed using two sections of N type material and one section of P type material. The emitter and collector are of N type and the base is of P type.
- **Non-sinusoidal :** (1) Any waveform that is not a sine wave, it therefore contains a sine wave plus harmonics. (2) A repetitive waveform which is a shape other than a pure sine wave.
- **N-Type :** (1) An extrinsic semiconductor in which the conduction electron density exceeds the hole density. (2) Semiconductor material in which electrons are the majority carriers and holes are the minority carriers.
- **Notched :** Pulses of equal length.
- **Offset :** The measure of imbalance between halves of a symmetrical circuit.
- **Offset Voltage Drift :** The amount of voltage drift that occurs between the balanced inputs of an operational amplifier.
- **One Shot Multivibrator :** See Monostable Multivibrator.
- **OP-AMP :** See Operational Amplifier.
- **Open-Loop :** Control system in which no information regarding the controlled quantity is known to the controlling element.
- **Open Loop Gain :** The gain present in an operational amplifier that does not have feed-back.
- **Operational Amplifier :** An amplifier that performs various mathematical operations. Also usable as a d.c. amplifier.
- **Operating Point :** Also called quiescent point and Q point. The point along a load line where an active device operates with only DC voltages applied.
- **Orbit :** The path that an electron takes around the nucleus of an atom.
- **Oscillator :** An electronic circuit which generates AC power at a frequency determined by the values of the certain constants in its circuit. An oscillator may be considered an amplifier that has positive (regenerative) feedback.
- **Output Signal :** The current, voltage, power or other driving force that is present at the output terminals of the circuit or device.
- **Over-Damped :** Damping greater than that required for critical damping.

- **Over-Damping :** Any periodic damping greater than the amount required for critical damping.
- **Overlap Angle :** Commutation period in converters during which time two or more devices conducting simultaneously.
- **P-type :** An extrinsic semiconductor in which the conduction hole density exceeds the electron density.
- **Package :** The case that contains and protects a transistor or other device.
- **Packaging :** The physical process of locating, connecting and protecting devices, components, etc.
- **Parallel Capacitor :** Connection of a reverse charged capacitor in parallel with a thyristor to facilitate turn off.
- **P-Channel :** The resistive bar (channel) in a FET that is constructed from P-type material.
- **Peak Inverse Voltage :** The peak AC voltage which a rectifying cell or PN junction will withstand in the reverse direction.
- **Peak Point :** In a zener diode or other thermistor, the maximum forward current that a diode can conduct when a varying current is present as in AC operations.
- **Peak Repetitive Forward Blocking Voltage :** (Abbr. PFV). The maximum instantaneous cyclic voltage which a forward biased thyristor can withstand. Normally a thyristor is chosen to have a value twice that of the peak forward voltage experienced by the thyristor in the working circuit.
- **Peak Reverse Voltage :** See Peak Inverse Voltage.
- **Peak Transient Voltage :** Non-repetitive, occasional peak instantaneous voltage the device can withstand without breakdown.
- **Pentavalent :** Having five valence electrons.
- **Permissible Energy Level :** An energy level at which an electron can exist as it orbits an atom.
- **Phase :** The angular relationship between current and voltage in AC circuits.
- **Phase Angle Control :** AC load control in which regulation is by delaying conduction in each half cycle.
- **Photo-Diode :** A solid state device similar to an ordinary diode with the exception that when light strikes the junction the diode conducts.
- **Pinch-off Region :** Region at which channel current in an FET is minimum.
- **Pinch-off Voltage :** Amount of bias voltage present when FET enters the pinch-off region of its operation.
- **PIN Diode :** A diode whose junction acts like a variable resistance and whose resistance can be controlled by junction bias.
- **PMOS :** MOSFET device that has a P channel.

- **PN Junction :** The region of a transistor between P type and N type material in a single semiconductor crystal.
- **PN Junction Diode :** See Diode.
- **PNP Transistor :** A junction transistor formed using two sections of P type material and one section of N type material. Emitter and collector are P type and the base is N type.
- **Polarized :** Having non-symmetrical characteristic.
- **Positive Carriers :** Holes.
- **Positive Ions :** Ions that have a deficiency of electrons.
- **Potential Energy :** Energy due to the position of one body with respect to another or to the relative parts of the same body.
- **Potential Hill :** Forward bias required to start current in a PN junction.
- **Power Gain :** The ratio of output to input power.
- **Power Factor :** The ratio of mean power to the product of rms value of voltage and current.
- **Power Line Conditioner :** An active filter based on the principle of a PWM converter which absorbs harmonics and reactive current generated by controlled rectifiers.
- **Power Transistor :** A junction transistor designed to handle high currents and power. Used chiefly in low frequency (audio) and switching applications.
- **Programmable UJT :** A four-layer switch that operates at very low current levels that has only one anode gate for control of triggering.
- **Proton :** The positively charged particle that exists in the nucleus of all atoms.
- **PRV :** See Peak Inverse Voltage.
- **P-Type Material :** Semiconductor material in which holes are the majority carriers and electrons are the minority carriers.
- **Pulse :** (1) The variation of a quantity having a normally constant value. This variation is characterized by a rise and decay of a finite value. (2) An abrupt change in voltage either positive or negative, which conveys information to a circuit.
- **Pulse Number :** Repetition cyclic rate in the output voltage waveform of a converter as a multiple of the supply frequency.
- **Pulse Repetition Frequency (PRF) :** The rate (usually given in frequency or pulses per second) at which a series of pulses occurs.
- **Pulse Recurrence Time (PRT) :** The time that lapses between the start of one pulse to the start of next pulse.
- **Pulses Per Second (PPS) :** Number of pulses that occur in one second.
- **Pulse Width (PW) :** The time interval between the points at which the instantaneous value on the leading and trailing edges bear a specified relationship to the peak pulse amplitude.
- **Pulse Width Modulation :** A square wave sinusoidally modulated to give varying on and off periods within the cycle, so as to eliminate the low order harmonics.

- **Q-Factor :** A figure of merit for an energy storing device. Equal to the reactance divided by the resistance. Shows the rate of decay of stored energy.
- **Q-Point :** See Operating Point.
- **Quasi-Square Wave :** Similar to a square wave, but with two equal two periods in each cycle.
- **Quiescent Point :** See Operating Point.
- **Radio Frequency Interference :** Undesired electromagnetic radiations of energy in the communication frequency bands.
- **Ramp :** Quantity rising linearly with time.
- **RC Oscillator :** An oscillator in which the operating frequency is determined by the resistance-capacitance elements.
- **Recombination :** The simultaneous elimination of both an electron and a hole in a semiconductor.
- **Recovery Angle :** Angle after turnoff in which a thyristor experiences a reverse voltage in a converter.
- **Rectangular Wave :** A periodic wave which alternately assumes one of two fixed values, the time of transition being negligible in comparison with the duration of each fixed value and each fixed value having a different duration.
- **Rectifier :** A circuit which converts AC to DC.
- **Regeneration :** Control or adjustment. Characteristic of regulated load.
- **Repetitive Peak Inverse Voltage :** The maximum allowable instantaneous value of the reverse voltage that may be repeatedly applied to the anode of an SCR with the gate open.
- **Resonance :** (1) Any situation in which energy oscillates between two or more different energy storage components. (2) The circuit condition that exists when $X_C = X_L$. This is usually represented by a single frequency or very narrow band of frequencies.
- **Resonant Frequency :** The centre frequency at which a circuit or device resonates.
- **Restriking Voltage :** The voltage that seeks to re-establish conduction.
- **Rest Time :** The time between the end of one pulse and beginning of the next pulse.
- **Reverse Bias :** An external voltage applied to a PN junction that reduces the flow of current through the junction.
- **Reverse Conducting Thyristor :** An integrated device incorporating a thyristor and an antiparallel diode on the same silicon wafer.
- **Reverse Current :** See Minority Current.
- **Reverse Recovery Charge :** The charge carrier quantity stored in the junction, giving rise to a reverse current before the junction recovers its blocking state, when current reduction is fast at turn off.
- **Ringing :** An oscillatory transient.
- **Ripple Factor :** Ratio of rms value of the alternating component to the mean value of a direct voltage waveform.

- **Rise Time :** The amount of time required for a pulse to rise from 15% of peak to 90% of its maximum amplitude.
- **RMS Current Rating :** Maximum possible forward rms current.
- **Safe Operating Area :** The area within the collector current versus collector-emitter voltage characteristic in which the power transistor can be operated out of saturation during switching.
- **Saturable Reactor :** An iron core reactor in which the flux reaches saturation below the rated current level.
- **Saturation Voltage :** Collector-emitter (or base-emitter) voltage when transistor is saturated at defined levels of collector and base currents.
- **Sawtooth Wave :** A periodic wave, the amplitude of which varies linearly between two values.
- **SBS :** See Silicon Bilateral Switch.
- **Schmitt Trigger :** A bistable pulse generator in which an output pulse of a constant amplitude exists only as long as the input voltage exceeds certain DC value.
- **SCR :** See Silicon Controlled Rectifier.
- **SCS :** See Silicon Controlled Switch.
- **Self Bias :** The bias developed by current flow through a resistor connected in series with the emitter of the transistor.
- **Semiconductor :** An element that is neither a good conductor nor a good insulator.
- **Shell :** See Energy Level.
- **SI (Static Induction) :** Relates to a new family of devices which can switch at very high frequencies.
- **Signal :** Intelligence into and/or extracted from an active device such as an amplifier.
- **Silicon :** A metallic element that in its pure state is used as a semiconductor.
- **Silicon Controlled Rectifier (SCR) :** (1) An expression used for thyristor before the name thyristor was adopted. (2) A four layer PNPN device, that when in normal state, blocks applied voltage to a gate terminal enables the device to conduct in the forward direction.
- **Silicon Controlled Switch (SCS) :** A four terminal PNPN semiconductor switching device that can be triggered into conduction by application of either positive or negative pulses.
- **Silicon Bilateral Switch (SBS) :** A device that has characteristic similar to the SCS but that is capable of conduction in either direction.
- **Single-way :** See half-wave.
- **Sinusoidal :** (1) Varying in proportion to the sine of the angle or time function. Normally a sine wave. (2) A waveform which is a pure sine wave in shape.
- **SIT (Static Induction Transistor) :** A voltage controlled transistor, normally on; turned off by application of reverse base voltage.
- **SITH (Static Induction Thyristor) :** A voltage controlled thyristor normally on; turned off by the application of reverse gate voltage.

- **Slew Rate :** The maximum rate of change of output voltage of an amplifier operated within its linear region.
- **Smoothing :** Attenuation of the ripple in the direct voltage waveform.
- **SMPS (Switch Mode Power Supply) :** Uses the principle of rapid on/off switching off the devices as the control philosophy.
- **Snubber :** RC series network placed in parallel with a device to protect against overvoltage transients. Also any circuit used to attenuate changes and afford protection or shape waveforms.
- **Soft-Start :** The gradual application of power when switching in a load.
- **Solid State :** Pertaining to circuits and components made of or using semiconductors.
- **Source :** The element of a field effect transistor that compares to the collector of a bipolar transistor.
- **Space Charge Region :** The region where the net charge density of a semiconductor differs significantly from zero (also see depletion layer).
- **Square wave :** A periodic wave which alternately assumes two fixed values for equal length of time, the transition being negligible compared to the duration of each fixed time.
- **Subharmonic :** A harmonic at a fractional ratio of the exciting frequency. Occurs in the current associated with integral cycle control.
- **Substrate :** The supporting material on or in which the parts of a semiconductor device or integrated circuits are made or attached.
- **Sub-synchronous :** Below synchronous speed.
- **Super-Synchronous Speed :** Above synchronous speed.
- **Suppresser, Surge :** A device that responds to the rate of change of current or voltage to prevent a rise above a predetermined level.
- **Surge-Current :** Sudden current change in the circuit.
- **Surge Current Rating :** The peak value of a single sine wave current of specified length (say 10 ms) which a device can tolerate with the junction temperature at rated value at the start of the surge.
- **Sustaining Voltage :** Maximum rated collector emitter voltage with the base open circuited.
- **Switching Loss :** The energy dissipated within a device during switching from off to on state or vice versa.
- **Synchronous :** In step with the exciting frequency.
- **Synthesis :** Putting together component parts to form the whole.
- **Temperature, Maximum Junction :** Maximum operating junction temperature.
- **Tertiary Winding :** The third winding of a transformer normally an output winding.
- **Thermal Resistance :** Ratio of temperature difference to the heat power flow between two interfaces.

- **Thermal Runaway :** A condition in which the dissipation in a transistor or other device increases so rapidly with higher temperature that the temperature continues to rise.
- **Thyristor :** A bistable device comprising three or more junctions.
- **Threshold Voltage :** The level of voltage at which a PN junction begins to conduct.
- **Timer :** An assembly of electric circuits and associated equipment which provides the following : trigger pulses, sweep voltage, intensifier pulses, gate voltage and blanking voltages.
- **Timing Pulse :** A pulse used to synchronize the circuit.
- **Trailing Edge :** The transition of a pulse that occurs last.
- **Transient :** A sudden change. Short lived phenomenon.
- **Transistor :** An active semiconductor device, usually made of silicon or germanium, having three or more electrodes.
- **Transit Interval :** The amount of time required for a pulse to rise from zero to maximum value or to fall from maximum value to zero.
- **Trapezoidal Wave :** A trapezoidal-shaped waveform.
- **Triac :** A five layer NPNPN device that is equivalent to two SCRs that can be used to switch either polarity of applied voltage. Operation can be controlled in either polarity from the single gate electrode.
- **Trigger :** A pulse that starts an action.
- **Trigger Generator :** A pulsed oscillator designed to generate single pulses at a predetermined frequency.
- **Triggering :** (See also firing) To initiate a sudden change.
- **Trivalent :** Having three valence electrons.
- **Tunnel Diode :** A highly doped PN diode which when forward biased, exhibits a region of negative resistance as part of its operational characteristics.
- **Tunnel Effect :** Piercing of rectangular potential barrier in a semiconductor by a particle that does not have enough energy to go over the barrier.
- **Turn-Off Time :** (1) The time that switching circuit takes to stop the flow of current in the circuit it is controlling. (2) The time between the reduction of current to zero and the reapplication of forward voltage. A thyristor or triac has a minimum rated value.
- **Turn-On Time :** (1) The time that a switching circuit takes to start the flow of current in the circuit it is controlling. (2) The time from the moment turn on is initiated to when the device is fully conducting.
- **Uncontrolled Rectifier :** Rectifier with diodes only.
- **Undamped :** No damping.
- **Underdamped :** Damping less than that required for critical damping. Transient response is oscillatory.
- **Underdamping :** The condition where damping is so small that excessive overshoot is present.

- **Unidirectional :** Flow in one direction only.
- **Unijunction Transistor (UJT) :** A three terminal semiconductor device exhibiting stable, open circuit, negative-resistance characteristics.
- **Unilateral :** Conductivity in one direction only.
- **Unity Power Factor :** Power factor has value of one.
- **Valence :** A number that represents the chemical activity of an element.
- **Valence Band :** The area, within an element, just below the conduction band.
- **Valence Orbit :** The outermost orbit in an atom.
- **Valence Shell :** The electrons which form the outermost shell of an atom.
- **Valley Point :** In a tunnel diode, the point on the characteristic curve at which junction current is minimum prior to beginning its rise and after having passed through the negative resistance region.
- **Valley Voltage :** In a tunnel diode the voltage at which junction current is minimum prior to beginning its rise and after having passed through the negative resistance region.
- **Varactor :** A diode whose junction capacitance can be controlled by a reverse bias voltage.
- V_{CB} **:** Voltage drop - collector to base.
- V_{CE} **:** Voltage drop - collector to emitter.
- V_{EB} **:** Voltage drop - emitter to base.
- **VMOS :** Any MOS device whose gate is V-shaped.
- **Voltage Controlled Oscillator :** An oscillator whose frequency can be controlled by a changing voltage.
- **Voltage Gain :** The ratio that exists between the change in output voltage and the change in input voltage of an amplifier.
- **Zener Diode :** (1) Also called voltage regulator diode. A two-layer device that, when reverse biased, reaches a point where current increases rapidly with little change in voltage. Used as a voltage regulator. (2) A special type of diode in which the reverse avalanche breakdown voltage is almost constraint, irrespective of current. Used for regulation and voltage limiting. May be considered an avalanche diode.

www.ingramcontent.com/pod-product-compliance
Lightning Source LLC
Chambersburg PA
CBHW080242170426
43192CB00014BA/2538